Investment
Management

Founded in 1807, John Wiley & Sons is the oldest independent publishing company in the United States. With offices in North America, Europe, Australia, and Asia, Wiley is globally committed to developing and marketing print and electronic products and services for our customers' professional and personal knowledge and understanding.

The Wiley Finance series contains books written specifically for finance and investment professionals as well as sophisticated individual investors and their financial advisors. Book topics range from portfolio management to e-commerce, risk management, financial engineering, valuation, and financial instrument analysis, as well as much more.

For a list of available titles, visit our Web site at www.WileyFinance.com.

Investment
Management

Portfolio Diversification, Risk, and Timing—Fact and Fiction

ROBERT L. HAGIN

WILEY

John Wiley & Sons, Inc.

Published by John Wiley & Sons, Inc., Hoboken, New Jersey.
Published simultaneously in Canada.

For general information on our other products and services, or technical support, please contact our Customer Care Department within the United States at 800-762-2974, outside the United States at 317-572-3993 or fax 317-572-4002.

Wiley also publishes its books in a variety of electronic formats. Some content that appears in print may not be available in electronic books.

For more information about Wiley products, visit our web site at www.wiley.com.

Library of Congress Cataloging-in-Publication Data:
Hagin, Robert L.
    Investment management : portfolio diversification, risk, and
timing—fact and fiction / by Robert L. Hagin.
        p.   cm.
    ISBN 0-471-46920-3 (CLOTH)
    1. Investments.   2. Portfolio management.   3. Investment analysis.   I. Title.
    HG4521 .H2247   2003
    332.6—dc21   200314215

Printed in the United States of America.

10   9   8   7   6   5   4   3   2   1

To my wife
Susie
and our daughters
KC and Tory

Acknowledgments

Having spent a long and rewarding career in the investment management business, I am indebted to many people. The first is my father. Many years ago, with my "junior" driver's license in hand, I bought a 1929 Model A Ford. (At the time the car was 19 years old; I was 14 and a half.) My father's admonition was that I could drive the car only after I had taken it *completely* apart and put it back together. My father's lesson—that whatever I do I should take apart and put back together before I "drive" it—has served me well.

In the early 1960s I was fortunate to be awarded a fellowship from IBM to pursue doctoral studies at UCLA. My thanks to IBM for finding my proposal to use computers to study financial markets worthy of funding and launching me in a career no one could have imagined.

At UCLA I had an opportunity to work with many distinguished scholars. I owe a debt of gratitude to all of them. One person who stands out from this elite group is Benjamin Graham (considered to this day to be the "father of security analysis"). He remained a mentor, friend, and frequent luncheon companion until his death in 1976. His legacy to me was, "No beliefs—particularly those that are most strongly held about the 'proper' ways to invest—should be safe from inquiry. Never let what you think you know get in the way of learning."

After graduation and a teaching stint at UCLA, I joined the faculty of the Wharton School at the University of Pennsylvania. Of my many colleagues at Wharton the person who was the "invisible hand" on this book was the late Chris Mader—with whom I collaborated in writing three earlier books.

Moving from Wharton to Wall Street in the early 1970s was eye-opening—to say the least. Armed with my first book, *The New Science of Investing*, I quickly discovered the chasm that to this day separates science from seat-of-the-pants guesswork in most firms. Bridging this gap has been an almost lifelong crusade.

I am by no means alone in this quest. There is an invaluable network of colleagues, many of whom are cited in the following chapters. Over the years we have gathered at Center for Research into Security Prices (CRSP) seminars at the University of Chicago (now effectively replaced by the Chicago Quantitative Alliance); Barra research seminars in Pebble Beach; Berkeley Program in Finance conferences in California; Cambridge Center for Behavioral Studies seminars at Harvard; meetings at the Society of Quantitative Analysts in New York (where I have served as president and remain a board member); and last, but by no measure least, the Institute for Quantitative Research in Finance (Q-Group) seminars. The interactions and friendships afforded me by my membership in the Q-Group (where I am privileged to be a board member and serve on the program committee) have been particularly valuable. I owe particular thanks to Jim Farrell, Bill Fouse, and Dale Berman, whose combination of commitment and flexibility has allowed the Q-Group to evolve into a premier organization dedicated to the discussion and dissemination of the most recent quantitative research.

I owe a special thanks to Jon Jankus at Guardian Life Insurance Company of America and Wayne Wagner at Plexus Group, Inc., who helped me with certain chapters as well as offered helpful suggestions on the entire manuscript.

I received invaluable suggestions on early drafts of this book from Ted Aronson at Aronson + Johnson + Ortiz, LP; Jack Bogle at Bogle Financial Markets Research; Charley Ellis at Greenwich Associates; Jon Ender at ABN AMRO Asset Management; Brian Hersey at Watson Wyatt Worldwide; Marty Hertzberg at Spring Mountain Capital; Frank Jones at San Jose State University; Mark Kritzman at Windham Capital Management; Marty Liebowitz at TIAA-CREF; Philip Nelson at Baseline; Jerry Pinto at Association for Investment Management and Research; Stephanie Pomboy at Macro Mavens; Katy Sherrerd at Association for Investment Management and Research; Bob Shultz at TSW Associates; Arnie Wood at Martingale Asset Management; and my daughters, KC and Tory Hagin, whose suggestions were invaluable.

Special thanks are due to several people who worked on the production of the manuscript. Laura Thomas tirelessly typed myriad drafts, checked references, sought permissions, and diligently managed each step of the production process. Lois Stewart—who edited a research report that I wrote upon my arrival at Kidder Peabody & Co., Inc., in 1980—has improved the grammar and clarity of almost everything that I have written in the intervening years. At Morgan Stanley Investment Management Kris Rouff downloaded data and constructed spreadsheets; Linda Johnson-Barth (an artist and potter who works as a librarian) tracked down copies of articles; and Doug Kugler gathered data.

Thanks also to Ralph Rieves, at Farragut, Jones & Lawrence, who led the charge for this, our fourth investment book; and Pamela van Giessen, Jennifer MacDonald, and Mary Daniello at John Wiley & Sons for their experienced guidance and counsel. And last but certainly not least, thanks to the very talented people at Cape Cod Compositors. Their careful review of every word coupled with a keen understanding of the subject added to the clarity.

Any errors are mine alone. Three final things: First, the opinions expressed here are my own and not necessarily shared by the people I have mentioned. Second, my quest is to simplify academic research papers that usually incorporate equations and tests of statistical significance for an important reason—to make the message indelibly clear. Summarizing the conclusions of such papers carries the risk that an important part of the author's message is lost. Third, I take full responsibility for any important papers not included. Be assured that any such omissions result from my oversight and the rush to meet publisher deadlines—not a conscious decision to leave out any relevant research.

ROBERT L. HAGIN

Haverford, Pennsylvania
November 2003

Contents

PART TWO

Avoiding Torpedoes

PART THREE

Landmark Insights

Getting Started— Your Tool Kit

CHAPTER 1

Introduction

My reason for writing this book is straightforward. After more than 40 years of investment research and practice I have seen first hand how misconceptions about investing adversely affect the well-being of countless people. The purpose of this book is to replace those fictions with facts.

This book is written for both buyers and providers of investment-management services. Fiduciaries—assisted by consultants—shoulder enormous responsibilities. Their decisions have by far the most impact on the futures of the trusts, endowments, foundations, and public and private pension funds they administer.

Investing is an extremely complex business. The skills that lead to success in most human endeavors are not necessarily the skills that lead to investment success. Myths about investing abound.

As you begin to look at "investing" from a fresh perspective it is instructive to recall a quotation from President John F. Kennedy's commencement address at Yale University on June 11, 1962: "The greatest enemy of truth is very often not the lie—deliberate, contrived, and dishonest—but the myth—persistent, pervasive, and unrealistic."

What you will find ahead is not the debunking of lies—"deliberate, contrived, and dishonest." I fervently believe that, with rare exceptions, today's financial markets are organized to protect investors against abuses. In no way do I seek to minimize the financial catastrophes brought upon investors and employee-shareholders by the likes of Enron and WorldCom, but there have always been scoundrels who pilfer the coffers of their businesses and exploit the public's trust. Today, as in yesteryear, these events prompt public outcry that, in turn, heightens vigilance and should deter other would-be criminals who consider following the path of deceit.

What lies ahead is much more subtle. There are legions of honest, hardworking investment professionals. These people toil diligently to provide value-added services to their clients. One of the "persistent, pervasive, and unrealistic" myths that needs to be debunked is that these hardworking, diligent men and women—while competing feverishly with one another—can somehow provide all of their clients with above-average investment returns.

The quest to attain above-average returns, or instead to settle for average returns, has spawned two fundamentally different ways to invest. If you are an "active" investor you try to earn above-average returns, and, in so doing, you expose yourself to the not insignificant risk of earning below-average returns. In this very competitive I-am-a-smarter-investor-than-you contest everyone cannot be above average. The returns of investors who earn above-average returns must be offset by the returns of other investors who earn the offsetting below-average returns.

If you are a "passive" investor you seek to match the return of broad-based market indexes. In so doing you forgo the possibility of earning above-index returns, and, simultaneously, you avoid the risk of earning below-index returns. If you are a passive investor you have no need for up-to-the-minute information.

In turn there are two very different types of active investors. On one hand are investors who stay abreast of the advances in our understanding of financial markets that come primarily from university researchers and who apply these insights to their day-to-day investment decisions. On the other hand, by far the majority of private and professional investors use a hodgepodge of investment techniques that stand little chance of rewarding themselves or, in the case of professional investors, their clients.

A dozen scholars have been awarded the coveted Nobel Prize in economic sciences for insights that have a direct bearing on the investment profession. Similarly, there is a long list of academics who—without bias or axes to grind—have significantly increased our understanding of how investment markets work. Yet most professional investors—and the fiduciaries who supervise them and set critically important investment policies—are not able to name any of the Nobel laureates or prominent academic researchers, summarize the essence of their contributions, and describe how and why these insights affect, or do not affect, their investment decisions.

At the outset I should also make the distinction between two very different kinds of research. Academics and a limited number of investment professionals publish research on how to make rewarding—and how to avoid making unrewarding—investment decisions. Economists and security analysts publish research on the economy, industries, and individual companies. This book is concerned with the research that bears on how to make better investment decisions.

My premise is that because those of us who are academics or quantitatively oriented professionals usually write and speak in our own equation-and-jargon-riddled language it is difficult for outsiders to understand many useful facts. As a result, many extremely important insights are hidden from most investors. Yet it is the very precise nature of these presentations, the process of having anonymous referees scour every detail of the papers before they are accepted for publication in the learned journals, and the open nature of the research allowing colleagues and students to critique these works that assure their credibility.

Most people agree that there must be something to learn about investing from Nobel laureates, dedicated academics, and quantitative practitioners, who have provided us with truly landmark insights, if this body of knowledge can be presented in a clear and meaningful way. Here you will see that the findings from this research are not abstruse because of their messages; they are abstruse because of the way the findings are presented. There is no question that successful investors—like successful physicians, airline pilots, and accountants— after completing a significant amount of initial training must continuously "retool." In the case of successful investors, by "retooling" I do not mean staying abreast of the latest product, industry, and economic trends. I mean continuing to stay abreast of what we continue to learn about the *process of investing*.

Hence, the goal of this book, first and foremost, is to translate an often complex body of knowledge into understandable and practical investment advice. You will discover that these insights have profound implications for those of you who are sophisticated amateur and professional investors as well as for the fiduciaries and consultants who have taken on the enormously important responsibility of hiring, supervising, and sometimes firing professional investment managers.

Over the course of your lifetime you have acquired a lot of

knowledge about investing. Some of it is good and some of it is bad. When you invest, or when you supervise professional investors as a fiduciary, you rely on the considerable knowledge you have gained along the way.

Geography is another field in which you have gathered a lot of knowledge. Most of it is very reliable as we successfully navigate our way around the globe. Most readers, for example, can answer the following geography questions (without consulting a map)—and do so with a high level of confidence. Similarly, most readers can do a surprising amount of arithmetic in their heads.[1]

Question 1.1. If you flew from Los Angeles, California, to Reno, Nevada, your compass setting would be:
   a. 20 degrees west.
   b. 10 degrees west.
   c. Due north.
   d. 10 degrees east.
   e. 20 degrees east.

Question 1.2. How confident are you that your answer to the foregoing question is correct?
   a. Very confident.
   b. Reasonably confident.
   c. Uncertain.
   d. No confidence—guessed.

Question 1.3. Rome, Italy, is closest in latitude to which U.S. city? (Latitudes are the measures around the globe that are parallel to, above and below, the equator.)
   a. Boston.
   b. New York.
   c. Atlanta.
   d. Miami.
   e. San Juan, Puerto Rico.

Question 1.4. How confident are you that your answer to the foregoing question is correct?
   a. Very confident.
   b. Reasonably confident.

c. Uncertain.

d. No confidence—guessed.

Question 1.5. *Add these numbers (in sequence) in your head: Begin with 1,000. Add 40. Now add another 1,000. Add 30. Now add another 1,000. Add 20. Now add another 1,000. Add 10. Your answer is:*

a. 4,000.

b. 5,000.

c. None of the above.

Most of you will be comforted to know that 95 percent of the people who are asked these questions believe that Reno, Nevada, is 20 degrees east of Los Angeles and that Rome, Italy, is closest in latitude to Atlanta or Miami. Moreover, when asked to rank your confidence that these answers are correct, most of you report that you are "very confident" that your answers are correct. As one person said, "After all, west of Los Angeles is water."

These popular answers are fascinating because they are wrong! Contrary to what most people believe, your compass setting to travel from Los Angeles to Reno, Nevada, is 20 degrees west;[2] the latitude of Rome, Italy, is closest to that of Boston.[3] What is even more interesting is that even after being told that Reno is west of Los Angeles and that Rome is on a latitude that is close to Boston's it is still very difficult for most people to accept these truths.

For the "add these numbers in your head problem" you are in the majority if your answer is "b"—5,000. Even though most of us quickly arrive at 5,000, it is wrong. The correct answer is "c"— none of the above. Here, if you are typical of most readers you will need to write down the numbers and add them on paper before you are convinced that the correct total is 4,100.

What has happened? How can most of us be so wrong? Why? We did not learn this in school. Yet for some inexplicable reason most of us just plain "get it wrong." Moreover, we "get it wrong" in the same direction—we think that Reno is east of Los Angeles, that Rome is significantly south of Boston, and that the total of an ordinary sequence of numbers is 5,000.

There is an old adage: "The problem is not what you don't know; it is what you do know." On the following pages you will discover that investors' misconceptions abound. Just as most people make mistakes when asked the foregoing questions about geography and simple addition, many amateur and professional investors frequently make costly investment mistakes. The fictions that drive these mistakes are insidious. You often don't have a clue that what you are doing is so damaging to your investment success.

This book explains the evolution, meaning, and practical significance of investment facts that have been gleaned from hundreds of scientific research studies conducted by Nobel laureates, university researchers, and quantitatively oriented investment professionals. Several chapters contain counterintuitive findings from my own research.

The occasionally formidable math and jargon that characterize academic research are gone. I have replaced them with easily understood explanations. Technical details have been kept to the barest minimum, and no special knowledge or educational level is assumed. The result is an accurate, yet easily understood, presentation of the subject matter of an advanced investment course.

This book is published at a propitious time. The recent bear market and poor investment strategies have combined to inflict catastrophic losses on many investors. The sight of once lush portfolios drained of value has prompted many investors to leave the market. Many of these investors have blindly placed their remaining investable funds into what presumably are safe havens offering relatively unattractive yields and no appreciation possibility—and no escape from the steady erosion of inflation. If continued, this head-in-the-sand approach to investing will destroy the financial security and independence of millions of American families. To these families, and the financial advisers and investment managers they employ, this book provides the knowledge and direction needed to devise and implement a successful long-term investment strategy.

To increase the relevance of my message I have organized the book around questions and answers. Knowing the correct answers to these questions will significantly increase your effectiveness as a hands-on investor and as a fiduciary.

In spite of the fact that at the end of any day, week, month, or year not everyone can turn in above-average investment results, I fervently believe there is a small number of professional and skilled amateur investors who can consistently deliver above-average investment results. It is *not easy* to provide such returns; it is *not easy* to find people who can. For many people, there is a wonderful easy-to-implement alternative strategy.

The following chapters focus on investing in stocks. This does not mean that bonds and other investment vehicles are not important. The omission is due solely to time and page-count constraints.

> *Part One: Getting Started—Your Tool Kit* covers what you need to know to be a successful investor; contrasts noise with information; and explains the notion of an efficient market.
>
> *Part Two: Avoiding Torpedoes* examines earnings; explains the "torpedo effect"; and shows its relationship to the price/earnings and size effects.
>
> *Part Three: Landmark Insights* explains the everyday importance of work by Nobel laureates and other distinguished academics.
>
> *Part Four: Dissecting Returns* shows how to discern luck from skill; contrasts the returns earned by indexes versus the returns earned by investors; and examines the risk-reward trade-offs for market-timing strategies.
>
> *Part Five: Putting the Pieces Together* looks at the risk of low-risk investments; addresses the active versus passive debate; summarizes my views on how "to win the active game"; and concludes with a retrospective look at the lessons learned from the Long-Term Capital Management debacle.

I welcome your comments, criticisms, and inquiries. I shall make every effort to reply. Correspondence or e-mails should be addressed to:

Robert L. Hagin
President
Hagin Investment Management and Research, Inc.
9 Tunbridge Circle, Suite 200
Haverford, PA 19041–1031
Robert.Hagin@HaginGroup.com

Enjoy the journey.

CHAPTER 2

What You Need to Know

Question 2.1. *Imagine you are a portfolio manager who buys and sells stocks over time in your quest for above-average investment returns. Also, imagine that you have a system at your disposal that can provide you with any up-to-the-minute data on the economy, your portfolio, or individual securities. (Given today's technology and the myriad sources for historical and up-to-the-minute financial data, this is not a hypothetical question.)*

    a. Make a list of the data items that you would like to have to guide your quest for above-average investment returns.

    b. Note on your list, as precisely as possible, how you intend to use the data once it is received.

As you answer these questions there are two important caveats. First, the data you request cannot include peeks into the future. Asking, for example, for all of the stocks that will appreciate by more than 20 percent over the next 12 months is not a legitimate request. Second, your "would like to have" list cannot include inside information. Given the vigilance of today's regulators, if you attempt to procure and use information that is not in the public domain it is not likely you will be around long enough to finish this book.

    Question 2.1—"what you need to know and why you need to know it" as well as the equally important corollary "what you do not need to know and why you do not need to know it"—cuts to the heart of the puzzle faced by all investors. The answers to this fascinating question will unfold in the chapters that lie ahead. I can promise that when you reach the last page you will be armed with keen understanding of "what you need to know" and "what you do not need to know" to make better investment decisions.

Question 2.2.   What is your biggest problem when making invest-ment decisions?
   a. Not enough information.
   b. Not receiving information fast enough.
   c. Too much irrelevant information.
   d. All of the above.
   e. None of the above.

There is a huge paradox in the way most people approach in-vesting. If you are a typical investor, even though you rank financial success and security among your most sought-after goals, you pur-sue this goal with a mixture of guesswork and wishful thinking. You routinely watch your favorite news channel and listen to your fa-vorite radio station for market updates. Paradoxically, however, it is most likely that you are not up-to-date on the *knowledge* that you need to reach your financial goals. Similarly, if you are a typical fiduciary, you are bombarded by a barrage of usually conflicting in-formation about how best to fulfill your responsibilities to the bene-ficiaries you serve.

In an insightful article written at the dawn of the information age (1967) Russell Ackoff[1] (at the time a colleague of mine at the Wharton School of the University of Pennsylvania) posited that the universal problem facing all decision makers—in disparate fields from weather forecasting, to medicine and, especially, in-vesting—is that we all suffer from an "overabundance of irrele-vant information." Ackoff coined the term "management misinformation systems" to describe information systems that are designed to provide decision makers with more information, de-livered faster, and that fail to take into account how the informa-tion will be used. Answers "a" and "b" to Question 2.2 are incorrect because they each describe elements of a "management misinformation system." The correct answer is "c"—you have too much irrelevant information.

My favorite description of a management misinformation sys-tem was provided by Norman, one of my Wharton students in the late 1960s. Norman had a weekend job in the data-processing de-partment of a large, well-known Philadelphia company. Each week-end his task was to run, print, and bind a report that was described to him as the "backbone" of a key division.

This was the era when data-processing output was printed on wide sheets of continuous paper with spindle holes running along both sides of each page (which kept the paper from jamming in the high-speed printers of the time). Dutifully each week Norman would replace the old pages with the new and put the updated books on a cart for delivery first thing Monday morning.

One Thursday evening Norman received an emergency call at his home. The caller, with terror in his voice, explained to Norman that they had lost the file that produced the report. They could reconstruct the file but it would take everyone working around the clock from Thursday evening until Monday morning.

At work Norman found catered meals (much better, he said, than the typical grad-student fare). The company had even borrowed cots, blankets, and pillows from the local armory. After considerable work the file was reconstructed and ready for distribution as usual on Monday morning.

Having studied "management misinformation systems," Norman asked his supervisor where the freshly bound books of up-to-date printouts went. The supervisor's response, showing little patience with the probing of a young graduate student, was, "They go to the cart."

Working virtually alone in the firm's basement each weekend, Norman had an idea. After all, he told me, he already had a job lined up when he finished his MBA.

Norman put a note inside one of the reports. It said something to the effect that he worked in the basement each weekend and if the reader would send him a note in reply he would be happy to buy him or her lunch at Arthur's—at the time an excellent restaurant near the company's offices. To Norman's dismay, no one called. And, sure enough, when the books came back to be purged of the old pages and filled with the new, his note was still there—apparently undiscovered.

As Norman neared graduation he became more bold. Fearing he might end up treating a small army to lunch, he repeatedly put several notes in each of a dozen or so books. No one ever responded; all of his notes appeared to have been undiscovered when the old books were returned. The report that the data processing minions believed was the backbone of the division apparently was never opened—a real management misinformation system.

Reflecting on the investment-management business, there is no doubt that the biggest problem that those of us who are individual and professional investors face is that we are inundated by an over-abundance of irrelevant information. It is as if hundreds of thousands of Normans toil in a basement somewhere producing mounds of data that some techie decided we needed. It is too bad someone did not ask how on earth we might use all this stuff.

CHAPTER 3

Information or Noise?

Question 3.1. Decision theorists make important distinctions in terms of meaning among knowledge, news, information, data, and noise. Which of the following statements are correct?

    a. Facts are descriptive measures of something that has occurred.

    b. Data are descriptive measures of something that has occurred.

    c. News is new data or new facts.

    d. Knowledge is required to translate facts, news, or data into useful, value-added information.

    e. Information results from processing facts, news, or data.

    f. Information can be used to make more accurate decisions.

    g. Noise is data, or news, that cannot be processed into useful information.

    h. All of the above.

The word "information" is used in a variety of misleading and confusing ways. To avoid this confusion, within the pages of this book I shall adhere to the narrow definition preferred by decision theorists.[1]

Following this convention, it is useful to think of "facts," "data," and "news" as the raw materials from which "information" is derived. There are billions of things going on around us every minute of every day. Data describing almost any of these events can be sensed, measured, recorded, and transmitted almost instantaneously to anyone anywhere on the globe. Within the realm of global financial markets there are transaction data describing changing prices of a myriad of securities, currencies, and commodities traded on exchanges around the world. Given our society's proclivity to count and measure virtually everything, various agencies produce countless statistics that seek to measure the pace of every conceivable aspect of economic activity. Prices of securities and measures of the state of the economy, such as the various forms of the consumer price index, are "data." They are not, by any stretch of one's imagination, "information."

Knowledge is required to translate data or news into information that can be used to make valued-added decisions. Information—by the definition used here—is always "useful."[2]

You receive the news that there is a 70 percent chance that it will snow three inches tomorrow. You may know from your experience that day-ahead weather forecasts are dreadfully unreliable. Guided by this "knowledge," you conclude that there is a 50–50 chance that it will snow six inches. Using this "information," you decide to drive your wife's four-wheel-drive car to work.

Someone gives you the news that yesterday the Dow Jones Industrial Average (DJIA) was up 95 points. As you will discover when we explain the investor implications of the random walk model, unless you have some remarkable gift of knowledge that can translate this news into information that will weigh meaningfully on a coming decision, this update on the DJIA is "noise."

Noise arrives in two ways. First, and most often, we do not know how to filter, and then translate, the mountains of "news" that bombard us each day into "information" that is used to make value-added investment decisions. Second, if the underlying data are spurious, no amount of knowledge can transform bad data into a value-added decision. In both cases it is just noise.

The late Fischer Black, a highly acclaimed academic and investment practitioner who is best known for his pioneering work on option-pricing theory (and the discovery of the Black-Scholes option pricing model), had a knack for putting forth stimulating ideas. One such idea was his presidential address before the American Finance Association in 1985 entitled simply, "Noise."[3]

In this landmark paper Black makes the important distinction between "noise" and "information." He labels persons who trade securities on the basis of a bewildering array of elements that, in fact, are not likely to be precursors of future prices, "noise" traders.

In such a world, Black asserts, "one trader's beliefs are as good as any other trader's beliefs."[4] That is, they are all useless.

Richard Bernstein, chief U.S. strategist and chief quantitative strategist at Merrill Lynch, courageously entitled his 2002 book *Navigate the Noise: Investing in the New Age of Media and Hype.* In this wonderful book Bernstein sets forth his view that much of the palaver to which we are subjected is designed to urge us to act quickly and frequently. In Bernstein's words, "If you have invested intelligently, today's news will have little impact on [your] retirement account or portfolio performance."[5]

Returning to Question 3.1, the correct answer is "h"—all of the above. It is correct that facts are descriptive measures of something that has occurred; data are descriptive measures of something that has occurred; news is new data or new facts; knowledge is required to translate facts, news, or data into useful, value-added information; information results from processing facts, news, or data; information can be used to make more accurate decisions; and noise is data, or news, that cannot be processed into useful information.

In this context I remember Herb Simon telling me that he never read newspapers or listened to radio or television news programs. This truly remarkable man made significant contributions to such diverse fields as psychology, information sciences, applied mathematical statistics, operations analysis, and economics. In 1978 he was awarded the Nobel prize for his pioneering research into the decision-making process within economic organizations. He accomplished all of this, I have always remembered, without reading newspapers or listening to radio or television news programs—or possibly because he was *not* distracted by newspaper, radio, and television news.

Similarly, Richard Bernstein, in his capacity as the chief U.S. strategist at Merrill Lynch, has revealed: "People are often surprised to hear that I do not regularly read certain daily financial newspapers. They are shocked that I do not want to keep up with what is going on in the markets [but I believe] . . . the more you attempt to keep up and be aware of everything that is going on, the more susceptible you are to trading on noise."[6]

My goal in the following pages is to provide you with surprising insights into how financial markets work. This "what you need to know and why you need to know it" and "what you do not need to know and why you do not need to know it" approach will teach you how to earn above-average investment returns.

The first step: When you make any decision, train yourself to ask: "Can I articulate how these facts or these news items relate to the decision at hand?" If you cannot, they are *noise*.

CHAPTER 4

Intuition

As you answer successive questions throughout this book you will have a strong tendency to think "something is up"—especially if you were burned on a recent question. You will benefit most from these questions if you set aside your suspicions and approach each question as something new.

Question 4.1.   Suppose someone offers you a bet. If two or more people out of the next 25 people that you meet have the same birthday (month and day) you forfeit your wager. If two or more of the next 25 people you meet do not have the same birthday you are paid double your wager. (Tip: If you believe there is at least a 51 percent chance that two of the next 25 people you meet will not have the same birthday, you should accept the bet.) Will you accept a bet whereby you forfeit your wager if any two (or more) of the next 25 people you meet have the same birthday?
   a. Yes.
   b. No.

Most people who are offered this bet reason that, excluding leap year, there are 365 possible birthdays and there could be at most only 25 birthdays for 25 randomly selected people. You might even calculate that 25 is only 6.8 percent of 365. Intuitively, it seems very unlikely that any two of the next 25 people you meet will have been born on the same day of the year. Hence, if you are like most people, you will accept a bet that will double your money if two people out of the next 25 people you meet do not have the same birthday.

Question 4.2. *Will you accept a bet whereby you forfeit your wager if any two (or more) of the next 50 people you meet have the same birthday?*
   a. Yes.
   b. No.

Of the next 100 people?
   a. Yes.
   b. No.

Of the next 180 people?
   a. Yes.
   b. No.

If you are like most people you will accept this wager until the number of people reaches 180—which most people perceive as the point at which there is close to a 50–50 likelihood (i.e., 180 out of 365) that two (or more) of the next 180 people you meet will have the same birthday.

The correct answer for all of the questions is "b"—No, you should not take any of the bets! Even with only 25 randomly selected people it is more likely than not that two of them will have the same birthday. If you are typical of most people, even though you have been told that there is better than a 50–50 chance that two (or more) out of 25 randomly selected people are more likely than not to have the same birthday, you are more comfortable trusting your intuition and find it almost impossible to refuse the wager.

The birthday wager can be explained by noting that each person you meet has a *progressively better chance* of having a matching birthday. Working backward, when the 25th person is added, that person's birthday can match the birthday of any of the 24 people who preceded her. When the 24th person is added, that person's birthday can match the birthday of any of the 23 people who preceded him. Thus, instead of each of the last two people having only one chance to have a matching birthday, when persons numbered 25 and 24 are added they (together) have 47 (24 plus 23) chances to match someone else's birthday. In fact, with as few as 23 people there is a better than 50–50 chance that two people will have matching birthdays. With 50 people there is a 97 percent chance that two people will have the same birthday. Unintuitive, but true! (See Table 4.1.)

TABLE 4.1 Likelihood of Matching Birthdays for Different Numbers of People

Number of People	10	20	22	23	25	30	40	50
Likelihood of two (or more) matching birthdays	12%	41%	48%	51%	59%	71%	89%	97%

Later you will see that examples of poor intuition are not limited to the birthday wager. You will find that much of the information in this book is contrary to your intuition, age-old tenets of Wall Street, or both. You will discover that the key to becoming a successful investor is to set aside what you "know" about investing and take an objective look at what is "known" about investing. I begin with a look at the laws of chance that underlie much of our intuition about gambling and also investing.

CHAPTER 5

Random Occurrences

Peter Bernstein in his outstanding book *Against the Gods: The Remarkable Story of Risk* asks:

> What is it that distinguishes the thousands of years of history from what we think of as modern times? . . . the revolutionary idea that defines the boundary between modern times and the past is the mastery of risk; the notion that the future is more than a whim of the gods and that men and women are not passive before nature. Until human beings discovered a way across that boundary, the future was a mirror of the past or the murky domain of oracles and soothsayers who held a monopoly over knowledge of anticipated events.[1]

Bernstein's book tells the story of:

> a group of thinkers whose remarkable vision revealed how to put the future at the service of the present. By showing the world how to understand risk, measure it, and weigh its consequences, they converted risk-taking into one of the prime catalysts that drives modern Western society. . . . The transformation in attitudes toward risk management unleashed by their achievements has channeled the *human passion for games and wagering* [emphasis added] into economic growth, improved quality of life, and technological progress.[2]

An essential step toward successful investing is understanding the differences between *random* and *nonrandom* occurrences. These differences are best explained by examining games of chance.

*Question 5.1.[3]   I have just tossed a coin six consecutive times
and recorded the outcome using H for heads and T for tails. I
have also made up two six-letter combinations of Hs and Ts. The
three six-letter sequences of Hs and Ts—one real and two made
up—are:*
   a. HHHHTT.
   b. HTHTTH.
   c. TTTTTT.
*Assume that you have agreed to the following wager: If you can dis-
cern which sequence of Hs and Ts is the record of my actual coin
tosses, I will pay you $20. If you select one of my made-up se-
quences, you must pay me $10. What is your choice?*

Before learning which of the sequences is the real sequence you
may not be surprised to know that answer "b" is the overwhelm-
ing favorite of people who are asked this question. Their reason:
"b" *looks like a real sequence.* Let's examine the popular answer
by using coin tosses to review the concept of randomness, or statistical independence.

Suppose you have bet $1.00 on heads on a single flip of a
coin. This is an even-money bet; heads and tails are equally likely.
About half the time you will win $1.00; half the time you will
lose $1.00. Now, suppose you have tossed two heads in a row.
What are your odds of tossing heads on the next bet? Are they
still 50–50?

Intuitively, gamblers know that a run of three heads in a row
does not occur very often. This is true. Similarly, roulette players
know that a run of three "blacks" in a row does not occur very often. But do these runs alter the odds of winning the *next* coin toss or
the *next* spin of the roulette wheel? How might a gambler use this
knowledge for the next bet? The proper use of knowledge of this
kind—and, more important, how similar decisions arise in selecting
investments—comes from understanding what is, and is not, predictable about random events.

A random (or a statistically independent) event is an occurrence
whose outcome cannot be predicted from preceding events. Examples of random events are the result of a coin toss and the spin of a
roulette wheel. For such events, the outcome of any single trial is determined by chance and is impossible to predict. For example, if you

toss a fair coin it is impossible to know in advance whether that particular coin will fall heads or tails.

Let's return to the question of a gambler's odds after observing a run (a sequence of one kind of outcome). Gamblers often devise betting schemes based on "reversals" or "runs." After observing a sequence of one result—say, three consecutive coin tosses that land heads or three consecutive spins of a roulette wheel that land on black—they adopt a particular betting strategy. Some gamblers infer that it is not a good bet to expect still another head after two heads have been tossed. After all, they reason, everyone knows three heads in a row is a relatively rare occurrence. Thus, they reason, heads are "used up." Conversely, other gamblers reason that the game is "running hot" and that heads has a better than normal chance on the next toss. Assuming that the coin or roulette wheel is fair and unbiased, *both gambling systems are useless!*

The futility of both "it is time to reverse" and "it is running hot" betting systems will become clear if you analyze the game of coin tossing. Each toss has two possible outcomes: heads or tails. When heads occurs, tails cannot, and vice versa. The probability, or likelihood, that a fair coin will fall heads is one-half. This means that, *in the long run*, you expect half of the outcomes to be heads.

You need to remember two points:

1. It is impossible to predict which outcome will occur on any particular toss.
2. Over many repetitions, about half of the outcomes will be heads and half tails.

Consider the four possible results of two successive coin tosses. These are indicated by:

$$HH, HT, TH, TT$$

Here, HH means that the coin landed on heads on the first toss and also landed on heads on the second toss; HT means a heads followed by a tails; and so on. No other combinations of heads and tails are possible from two successive tosses. This situation is depicted in Figure 5.1.

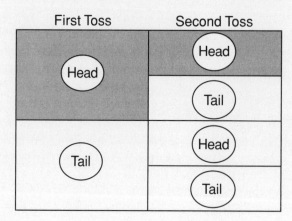

FIGURE 5.1   Four Possible Results from Tossing a Coin Twice

The occurrence of two heads in a row is shown in the shaded area. Tossing heads twice is one of the four possible outcomes. Now assume that, having just tossed two heads, your friend says, "I'll bet you can't toss another head." What are your chances?

In games of chance such as roulette, dice, or coin tossing the consecutive plays are called *independent* events. The roulette wheels, dice, or coins do not have memories. Having just been tossed two times, the coin does not "remember" which of the four possible sequences shown in Figure 5.1 has taken place. Whatever has gone on before cannot influence the coin. There remains a 50 percent chance that the next toss will be heads and a 50 percent chance that it will be tails. After two heads in a row the probability a coin will land heads is no greater or less than it was on the preceding tosses—it's still an even bet. Knowing what has happened in the past is *useless* in predicting the *next event*.

Most gamblers have difficulty reconciling the fact that what has happened in the past is useless with the other fact that everyone knows three heads in a row is an unlikely occurrence. To resolve this point of confusion, let us expand Figure 5.1 (which shows the four possible outcomes from two coin tosses) to show in Figure 5.2 the eight possible outcomes from three coin tosses. Notice that if each of the four possible outcomes that are shown in Figure 5.1 can, in turn, be followed by either a head or a tail, thus there are eight possible outcomes from tossing a coin three times.

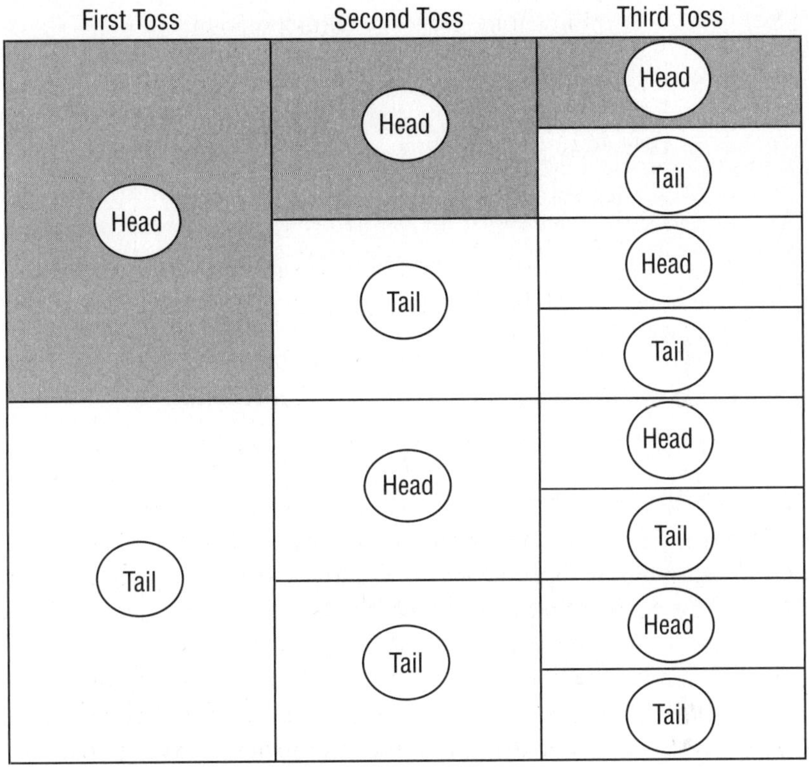

First Toss	Second Toss	Third Toss

FIGURE 5.2 Eight Possible Results from Tosssing a Coin Three Times

Now we can separate the *two questions* that together produce what is known as the "gambler's fallacy." First, we can ask what is the probability of tossing three heads in a row. Three heads in a row is one of eight equally likely possibilities. Therefore, the probability of three heads is one in eight or 12.5 percent. A probability of one in eight means that if you repeat a *large number* of three-coin-toss events, you expect to have an all-heads sequence about one-eighth of the time.

A second and quite different question is: What is the chance of tossing a head after two heads have *already* been tossed? The difference between these two questions is subtle and has eluded some gamblers for years. The chance of tossing a head after having just tossed two heads, or *any* number of heads, with a fair coin, is unaltered—tossing a head is still a 50–50 bet. Each successive coin toss is statistically independent of every toss that has gone before. As

Figure 5.2 indicates, even though two heads have *already* been tossed, the fact is that the two possible outcomes are equally likely on the *next* toss. It is true that tossing three heads in a row is unusual (one in eight). However, tossing a third head after two heads have already been tossed is not (one in two).

Remember: If events are random, as in coin tossing or roulette, *historical information cannot be used to predict a subsequent event.* In later chapters we will raise, and answer, the question: Are day-to-day stock price changes random events? If they are, patterns of historical price changes cannot be used to predict the magnitude or direction of subsequent price movements.

In addition to randomness, or statistical independence, two important concepts that investors need to understand are *expected values* and *variance.* Essentially, these concepts boil down to knowing what to expect and knowing the risk of not getting what you expect. Thus, risk can be defined as unpredictability, or the extent to which results do not match expectations. This can be illustrated by extending our coin-tossing experiment to learn about risk and variance.

To illustrate risk, or variations from expectations, the results of many three-coin-toss events are tabulated in the tables that follow. (In all honesty, I did not toss coins thousands of times but rather simulated the experiment on a computer.) As explained earlier, we expect each of the eight possible outcomes of a three-toss event to occur with equal likelihood (about one-eighth of the time).

The results of eight trials of our coin-tossing experiment are shown in Table 5.1. Notice that some of the possible outcomes did not occur at all! Also, notice that one outcome (TTT) occurred two times more often than we had expected. It should be emphasized that with only eight trials of the three-toss experiment such wide variations between expected and actual results are going to occur. In this case, the percent difference between the expected and actual results was as high as 200 percent.

Fortunately, statisticians understand the variability of such results. Probability theory tells us what to expect from chance events, *as well as the likely variations from these expectations.* It also tells us that the percent difference between what is expected and what actually happens tends to shrink the longer we play the game.

People who are unarmed with the knowledge that actual results

TABLE 5.1   Results of Three-Toss Sequences

Event	Expected Frequency	Actual Frequency	Percent Difference
HHH	1	1	0
HHT	1	0	−100
HTH	1	1	0
HTT	1	1	0
THH	1	0	−100
THT	1	2	+100
TTH	1	0	−100
TTT	1	3	+200
Totals	8	8	0

vary naturally from expected results see a different phenomenon in Table 5.1. They might notice, for example, that the TTT sequence has occurred three times. Does this mean that Ts are "running hot"? Or does it mean that Ts have been "used up"? Both notions are gamblers' fallacies.

To verify the point that the longer you play the game the closer your expected and actual outcomes will be, I increased the number of three-toss trials. Results of 80 separate three-toss events are recorded in Table 5.2. The "percent difference" column again is the difference between what was expected and what actually occurred.

The laws of chance state that as the number of actual trials

TABLE 5.2   Results of 80 Three-Toss Sequences

Event	Expected Frequency	Actual Frequency	Percent Difference
HHH	10	9	−10
HHT	10	8	−20
HTH	10	14	+40
HTT	10	11	+10
THH	10	8	−20
THT	10	11	+10
TTH	10	8	−20
TTT	10	11	+10
Totals	80	80	0

TABLE 5.3   Results of 800 Three-Toss Sequences

Event	Expected Frequency	Actual Frequency	Percent Difference
HHH	100	99	−1
HHT	100	109	+9
HTH	100	107	+7
HTT	100	94	−6
THH	100	94	−6
THT	100	102	+2
TTH	100	99	−1
TTT	100	96	−4
Totals	800	800	0

increases the percent variations between the expected and actual frequencies will decrease. Indeed, the percent difference figures in Table 5.2 are much smaller than before—dropping from a high of +200 percent to a high of +40 percent. Now the "hottest" sequence, with 14 occurrences, is head-tail-head. But this "information" is totally *useless*. You can safely bet on only one thing in this game: The longer you play, the smaller the deviations between the expected and actual results will become. However, in no case can you use data on historical patterns of tosses to predict the result of the next toss.

Table 5.3 shows the results of 800 three-coin-toss trials; Table 5.4 shows the results of 80,000 three-toss trials. Notice that the percentage differences between the expected and actual results become progressively smaller as the number of trials increases. With 80,000 trials recorded in Table 5.4, the outcome of this game is predicted within *less than 1 percent*.

Coin tossing is obviously not big sport on Wall Street, or even in Las Vegas. But in order to prepare better for the former it is useful to consider what happens on the roulette tables of the latter. The American double-zero roulette table has 38 equal-size numbered compartments around its circumference. A little white ball is whirled around it and ultimately comes to rest. On a single-number bet one wagers on any of the 38 possible outcomes. The payoff for a

TABLE 5.4 Results of 80,000 Three-Toss Sequences

Event	Expected Frequency	Actual Frequency	Percent Difference
HHH	10,000	9,965	−0.4
HHT	10,000	10,020	+0.2
HTH	10,000	10,045	+0.5
HTT	10,000	10,026	+0.3
THH	10,000	9,995	−0.1
THT	10,000	10,041	+0.4
TTH	10,000	9,990	−0.1
TTT	10,000	9,918	−0.8
Totals	80,000	80,000	0.0

single-number roulette bet is 35 to 1. Thus, if you wager $1 on one of the 38 possible outcomes and win, the croupier will return your $1 bet, plus the $35 you won.[4]

Laws of chance, which are based on probability theory, can reveal *what to expect* from a long series of chance events *but not what will actually happen on the next event*. A bettor might place only one roulette bet and win on that particular turn of the wheel. In fact, probability theory tells us to expect this to happen once out of every 38 times.[5] It is also possible to win twice in a row. Winning two single-number roulette bets is expected once in every 1,444 (38 times 38) two-try sequences. Even though no one can predict individual events, the more you play *the closer the total result will approach what is expected.*

Unlike the immutable law of gravity, which accurately predicts each outcome, the laws of chance cannot predict the outcome of any *single* event. This does not, however, diminish their usefulness. Probability theory and statistical inference are the *sine qua non* of scientific inquiry. These tools, based on the laws of chance, allow scientists to specify quite precisely when groups of events are *not* happening in accordance with chance expectations.

You may be asking yourself: What do coin tossing and roulette have to do with investing? Simply stated, understanding the difference between chance occurrences and predictable events will help you understand, despite your intuition, important research results described in the following chapters. For example, how would stock prices move if the sequence of day-to-day price changes were completely independent of preceding price changes?

To find patterns in roulette-wheel performance, one first assumes that the wheel's outcomes will be purely random and then compares the actual performance with this benchmark. Similarly, in the coin-tossing example we can expect some percent difference between the anticipated and observed results. Hypothesizing that stock-price changes occur randomly enables them to be studied for deviations from random behavior. Then, by means of the techniques of statistical inference, any discrepancies can be classified as either *statistically significant* or *chance* fluctuations. This approach permits the researcher to isolate any predictable patterns that might be useful for investment strategies.

Having armed you with an understanding of statistical independence, expected values, and variance, I can now return to Question 5.1, in which you were asked to select the real coin-toss sequence from the two made-up sequences. Your choices were:

  a. HHHHTT.
  b. HTHTTH.
  c. TTTTTT.

When people are asked to discern the real sequence from the two made-up sequences, the hands-down favorite for the real sequence is "b"—HTHTTH. In truth, however, each sequence is just as likely to occur as any other. Six consecutive tosses will land in one of 64 *equally likely sequences.*[6] The popular answer has everything to do with behavioral economics—people's perception of how real coin-toss sequences should look—and absolutely nothing to do with statistical probability.

CHAPTER 6

Law of Small Numbers

Having learned the probabilities associated with certain sequences of coin tosses, I offer some particularly important questions about the likelihood of certain clustered outcomes.

Caution: Even if you believe you have answered enough coin-tossing questions, do not skip these questions.

Question 6.1.[1] Jack and Jill have played a coin-tossing game each day for 1,000 consecutive days spanning most of the past three years. Jack always bet heads; Jill always bet tails. It was a fair coin and Jack and Jill were equally likely to win.

Jack was ahead on any given day if the tally of the number of heads exceeded the number of tails. Jill was ahead on any given day if the tally of the number of tails exceeded the number of heads.

Which of the following is the most likely description of their game?

a. Over time the lead changed frequently between Jack and Jill as their winning percentages seesawed back and forth between 48 and 52 percent.

b. One of the players moved ahead quickly—and stayed ahead—for more than 96 percent of the tosses.

As discussed earlier, on any toss of a fair coin the likelihood of the coin's landing heads versus tails is exactly 50–50. Unequivocally, the more tosses the more the percent deviation from the expectation shrinks.

Yet even in a perfectly random game such as coin tossing winners and losers emerge. Moreover, once the winners are ahead they are unlikely to relinquish their winning positions. Talk about counterintuitive! The correct answer to Question 6.1 is "b"—one of the players moved ahead quickly—and stayed ahead—for more than 96 percent of the tosses. The lesson to be learned from this example is that even though one player appears to have superior skill it is an illusion. You have been fooled into thinking there is a pattern in a sequence of undeniably chance outcomes.

Question 6.2.[2] *You and a friend toss a coin once a day. You always bet on heads; your friend always bets on tails. After about two months you and your friend both have a better-than-even chance of winning how many tosses in a row?*
  a. One.
  b. Two.
  c. Three.
  d. Four.
  e. Five.

Question 6.3. *Anyone who watches basketball knows that players have "hot" and "cold" streaks. That is, after making a couple of shots, hot players get in a groove and are more likely to score successive points. Conversely, players who miss several shots are said to be "cold" and are less likely to score on successive shots.*
  a. True.
  b. False.

The correct answer to Question 6.2 is "e"—after 60 coin-tossing games, two players each have a better-than-even chance of winning five tosses in a row.

Turning to the basketball question, a study by Gilovich, Vallone, and Tversky found that 91 percent of the knowledgeable basketball fans who were interviewed thought that a player has a "better chance of making a shot after having just made the previous two or three shots than after having just missed the previous two or three shots."[3] (Given that the fans who were interviewed were from Boston and Philadelphia, it is easy to understand that the word "fan" is derived from the word "fanatic.")

Contrary to what these fans believe—and the players whose shooting records were analyzed believe—the data show that basketball players are no more likely to make a shot after making their last one, two, or three shots than after missing their last one, two, or three shots. Perhaps hot streaks are perfectly compensated for by the tendency of "hot" players to attempt more difficult shots or to be more closely guarded.

Even though the relevant statistical tests indicate that there are no hot or cold streaks, fans simply refuse to believe the analysis. Siding with the fans, the analysis did not take into account the difficulty of the shot and the amount of defensive pressure.

One segment of basketball where shot difficulty and the amount of defensive pressure are not factors (particularly if you segregate home and away games) is free throws. Gilovich, Vallone, and Tversky's analysis of two seasons of free-throw statistics by the Boston Celtics showed that players did not run hot or cold. On average, Boston Celtics players made 75 percent of their second free throws after making their first and 75 percent after missing their first.

Hence, the correct answer to Question 6.3 is "b"—false. There is no evidence that basketball players have hot or cold streaks when shooting free throws.

The lesson here is that we expect random sequences—such as those produced by coin tosses—to alternate between heads and tails; however, in truth, truly random sequences have far more repetitions of one outcome than our intuition leads us to expect. Streaks of four, five, or six heads or tails in a row clash with our expectations for alternating heads then tails then heads sequences. Yet in a series of only 20 coin tosses there is a 50–50 chance of getting four heads in a row, a 25 percent chance of five in a row, and a 10 percent chance of a streak of six.[4]

I should emphasize that this research in no way implies that whether a basketball shot goes in the hoop is a random phenomenon. Whether a high or low percentage of a player's shots go in the hoop is a function of the player's offensive skill and the defensive skill of the players on the other team.

What the research here does show is that whether a basketball shot goes in the hoop or does not go in the hoop cannot be derived from studying the in-the-hoop or the not-in-the-hoop sequences in the player's previous shots.

Question 6.4.[5] *I show you and a large group of diehard basketball fans the following sequence:*

OXXXOXXXOXXOOOXOOXXOO

You and the fans are told the Xs stand for shots made and the Os stand for the shots missed in an actual National Basketball Association game.

What percentage of the fans believe there are hot streaks in the data?

Do you believe there are hot streaks in the sequence?

Most basketball fans see hot streaks in the sequence. In Gilovich, Vallone, and Tversky's study using this sequence 61 percent of the fans saw hot streaks. Frankly, I would have guessed a much higher percentage. After all, in the first eight symbols there are six Xs and only two Os. If Alan Iverson of the Philadelphia 76ers made six of his first eight shots, the announcer would certainly say something like "Alan is on fire in the opening minutes." The rub is, as you may have guessed, that the Gilovich, Vallone, and Tversky sequence was constructed to meet the precise definition of random.

Behavioral economists call our tendency to see patterns where none exist a "clustering illusion." Thomas Gilovich emphasizes that the importance of this insight "lies in the inescapable conclusion that our difficulty in accurately recognizing random arrangements of events can lead us to believe things that are not true and to believe something is systematic, ordered, and 'real' when it is really random, chaotic, and illusory."[6]

Again quoting Gilovich, "We are predisposed to see order, pattern, and meaning in the world; we find randomness, chaos, and meaninglessness unsatisfying. Human nature abhors a lack of predictability and the absence of meaning."[7]

Question 6.5.[8]   *One of the following sequences is an actual sequence that was derived from spinning the needle on the (unbiased) wheel shown in Figure 6.1. (R stands for red and G stands for green.) The two other sequences are made up. Notice that the likelihood the needle will stop on green is four out of six (66.7 percent); the likelihood the needle will stop on red is two out of six (33.3 percent).*

Which of the following series has the highest probability of being the real sequence?

    a. RGRRR.

    b. GRGRRR.

    c. GRRRRR.

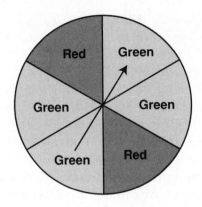

FIGURE 6.1 Random-Sequence Generator

Question 6.6.   Note that the R G R R R sequence in choice "a" is imbedded in the G R G R R R sequence in choice "b." Does this change your answer?
  a. Yes.
  b. No.

When a broad cross section of people is asked Question 6.5, roughly 65 percent select answer "b"—G R G R R R. Furthermore, the propensity for people to select "b" does not change markedly when it is pointed out that sequence "a" is embedded in sequence "b."

To find the correct answers think about what happens as we move from five spins of the needle to six spins of the needle. (The number of spins is especially important when you note that sequence "a" is embedded in sequence "b.")

When you examined the relative likelihood of certain coin-tossing sequences you saw that the probability of tossing consecutive heads is equal to the probability of tossing a head on one toss ($\frac{1}{2}$) times the probability of tossing a head on the next toss ($\frac{1}{2}$) and so forth for each successive toss. Thus, whatever the probability that the spinner will land on R G R R R on five consecutive spins, that probability is reduced to two-thirds if we bet that the next spin will land on G and to one-third if you bet that the next spin will land on R.

As you saw in the coin-tossing illustration, the reason people give for selecting sequence "b" as the one most likely to be real is that is appears more balanced or more typical. The correct answer to Question 6.1, however, is "a"—R G R R R. Question 6.2 essentially points out that sequence "a"—which has a much higher likelihood of occurring by chance—is embedded in sequence "b."

This illusion is another example of the "law of small numbers." Thus, although the calculus of probability rests firmly on the "law of large numbers," most people's intuition leads them to expect normal results in even very brief sequences.

There are important reasons why we, and our ancestors, have learned in some cases that once is enough. I can say with confidence that none of our ancestors dined on hemlock. Seeing someone become ill and die after eating hemlock did not prompt our ancestors to run a blind comparison of 50 people who ate hemlock and 50 people who ate a placebo. Once was enough.

This said, remembering the tendency to see order where there is none will be invaluable as we examine how investors attribute order to sequences of stock price changes in cases where there is none.

CHAPTER 7

Average Is Average

The answers to the following two questions are among the easiest to answer and, at the same time, are among the most overlooked.

Question 7.1. At the end of a month, quarter, or year among the myriad securities that compose the market, what percentage (properly weighted by the market value of each security) will have returns that are above average and what percentage will have returns that are below average?[1]
   a. Half above and half below.
   b. Something other than half above and half below.

One of the most useful things for investors and fiduciaries to remember is "the average is the average." You should approach each investment decision knowing that—over whatever time interval you choose—half of the securities that compose the market (properly weighted by the market value of each security) will earn above-average returns, and half will earn below-average returns. Hence, the correct anwer is "a"—half above and half below.

Question 7.2. What is the overarching difference between the average return derived from a large number of professionally managed portfolios and the average return of an index of the securities that compose the professionally managed portfolios?
   a. The average return of professionally managed portfolios will be *above* the average return of an index of the securities that compose the professionally managed portfolios.
   b. The average return of professionally managed portfolios will be *almost the same as* the average return of an index of

the securities that compose the professionally managed portfolios.

c. The average return of professionally managed portfolios will be *below* the average return of an index of the securities that compose the professionally managed portfolios.

It is important to remember that when investors—amateur and professional—actively buy and sell the securities that make up their portfolios, they incur costs. They incur commission and market-impact costs each time they buy and sell securities. Professional managers charge fees. These costs push the average return of all actively managed portfolios, as a group, below that of the market averages. Hence, "c" is the correct choice. The average return of professionally managed portfolios will be well below the average return of an index of the securities that compose the professionally managed portfolios.

Going forward, it is important to differentiate between the average returns of various market indexes (such as the S&P 500) and the average returns that are derived from portfolios that actively buy and sell the securities that compose the index. The distinction is that there are fees associated with actively managed portfolios; there are no fees associated with market indexes.

The following questions, which you may find relatively easy to answer, are included here because so many people, particularly newscasters, behave "as if it isn't so."

Question 7.3.   On the evening news the announcer says: "There were no buyers in today's market as the Dow tumbled 240.16 points."

a. The announcer is right: If there are no buyers—as during the collapse of the dot-com bubble early in 2002—the Dow will tumble.

b. It always "takes two to tango"; prices are set when people trade, and when people trade there cannot be an imbalance between buyers and sellers.

Every few years I spend an afternoon visiting with friends on the floor of a major stock exchange. It is always a remarkable experience. There representatives of buyers and sellers—who at the moment are diametrically opposed to one another as to the wisdom of owning specific securities—meet and pay commissions to trade their securities at mutually agreed-upon prices.

It is useful to remember that *the investment industry is built on disagreement.* With equal access to the same material facts, sellers and buyers hire representatives to meet—electronically or in person—to trade securities. Sellers pay commissions for satisfaction of no longer owning the security; buyers pay commissions to fulfill their desire to own exactly the same security.

It is also useful to remember that we are not talking about a few people meeting under the buttonwood tree of old. On a typical day, the New York Stock Exchange processes trades for 1.6 billion shares. At the end of each transaction the buyers were satisfied with the prices they paid; the sellers were satisfied with the prices they received; and the intermediaries who handled the transactions were satisfied with their compensation for facilitating the trades.

Hence the correct answer to Question 7.3 is "b"—it always takes two to tango; prices are set when people trade, and when people trade there cannot be an imbalance between buyers and sellers.[2]

Question 7.4. What does it mean that stock prices are set "at the margin"?
   a. Margin traders set prices.
   b. Investors who own shares of the stock of a particular company but do not trade set prices.
   c. On a given day buyers and sellers who typically trade a relatively small number of shares—relative to the total number of outstanding shares—set prices.

It is useful to remember that on a given day buyers and sellers who typically trade a relatively small number of shares—relative to the total number of outstanding shares—set prices. Investors who own shares of the stock of a particular company but do not trade *do not* set prices. Thus, the answer to Question 7.4 is "c."

Question 7.5. Because "quants" (quantitatively oriented investors) typically agree among themselves as to the relative values in the market and traditional investors are more likely to agree among

themselves, markets frequently have quants on one side of trades and traditional investors on the other.
  a. Fact.
  b. Fiction.

Investors who believe that financial markets have evolved into "quants" versus "traditionalists" have forgotten the admonition that *the investment industry is built on disagreement.* There is ample disagreement as to the motivations to trade among quants and traditional investors alike. Therefore, the correct answer is "b"—it is a fiction to say that quants are on one side of trades and traditional investors are on the other.

Question 7.6.   Assume that at the beginning of last year you and 10,000 other investors each purchased one randomly selected stock from the S&P 500 index.[3] You and your shadow investors each held the stocks for one year.
  Which of the following statements are true?
  a. The average return earned by you and your 10,000 brethren will be very close to that of the S&P 500.
  b. The returns will vary around the mean return with some better and others worse than the average.
  c. The pattern of the returns around the mean will approximate a "fat-tailed" bell-shaped curve.
  d. All of the above.

Question 7.7.   How would the outcome change if, instead, you and the 10,000 other investors each randomly selected 25 stocks?
  a. The average return will be even closer to that of the S&P 500.
  b. The magnitude by which the winners won and the losers lost will be narrowed.
  c. The pattern of returns will be more clustered around the mean.
  d. All of the above.

Even though you and the 10,000 hypothetical investors selected your investments at random, some of you will perform better than others; some will perform worse than others. Barring a tie, one investor will outperform the others.

You hear much about so-and-so's "expert performance." The questions that you need to answer are: How much of the performance is attributable to luck and how much is attributable to astute investment selection? To answer these questions you need to know something about (1) what is considered average and (2) expected variations from average.

In Question 7.6 the average performance of the investors' selections will be close to that of the S&P 500 index. Also, the investors' returns will be distributed above and below the S&P 500's average return. The distribution of returns will appear as a fat-tailed bell-shaped curve, similar to Figure 7.1. Hence the correct answer is "d"—all of the above.

In Question 7.7, as the stocks per portfolio increase from 1 to 25, the average return will be even closer to that of the S&P 500; the spread between the winners and losers will narrow; and the return will cluster closer to the mean, as shown in Figure 7.1. Hence the correct answer to Question 7.7 is "d"—all of the above.

The results for the 25-stock investors—the same average performance but with less variation—do not reflect more accurate forecasts of the market. The investors in this case still could not, on

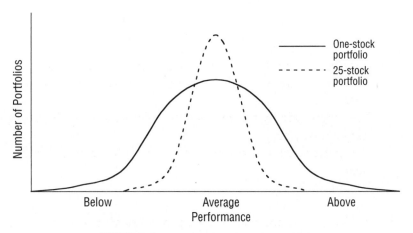

FIGURE 7.1 Randomly Selected Portfolios

average, beat the market. They were, however, able to avoid large negative variations through diversification.

Because the concept of a *standard deviation* plays an important role in modern finance, it is useful to understand the basics of this popular statistical measure. A standard deviation is a measure of variability around a mean. If it is assumed that the observations of a given characteristic, or value, cluster around the mean in a normal fashion, the computed standard deviation has a very convenient property: 68.0 percent of the values fall within plus or minus one standard deviation from the mean; 95.5 percent of the values fall within plus or minus two standard deviations from the mean; and 99.7 percent of the values fall within plus or minus three standard deviations from the mean.

Because 68.0 percent is very close to two-thirds (66.7 percent), a convenient rule of thumb is that the chances are two out of three that an expected value will fall within one standard deviation (plus or minus) of the mean. The key point to remember is that the smaller the standard deviation, the smaller the probability of a result that is far from the mean.

CHAPTER 8

Efficient Markets

Question 8.1. If financial markets are "efficient":
a. News is embedded[1] in prices so quickly that it becomes useless.
b. There is no differential advantage or disadvantage to trading with or without news.
c. Prices are always fair; they reflect all that is known at the instant of a trade.
d. All of the above.

If financial markets are truly efficient, they reflect the up-to-the-second composite judgment of millions of participants—in an environment characterized by many competing investors, each with similar objectives and each with equal access to the same material facts. In this context, "efficient" markets quickly digest new data on an economy, an industry, or the value of an enterprise and embed this data almost instantly into security prices. Thus, the answer to Question 8.1 is "d"—all of the above. This means that news is embedded in prices so quickly that it becomes useless; there is no differential advantage or disadvantage to trading with or without news; and prices are always fair and reflect all that is known at the instant of a trade.

Question 8.2. What features set the stage for an efficient market?
a. There are many active participants.
b. Participants have similar objectives.
c. Participants have equal access to the same material facts.
d. All of the above.

An efficient market is one in which many participants, each with similar investment objectives and each with equal access to the same material facts, actively compete. Global financial markets bring together millions of profit-motivated professional and private investors who continually search for attractive investment opportunities. Investors in these markets also have strikingly similar objectives. Each prefers a high rate of return to a low one, certainty to uncertainty, low risk to high risk. Finally, security law mandates that both parties to a transaction must have equal access to the same material facts. Thus, the correct answer to Question 8.2 is "d"—all of the above. All of the features listed set the stage for an efficient market.

As researchers over the years learned more and more about the behavior of prices in financial markets it became useful to split the notion of efficient markets into three progressively more rigorous forms. The weak form describes a market in which historical price data are efficiently digested and, therefore, are useless for predicting subsequent price changes. The semistrong form describes a market in which all publicly available information is fully reflected in prices and therefore all publicly available information is useless for predicting subsequent price changes. Finally, the strong form describes a market in which not even those with privileged inside information can use such information to obtain superior investment results.

Each of the three forms of the efficient market hypothesis provides a useful benchmark that allows researchers to determine how efficiently or inefficiently various types of information are embedded into security prices. This categorization is extremely important because, armed with knowledge gained from tests of each of the three forms of the efficient market hypothesis, investors can avoid analyzing useless, fully discounted information—the first step on the road to successful investing.

Before looking at the research into the three forms of the efficient market hypothesis, it will be useful to discuss the parallels between the weak and semistrong forms of efficient markets and the technical and fundamental approaches to security analysis.

Question 8.3. What is the difference between "technical" and "fundamental" investment analysis?
   a. Technical analysts use historical price (and volume) data to predict the direction and magnitude of price changes.

b. Technicians frequently chart historical price and volume data so that they can detect patterns that portend forthcoming price changes.
c. Fundamental analysts use data that are fundamental to a company's income statement and balance sheet to select investments that are expected to have better-than-average investment returns.
d. All of these descriptions are correct.

Market technicians believe that future movements of stock prices can be predicted from the diligent study of historical changes in stock prices and/or trading volume. Most technicians find it easier to see the patterns in the behavior of stock prices by charting the data and searching for patterns with such names as a "head and shoulders."

Fundamental investment analysts, in contrast, base their predictions of changes of stock prices on factors that are basic to a company and on the way a company's fundamentals are related to macroeconomic changes in the company's industry or the economy. A fundamental analyst might issue a purchase recommendation for a stock when the analyst deems the stock to be attractively priced because the company has consistently shown year-to-year earnings increases and is in an industry that the analyst believes will grow faster than the economy.

The answer to Question 8.3 on the difference between technical and fundamental investment analysis is "d"—all of these descriptions are correct. That is, technical analysts use historical price (and volume) data to predict the direction and magnitude of stock price changes; technicians frequently chart historical price and volume data so that they can detect patterns that they believe portend forthcoming price changes; and fundamental analysts use information that is fundamental to a company's income statement and balance sheet to select investments that they expect to have better-than-average investment returns.

Under the weak form of the efficient market hypothesis, we need to determine whether information derived from historical price and volume data can be used to predict either the magnitude or the direction of subsequent price changes. Thus, the weak form of the efficient market hypothesis is directly opposed to the basic premise of technical analysis. Similarly, the semistrong form of the efficient market hypothesis holds that there is no publicly available information, particularly forecasts developed from such data, that can be used for the accurate prediction of future prices. Thus, the semistrong form of the efficient market hypothesis is diametrically opposed to the concept of fundamental analysis.

One jab at believers in efficient markets is the story of a stockbroker who was walking a few steps behind an efficient-market disciple on Fifth Avenue in New York City on a busy Friday afternoon. The broker noticed that the true believer in efficient markets glanced to her feet, saw a $20 bill, and continued walking without breaking stride. The broker picked up the $20 bill and hurried to catch her.

The broker asks, "Why didn't you pick up the $20 bill?" Her reply: "It had to be an *illusion*. If it were real, someone else would have already picked it up."

Jokes aside, there are enormous implications for fiduciaries and investors if the preponderance of research supports either the weak form or the semistrong form of the efficient market hypothesis.

CHAPTER 9

Random Walk

Question 9.1. *What should you train yourself to do with the news of price changes (for both individual stocks and market indexes) that are reported on radio, television, and Internet sites throughout the day (and, of course, appear in your favorite newspaper on the following morning)?*

a. Buy individual stocks following large price declines.

b. Sell individual stocks following large price declines.

c. Buy individual stocks following large price increases.

d. Sell individual stocks following large price increases.

e. Both "a" and "d."

f. Both "b" and "c."

g. Nothing. Recent changes in stock prices are not a precursor of either the direction or the magnitude of forthcoming changes in those stock prices.

Historically known as the *random walk model,* the weak form of the efficient market hypothesis has received much attention. Early researchers described the random walk model with an analogy to a "drunkard's walk"—the pattern of whose steps cannot be forecast with any accuracy in either size or direction. I, along with numerous university researchers, investment practitioners, and students of the stock market, have devoted countless hours to searching for ways to use historical changes in prices to predict either the direction or the magnitude of subsequent price changes.

As if period-to-period price changes were coin tosses, the random walk model states that "any price change is independent of the sequence of previous price changes." Much of the confusion surrounding the random-walk model stems from overlooking the fact that, for each test of the model, the *intervals* over which prices change and the *market* (domestic stocks, financial futures, etc.) must be clearly specified. You can test, for example, the validity of the random walk model for day-to-day price changes, month-to-month price changes, or changes over any other interval. Over the years researchers have tested intervals that ranged from the shortest possible intervals (consecutive transactions shown on the ticker tape) to extremely long intervals of a year or more—and everything in the middle. Moreover, instead of reflecting fixed time periods, random walk intervals can be defined by the occurrence of particular events, such as a price reaching a new high, the formation of a certain pattern such as a head and shoulders, and so on.

It is important to remember that researchers cannot simply test the validity of the random walk model. Instead, researchers must ask, "Is the random walk hypothesis (or, if you prefer, the weak form of the efficient market hypothesis) valid within a specific market for a specific interval?" For example, is the relationship between day-to-day price changes on the New York Stock Exchange (NYSE) random? What about the week-to-week and month-to-month comparisons?

Also, it is important to remember that, even if the weak form of the efficient market hypothesis is true over most reasonable time intervals in the most popular markets, this does not deny the possibility that experts using other information can consistently achieve above-average returns. The random walk hypothesis simply states that investors cannot use information derived from historical price changes to predict the direction or magnitude of future price changes.

Tested against a long list of intervals, trigger events, and markets—with the exception of extremely short and extremely long intervals—there is persuasive evidence that the random walk model (a.k.a. the weak form of the efficient market theory) is a correct description of period-to-period changes in security prices.

Remarkably, the random walk model dates back to one of the first academic studies of speculative price behavior. In 1900 Louis Bachelier, a brilliant French mathematics student studying under the distinguished mathematician H. Poincaré, formulated and tested the random walk model of stock price behavior in his dissertation for the degree of doctor of mathematical sciences at the Sorbonne.

Bachelier's dissertation is an amazing document even today. Not only did he discover—over 100 years ago—something that is extremely important to investors, but his research contained other landmark contributions. For example, the equation Bachelier used to describe the random walk was identical to that developed by Albert Einstein, five years later, to describe Brownian motion.[1]

Bachelier's dissertation[3] bears on modern stock-market research in two significant ways. First, it provided an explicit statement of the random walk model. Second, Bachelier's tests of actual security prices corresponded closely to those predicted by the random walk model. In short, the prices he studied did not move in predictable trends, waves, or patterns. Thus, Bachelier showed, in 1900, that historical price data were useless for predicting future price changes. Either because Bachelier's work ran so counter to intuition or because it required an "Einstein" to understand it, his research findings fell into obscurity until they were rediscovered by Paul Samuelson and others at the Massachusetts Institute of Technology (MIT) in 1960.[2]

There is an important lesson to be learned from Bachelier's work. Even though a person with an intellect comparable to Einstein's could spend years studying the stock market and could develop a model that was to spark intellectual excitement 60 years later, there is no evidence that his research changed the investment behavior of his period.

With the benefit of 20/20 hindsight, a number of other studies performed early in this century raised doubts over the usefulness of historical prices in predicting price movements. The work of the Russian economist Eugene Slutsky[3] in 1927 is recognized as an independent rebirth of the random walk model. Slutsky, who was not aware of Bachelier's work, showed that randomly generated price changes resemble actual price movements and seem to exhibit cycles and other patterns. Unfortunately, 10 years passed before Slutsky's work was translated into English, and even in 1937 it did not spark the intellectual interest of either academicians or investment practitioners.

Although market technicians proliferated during the boom preceding the 1929 stock market crash, there were no rigorous attempts to test the validity of technical analysis during this period. Following the 1929 debacle, virtually all enthusiasm for investment advice evaporated. Memories of Black Tuesday (October 29, 1929); stock manipulation by investment pools; and suicides of suddenly impoverished investors persisted. Nor could the public forget the corruption exemplified by Richard Whitney, scion of the wealthy

Whitney family and former president of the New York Stock Exchange, who was jailed for misusing company funds.

Wall Street bore the stigma of these events for almost two decades, and both the general public and qualified researchers had little to do with the market. In fact, only two research studies that made material contributions to investment science were reported in the United States between 1930 and 1959.

In 1934, long before behavioral economists documented our proclivity to find patterns in meaningless data, Holbrook Working[4] of Stanford University demonstrated that artificially generated series of price changes form apparent trends and patterns. Working reported that investors could not distinguish between the real and the artificially generated series of prices. His studies, unfortunately, lacked both the mathematical rigor and empirical evidence needed to attract the attention of serious researchers.

In 1937 two distinguished researchers, Alfred Cowles and Herbert Jones[5] of the Cowles Commission (now Foundation) for Research in Economics, gave authoritative support to the case for technical analysis when they reported that stock prices indeed moved in predictable trends. As it happened, these findings were withdrawn in 1960 after an error in the analysis was discovered. For more than two decades, however, the widespread belief that Cowles had put the random walk theory to rest deterred would-be U.S. researchers from further examination of the subject. As a result, another 15 years passed until someone again questioned the presumption that stock prices move in discernible patterns.

While the seeds sown by early researchers lay dormant in the United States, Maurice Kendall[6] at the London School of Economics made significant advances in the study of the random walk model. In 1953 Kendall found, to his surprise, that stock prices behaved as if changes had been generated by a suitably designed roulette wheel. That is, each outcome was statistically independent of past history.

Using periods of 1, 2, 4, 8, and 16 weeks, Kendall reported that when price changes were observed at these intervals the random fluctuations from one price to the next were large enough to swamp any systematic patterns or trends that might have existed. He concluded that "there is no hope of being able to predict movements on the exchange for a week ahead without extraneous [that is, something besides price] information."[7]

In contrast to the widely quoted (but later shown to be erroneous) research by Cowles and Jones, Kendall's 1953 work was published in the rather obscure *Journal of the Royal Statistical Society* and received little attention. So, although there was scattered evidence challenging the practice, before 1959 no one seriously questioned the doctrine of technical stock-market analysis.

As we look at the dearth of financial research following World War II it is constructive to remember that the first computer— ENIAC (Electronic Numerical Integrator and Calculator), designed by J. Presper Eckert and John W. Mauchly at the Moore School of Electrical Engineering at the University of Pennsylvania—was not operable until 1945. It was not until 1946 that the blueprint for the full step to a true stored-program computer was provided by John von Neumann in his now-classic paper entitled "Preliminary Discussion of the Logical Design of an Electronic Computing Instrument." (Although there have subsequently been enormous technological improvements in computer hardware, the logical design is essentially the same as that outlined by von Neumann in his 1946 paper. Following ENIAC it took until April 1951 for the first commercially built computer—Remington Rand's UNIVAC I (Universal Automatic Computer)—to go into operation at the U.S. Bureau of the Census. It then took until 1954 before the first computer was installed in a commercial enterprise—a UNIVAC at General Electric's Appliance Park in Louisville, Kentucky.

Failing to anticipate the technological advances (from vacuum tubes to transistors to solid-state circuits) and software advances (from programming in machine language to higher-level programming languages), Remington Rand made its now-famous projection of the potential market for computers. Its estimate was 50. In this context it is easy to understand why using computers for the rigorous study of financial markets did not begin in earnest until 1959.

In 1959 a widely read paper by Harry Roberts[8] of the University of Chicago and another study by M. F. M. Osborne,[9] an astronomer at the U.S. Naval Research Laboratory in Washington, D.C., plus the discovery of Bachelier's 60-year-old dissertation by Professor Paul Samuelson and others at the Massachusetts Institute of Technology, kindled interest in using computers to study the random walk hypothesis.

After placing the earlier work of Holbrook Working and

Maurice Kendall in the context of the random walk model, Roberts showed that a series of randomly generated price changes would very closely resemble actual stock data. He was the first modern author to conclude that "probably all the classical patterns of technical analysis can be generated artificially by a suitable roulette wheel or random-number table."[10]

Osborne's paper developed the hypothesis that the subjective perception of profit is the same for a price change from $10 to $11 as one from $100 to $110. So that price changes such as these are treated alike one should study price changes in logarithmic form, which Osborne showed did conform to the random walk model. At long last the widely read papers by Roberts and Osborne planted the seed of the random walk controversy in the United States!

Research into the behavior of financial markets reached an important milestone as we entered the 1960s. In 1960 and 1961 Holbrook Working[11] and Sidney Alexander,[12] in turn, discovered independently that the process of averaging weekly or monthly stock prices causes period-to-period prices to appear to be correlated when, in fact, they are not correlated.

When Alfred Cowles realized that data composed of averages could produce his original results as a statistical artifact, he immediately withdrew his earlier findings.[13] This withdrawal was extremely important because in 1937 Cowles and Jones, both respected researchers, had provided weighty evidence in support of technical analysis. In the 1960 retraction Cowles concluded that there was no evidence that historical month-to-month price data could be used to predict the direction of price changes in subsequent months! Cowles' 1960 retraction, along with the ever increasing availability of computers, the introduction of higher-level programming languages, and the gathering of computer-readable price and return histories, provided the long-needed tools for detailed statistical analysis.

Even though one could conjure up an almost infinite number of so-called variable-time models of price behavior that rely on certain events—such as large price swings, specific chart patterns, and so on—all such schemes are based on the premise that the market repeats itself in patterns and that historical price changes can be used to predict the direction and magnitude of subsequent price changes. Directing their research at variable-time models, Sidney Alexander[14] at MIT and, independently, Hendrik Houthakker[15] at Harvard found no evidence to support the technical analysts' practice of using recent prices to forecast forthcoming price changes.

Even though the issue was almost unknown on Wall Street, by 1962 the academic debate on the validity of the random walk model had picked up momentum. Paul Cootner[16] at the Massachusetts Institute of Technology studied the random walk over 1-week and 14-week intervals. Underscoring the importance of specifying the time interval when talking about random walks, he found that over 1-week intervals price changes were random; over 14-week intervals they were not. Thus, by the early 1960s there was convincing evidence that information derived from recent price changes was worthless.

Further evidence came from Arnold Moore's 1962 doctoral dissertation[17] at the University of Chicago; Eugene Fama's 1965 doctoral dissertation,[18] also at the University of Chicago; and my own dissertation at the University of California at Los Angeles. Using a variety of different price histories, we found no evidence of trends in stock prices for any time interval we tested.

In 1966 Robert Levy's doctoral dissertation at the American University in Washington, D.C., was mistakenly described by *Fortune* magazine as a "decisive refutation of the random walk."[19] This obviously erroneous characterization overlooked the important fact that each definition of a random walk model requires an explicit definition of the time interval. Earlier researchers had shown that when price changes are studied over very long intervals (such as the six-month intervals studied by Levy) there is "some" evidence of price momentum.

To add a nail to the coffin, a careful follow-up study of Levy's work by Michael Jensen[20] revealed that Levy had overstated his returns. In another follow-up study Jensen and George Benington[21] tested two of Levy's "better" decision rules and concluded that, after allowance for transaction costs, Levy's trading rules were no more profitable than a simple buy-and-hold strategy.

Victor Niederhoffer, individually[22] and with Osborne,[23] studied the other end of the interval spectrum—successive transactions on the ticker tape. Research on this smallest possible interval between price changes provides striking evidence of dependence between successive stock transactions. Specifically, Niederhoffer and Osborne found a tendency for prices to reverse between trades especially at prices just above and below integers. There also is evidence of price persistence following two price changes in the same direction: The chance of continuing in that direction is greater than after changes in opposite directions. Unfortunately, these short-term and small-percentage relationships, although consistent, are eclipsed by transaction costs and provide no basis for successful trading strategies.

Returning to Question 9.1, What should you train yourself to do with the news of price changes (for both individual stocks and market indexes) that are reported on radio, television, and Internet sites throughout the day (and, of course, appear in your favorite newspaper on the following morning)? The correct answer is "g"—nothing.

Recent changes in stock prices are not a precursor of either the direction or the magnitude of forthcoming changes in those stock prices. Since the 1960s progressively more rigorous and more probing tests of the efficient market hypothesis have reaffirmed the validity of the random walk model (a.k.a. the weak form of efficient market model) for intervals from 1 to 30 days. The unwavering conclusion to this day is that any news of recent changes in stock prices is *noise*.

In no way contradicting the conclusion that news of recent price changes is noise, recent research shows there is useful information in the trading volume of individual securities. Two respected researchers, Charles Lee and Bhaskaran Swaminathan[24] at Cornell University, found that past trading volume provides an important link between "momentum" and "value" strategies. Specifically, they found that firms with high past turnover ratios exhibit many glamour characteristics, earn lower future returns, and have consistently more negative earnings surprises over the next eight quarters.

Conversely, they found that firms with low past turnover ratios exhibit many value characteristics, earn higher future returns, and have consistently more positive earnings surprises over the next eight quarters. They also found that past trading volume predicts both the magnitude and the persistence of price momentum. Specifically, price momentum effects reverse over the next five years, and high-volume winners experience faster reversals (conversely, low-volume losers experience slower reversals).

Avoiding Torpedoes

Perfect Earnings Forecasts

Question 10.1. *If you had year-ahead foresight and knew next year's earnings for a large number of actively traded stocks, could you use this information to attain above-average investment returns?*
  a. No. Markets of actively traded stocks are so efficient that next year's earnings are already reflected in today's prices.
  b. Yes. Looking ahead a full year, the market does not have a clue as to next year's earnings.

The degree to which the market correctly anticipates year-to-year earnings changes has enormous implications for portfolio managers. If today's stock prices correctly anticipate next year's earnings, there is no value in earnings forecasts. But, if the market is frequently surprised by next year's earnings and if unfolding earnings changes do in fact influence stock prices, then accurate year-ahead earnings forecasts should be extremely useful.

It is remarkable that many professional investors make and/or use earnings forecasts without ever quantifying their usefulness. In this chapter I examine the usefulness of perfect earnings forecasts. If perfect earnings forecasts are useful, the *big* next step will be to determine whether (and to what degree) less than perfect earnings forecasts can be used to attain above-average returns.

Table 10.1 shows 25 years of returns for between 500 and 800 stocks ranked into five quintiles on the basis of actual changes in earnings.[1] These companies were ranked *after the end of each year* on the basis of the earnings changes that occurred over the course of that year. Next, five portfolios (quintiles) were formed, with the 20 percent of the companies having the worst earnings changes (largest percent decrease or smallest percent increase) composing the first

TABLE 10.1 Universe Relative Returns (Percent)

Date			Number of Stocks	Actual Earnings Changes (Percent)				
				Worst 1	2	3	4	Best 5
3/77	to	3/78	500	−15.0	−4.4	−1.8	6.1	15.1
3/78	to	3/79	575	−12.6	−8.6	−4.9	8.1	18.1
3/79	to	3/80	720	−16.1	−10.1	−1.7	6.6	21.4
3/80	to	3/81	765	−15.8	−8.5	−5.5	10.5	19.3
3/81	to	3/82	765	−21.8	−2.7	3.0	14.1	7.3
3/82	to	3/83	760	−17.7	−5.5	−0.5	0.2	23.5
3/83	to	3/84	750	−5.6	−3.9	1.5	2.3	5.7
3/84	to	3/85	800	−22.5	1.2	8.8	11.4	0.9
3/85	to	3/86	800	−25.8	−10.7	−2.4	15.7	23.1
3/86	to	3/87	800	−8.9	−6.3	−3.3	3.7	14.8
3/87	to	3/88	800	−12.9	−4.0	2.1	1.6	12.2
3/88	to	3/89	800	−12.9	−2.7	1.4	4.0	10.1
3/89	to	3/90	800	−20.4	−5.6	2.0	10.8	13.1
3/90	to	3/91	800	−23.7	−7.9	2.8	10.4	18.4
3/91	to	3/92	800	−15.6	−7.4	−0.9	5.8	18.1
3/92	to	3/93	800	−22.4	−4.7	3.9	9.0	14.2
3/93	to	3/94	800	−7.5	−6.3	−2.1	4.3	11.6
3/94	to	3/95	800	−8.5	−5.2	−1.2	5.0	10.0
3/95	to	3/96	800	−9.8	−5.1	0.3	11.3	2.9
3/96	to	3/97	800	−12.7	−3.9	5.2	5.2	6.2
3/97	to	3/98	800	−17.7	−3.8	0.9	14.2	6.6
3/98	to	3/99	800	−14.2	−5.7	1.6	8.9	9.5
3/99	to	3/00	800	2.0	−6.9	−8.1	7.8	5.3
3/00	to	3/01	800	−23.5	−1.4	10.0	13.3	1.6
3/01	to	3/02	800	−13.0	−1.5	2.0	5.2	7.3
Twenty-Five-Year Average				−15.2	−5.3	0.5	7.7	11.6

Worst return during holding period.
Source: Hagin Investment Research, Inc.

portfolio (quintile) and the 20 percent of the companies having the best earnings changes (largest percent increase or smallest percent decrease) composing the fifth portfolio (quintile).

Then, to study the pattern of investment returns, I calculated the average 12-month return[2] for each of the five portfolios for the 25 corresponding 12-month holding periods (March 31 to March 31). The second column in Table 10.1 shows the number of stocks that were analyzed during each of the 25 12-month holding periods. In the first year of the study exactly 500 stocks had enough earnings forecasts to be included in the study. In later years, when the number of stocks with sufficient data exceeded 800, I limited this particular investigation to the 800 largest companies.[3]

The first column under the caption "actual earnings changes" shows the returns for the companies with the worst actual earnings changes; moving to the right, each column contains the returns for the companies with successively better earnings changes. The rightmost column contains the companies with the best actual earnings changes. For example, the 20 percent of these companies that had the worst earnings changes in 1977 had a return of –15.0 percent in the period from March 31, 1977, to March 31, 1978. The companies that had the best earnings changes had a return of 15.1 percent. The boxes indicate the portfolios with the worst return in each of the 25 12-month holding periods. The bottom row shows the 25-year average returns for each of the columns.[4]

Notice in Table 10.1 the remarkable consistency with which the companies with the worst earnings changes have the worst returns and the companies with the best earnings changes have the best returns. Notice in the first row, for example, that from the time you could have known the prior year's earnings (March 31, 1977) until the time you could have calculated the actual percent change in earnings 12 months later (March 31, 1978) stock prices changed in a very orderly pattern. Specifically, the returns tended to move down in the portfolios that experienced the worst earnings changes and up in the portfolios that experienced the best earnings changes.

This pattern tends to persist as we move down the columns. Notice that, with only two exceptions in 25 years, the portfolios in the two worst actual-earnings-change categories (columns labeled 1 and 2) had negative returns. Conversely, the portfolios from the two best actual-earnings-change categories (columns labeled 4 and 5) had positive returns for *each* of the 25 holding periods.

Also, notice the magnitude of the returns. For the portfolios with the worst earnings changes the returns over the 25 periods averaged –15.2 percent. The returns averaged 11.6 percent for the portfolios with the best earnings changes. I call this remarkably consistent pattern the "concurrent earnings-change/return-change" effect.

The concurrent earnings-change/return-change effect provides three extremely important insights. First, it shows, quite clearly, that accurate one-year-ahead information as to which stocks will have the worst and best earnings changes was not, over this 25-year period, accurately embedded in beginning-of-March stock prices. If the market had accurately anticipated and priced the forthcoming year-to-year earnings changes, there would be no discernible differences in the returns in Table 10.1. There is absolutely no doubt that if you knew next year's earnings for a large number of actively traded stocks you could use this information to attain significantly above-average investment returns. Hence, the answer to Question 10.1 is "b"—yes. When it comes to knowing (and correctly pricing) next year's earnings, the market does not have a clue.

Second, the concurrent earnings-change/return-change effect gives security analysts a reason to try to forecast earnings. If the market had been efficient in anticipating—and pricing—year-ahead earnings changes, attempts to forecast these changes would be a waste of time. But, happily for forecasters, the existence of the concurrent earnings-change/return-change effect shows that anyone who could have accurately grouped 500 to 800 of the largest-capitalization stocks into five portfolios on the basis of year-ahead relative earnings changes could have reaped extraordinary rewards.

Third, it is important that to have been successful such a forecaster did not have to have forecasted each company's actual earnings changes. To exploit the concurrent earnings-change/return-change effect a forecaster faced a much easier task. Such a forecaster merely would have had to build a portfolio of the approximately 150 stocks that would—in terms of relative earnings changes—fall into the best relative-earnings-change category one year later.

Question 10.2.   Can you use the concurrent earnings-change/return-change effect shown in Table 10.1 to build portfolios that will consistently provide above-average returns?
   a. Yes.
   b. No.

Academics make an important distinction between *ex post* and *ex ante*. *Ex post* means after the fact. As post meridiem means afternoon, the term *ex post* is used to refer to investment information that is known only after we invest. *Ex ante*, the opposite of *ex post*, means before the fact. Thus, as a poker player may "ante" before the cards are dealt, the term *ex ante* is used to refer to investment information that is known before we invest.

It is important to note that the concurrent earnings-change/return-change effect is an *ex post* phenomenon. That is, when we look back after the end of each year, the portfolios that had the worst and best relative earnings changes over the course of the past year also provided the worst and best relative investment returns. Because the actual earnings changes used to form these portfolios were not known until after the fact, the answer to Question 10.2 is "b"—no. You cannot profit directly from the concurrent earnings-change/return-change effect.

Question 10.3.   Has the power of the concurrent earnings-change/return-change effect diminished over time?
   a. Yes.
   b. No.

To answer this question I examined the concurrent earnings-change/return-change effect over five five-year periods. These results are shown in Table 10.2. Here there is little difference during the first three five-year periods. However, during the two most recent five-year periods the magnitude of the returns in the worst and best earnings-change categories appears to have diminished.[5] Hence, the answer to Question 10.3 is "b"—no. Even though there is some diminution in the strength of the concurrent earnings-change/return-change effect in the most recent five-year periods, the effect remains statistically significant.

TABLE 10.2 Universe Relative Returns (Percent)

Actual Earnings Changes	Five-Year Periods					25-Year Period
	3/77 Through 3/82	3/82 Through 3/87	3/87 Through 3/92	3/92 Through 3/97	3/97 Through 3/02	3/77 Through 3/02
Worst	−17.0%	−15.8%	−17.1%	−12.1%	−13.5%	−15.2%
2	−6.7	−4.9	−5.5	−5.1	−4.1	−5.3
3	−1.8	0.9	1.5	1.1	1.1	0.5
4	9.2	6.4	6.3	6.8	9.7	7.7
Best	15.9	12.7	14.3	9.1	6.2	11.6

[   ] Highest return for holding period.

Source: Hagin Investment Research, Inc.

Conclusion: The concurrent earnings-change/return-change effect provides a remarkable insight in how the stock market works. Efficient markets embed everything that is known today into today's security prices. However, with regard to knowing which companies will report the best and worst earnings changes 12 months down the road the market does not have a clue.[6]

CHAPTER 11

Can Analysts Forecast Earnings Changes?

The preceding chapter showed that anyone who can correctly forecast next year's earnings can reap extraordinary returns.

Question 11.1.   Can analysts, on average, correctly forecast changes in next year's earnings?
   a. Yes.
   b. No.

Figure 11.1 shows the format that I used to compare companies' forecasted earnings changes for the next 12 months with the companies' actual earnings changes 12 months later. The first step was to divide the forecasted earnings changes (in percentages) into five categories—each with 20 percent of the companies—ranging from the worst (largest negative or smallest positive) to the best (largest positive or smallest negative) forecast. This information was placed in the *rows* as depicted in Figure 11.1.

Similarly, the actual earnings changes that were recorded 12 months later were divided into five worst-to-best categories. This information was placed in five *columns*, as depicted in Figure 11.2.

As shown in Figure 11.3, if analysts are perfect forecasters 20 percent of the joint forecasted and actual classifications will fall along the diagonal from the worst-worst cell in the upper left-hand corner to the best-best cell in the bottom right-hand corner. That is, if a company for which analysts had a worst forecasted earnings change turned out—12 months later—to have a worst actual earnings change, the company would be classified in the worst-worst cell in the upper left-hand corner.

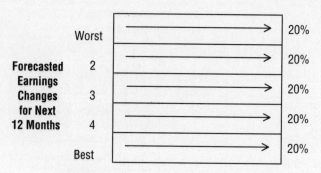

FIGURE 11.1   Forecasted Earnings Changes

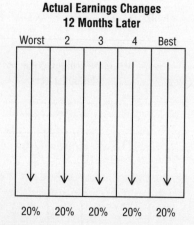

FIGURE 11.2   Actual Earnings Changes

Figure 11.4 depicts the percentage of companies that will fall into each cell if there is no relationship between the earnings forecasts for the next 12 months and the actual earnings changes 12 months later. That is, if forecasts and actual results are not related there will be approximately 4 percent of the companies in each of the 25 cells in the 5-by-5 classification scheme.

To determine whether analysts can, on average, correctly forecast earnings changes 12 months into the future, I compared the average 12-month-ahead earnings estimates in the Institutional Brokers Estimate Service (I/B/E/S) database with the actual percent earnings changes that occurred 12 months later. That is, starting

**Actual Earnings Changes
12 Months Later**

	Worst	2	3	4	Best	
Worst	20%					20%
2		20%				20%
3			20%			20%
4				20%		20%
Best					20%	20%
	20%	20%	20%	20%	20%	

Forecasted Earnings Changes for Next 12 Months

FIGURE 11.3 Perfect Forecasts

**Actual Earnings Changes
12 Months Later**

	Worst	2	3	4	Best	
Worst	4%	4%	4%	4%	4%	20%
2	4%	4%	4%	4%	4%	20%
3	4%	4%	4%	4%	4%	20%
4	4%	4%	4%	4%	4%	20%
Best	4%	4%	4%	4%	4%	20%
	20%	20%	20%	20%	20%	

Forecasted Earnings Changes for Next 12 Months

FIGURE 11.4 Useless Forecasts

from December 31, 1976, I compared the forecasted 12-month-ahead percent change in earnings for the 500 to 800 largest December-fiscal-year companies for which I/B/E/S had forecasts with the actual earnings changes that occurred 12 months later. I repeated this process for 25 one-year periods through December 31, 2001.

Figure 11.5 shows the percentage of companies that fell into each joint-classification cell. If there is no relationship between the

**Actual Earnings Changes
12 Months Later**

		Worst	2	3	4	Best	
Forecasted Earnings Changes for Next 12 Months	Worst	5.6	5.9	3.9	2.5	2.1	20%
	2	2.9	4.6	6.0	4.3	2.3	20%
	3	2.6	3.8	5.2	5.9	2.5	20%
	4	3.9	3.4	3.2	5.0	4.4	20%
	Best	5.0	2.3	1.7	2.3	8.7	20%
		20%	20%	20%	20%	20%	

FIGURE 11.5 Percentage of Companies
Percentages greater than 4% are in boldface type and are shaded.
Source: Hagin Investment Research, Inc.

12-month-ahead forecasted and actual earnings changes 12 months later, there would be approximately 4 percent of the joint classifications in each of the 25 cells. For ease of interpretation the cells in Figure 11.5 with frequencies that are greater than 4 percent are shown in boldface type and are shaded.

At a glance you can see that there is a relationship between forecasted and actual results. Clearly, the cells along the diagonal from the upper left-hand corner to the lower right-hand corner have frequencies greater than 4 percent. The cell in the upper left-hand corner shows, for example, that 5.6 percent of the companies that analysts predicted would be in the worst earnings-change quintile were actually in that quintile 12 months later.

Similarly, of the 20 percent of the companies with the best forecasted earnings changes in the bottom row, 12 months later 8.7 percent were classified in the best actual-earnings-change column. Even though far from the 20 percent of the forecasts that would cluster along the diagonal with perfect forecasts, this tendency for more than 4 percent of the forecasted-actual classifications to cluster along the diagonal is indicative that analysts have some degree of ability to forecast year-ahead earnings changes accurately.

Next, notice the cells in Figure 11.5 with the percentage of companies greater than 4 percent *that are above and to the right of the diagonal*. This shows that over the course of the last 25 years analysts were frequently surprised by better-than-forecasted results. For example, when analysts forecasted earnings changes in the worst (row) category 5.9 percent of these turned out 12 months later to be in actual-earnings-change category (column) 2. This better-than-forecasted pattern is so pervasive that each cell along the diagonal has an above-normal-frequency cell to its right (except, of course, for the cell in the bottom row).

Most of the other cells on both sides of the diagonal show percentages of companies below 4 percent. The notable exception appears in the lower left-hand corner.

Most experienced investors feel that during the past 25 years there have been more "torpedo" stocks—high-expectation stocks that have reported disappointing earnings—than there have been low-expectation stocks that have provided pleasant earnings surprises. The data in Figure 11.5 confirm this belief. Here, the tabulations over 25 years show that, on average, 5.0 percent of the companies fell into the extremely disappointing earnings cell in the lower left-hand corner of the grid. Conversely, only 2.1 percent of the companies fell into the extremely pleasant surprise cell in the upper right-hand corner.

Have analysts been able to forecast next year's changes in earnings per share accurately? One way to answer this question is to use contingency analysis to compare the actual frequencies that appear in Figure 11.5 with the frequencies that we would expect if there were no relationship between forecasted and actual percent earnings changes. The other is to use correlation and regression analysis to compare the forecasted and actual changes. Yes, there has been a statistically significant[1] relationship between beginning-of-year forecasted and year-later actual earnings changes.

Statistically speaking, the answer to Question 11.1 is "a"—yes, analysts can, indeed, correctly forecast next year's earnings changes.

CHAPTER **12**

Earnings Forecasts
(and Torpedo Stocks)

The preceding chapter showed that analysts can forecast next year's earnings.

Question 12.1. *What pattern of returns do you expect when portfolios are ranked on the basis of* forecasted *percent changes in earnings per share?*

    a. Portfolios with the *best* forecasted earnings growth rates will have the *best* returns.

    b. Portfolios with the *worst* forecasted earnings growth rates will have the *worst* returns.

    c. Portfolios with the *worst* forecasted earnings growth rates will have the *best* returns.

    d. Portfolios with the *best* forecasted earnings growth rates will have the *worst* returns.

    e. "a" and "b."

    f. "c" and "d."

In Figure 12.1, when the quintile rank of a forecasted earnings change matches the quintile rank of the actual earnings change 12 months later the cells are labeled as perfect forecasts. Note that the five cells along the diagonal are labeled "perfect."

The three cells in the upper right-hand corner contain the companies that had pleasant earnings surprises. These cells contain the companies that (1) were forecasted to have the worst earnings changes but, 12 months later, had actual earnings changes that ranked in the best or next-to-best column, and (2) were forecasted to

**Actual Earnings Changes
12 Months Later**

		Worst	2	3	4	Best
	Worst	Perfect	—	—	☺	☺
	2	—	Perfect	—	—	☺
Forecasted Earnings Changes	3	—	—	Perfect	—	—
	4	☹	—	—	Perfect	—
	Best	☹	☹	—	—	Perfect

FIGURE 12.1   Forecasted and Actual Earnings Comparison Framework

have next-to-worst earnings changes (in the second row) but, one year later, had actual earnings changes that ranked in the best column. I coded these pleasant earnings surprises in the three cells in the upper right-hand corner with a ☺ sign.

Similarly, the three cells in the lower left-hand corner contain the companies for which forecasts of best and next-to-best earnings changes in the bottom two rows gave way to changes over the ensuing year that ranked worst and next-to-worst in the two left-hand columns. These unpleasant surprises are coded with a ☹ sign in the three cells in the lower left-hand corner. The remaining cells are marked with dashes.[1]

Thus, the *rows* of Figure 12.1 contain forecasted earnings changes. The *columns* contain the actual earnings changes that occurred one year later. Finally, the symbols in the cells represent my hypothesized pattern of returns.

The torpedo effect—which I first documented in 1984[2]—occurs when a few high-expectation stocks "torpedo" and "sink" the return of an entire portfolio. The generating process for the torpedo effect requires: (1) there must be a sufficient number of unpleasant earnings surprises, and (2) these unpleasant surprises must have significantly below-average returns.

Because the ☺ symbol and the ☹ symbol in Figure 12.2 represent expected returns, I can merely add the symbols to derive the expected returns from the rows and columns. The leftmost column

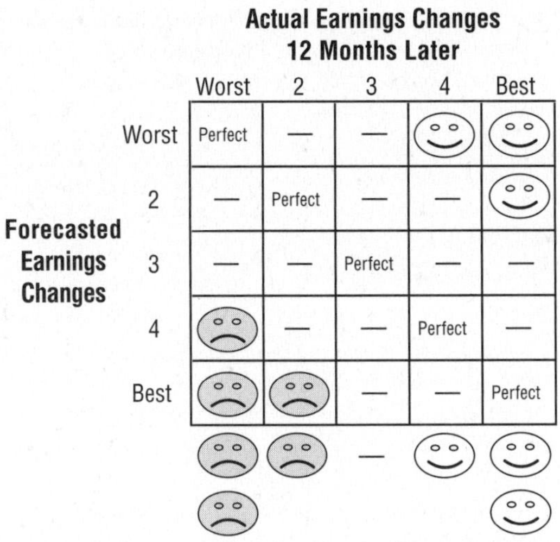

Actual Earnings Changes
12 Months Later

	Worst	2	3	4	Best
Worst	Perfect	—	—	☺	☺☺
2	—	Perfect	—	—	☺☺
3	—	—	Perfect	—	—
4	☹☹	—	—	Perfect	—
Best	☹☹	☹☹	—	—	Perfect
	☹☹	☹☹	—	☺	☺☺
	☹☹				☺☺

(Forecasted Earnings Changes — row labels at left)

FIGURE 12.2 Column Performance Expectations

contains, for example, two cells with a ☹ (representing below-average expected returns). Adding these symbols, the expected return from a portfolio made up of the stocks in the first column is two sad faces (☹ ☹). Moving to the right, the second column has an expected return of one sad face (☹).

The third column has no symbols. The fourth column has an expected return of one happy face (☺). Finally, the rightmost column has an expected return of two happy faces (☺ ☺). Thus, as we move from left to right the pattern of performance expectations for each column is symbolically ☹ ☹, ☹,—, ☺, and ☺ ☺. *It is important to note that this* ex post *hypothesized pattern of returns coincides perfectly with the concurrent earnings-change/return-change effect described earlier.*

The rows in Figure 12.3 symbolize the analysts' forecasted earnings changes. Again, I added the symbols that represent the performance that I expected from the stocks in each row. Here the hypothesized returns for the five portfolios are, from the top row to bottom row, ☺ ☺, ☺,—, ☹, and ☹ ☹.

Thus, if the performance that I hypothesize for each cell turns out to be correct, the row with the best performance (represented symbolically by ☺ ☺) will be derived from the stocks with the

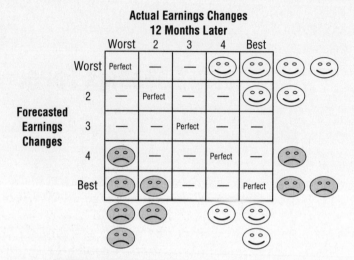

FIGURE 12.3 Overall Performance Expectations

worst forecasted earnings changes! Conversely, the worst performance (represented symbolically by 😟😟) will be derived from the stocks with the best forecasted earnings changes.

As mentioned earlier, for the torpedo hypothesis to be true, (1) there must be a high enough percentage of stocks in the unpleasant-surprise cells, and (2) the pattern of returns represented by the happy and sad faces must materialize.

Question 12.1 asked: What pattern of returns do you expect when portfolios are ranked on the basis of *forecasted* percent changes in earnings per share? With the proviso that there is a torpedo effect, the answer to Question 12.1 is "f"—portfolios with the *worst* forecasted earnings growth rates will have the *best* returns; portfolios with the *best* forecasted earnings growth rate will have the *worst* returns.

CHAPTER 13

Using Earnings Forecasts

The concurrent earnings-change/return-change effect described in Chapter 10 showed that someone who could have ranked companies into five portfolios based on the next year's earnings changes could have reaped extraordinary profits. Chapter 11 showed that the mean estimate in the I/B/E/S database is an accurate, statistically significant forecast. Even so, the possibility of the torpedo effect—described symbolically in Chapter 12—might turn the forecasting business upside down.

Question 13.1.   Can the consensus estimate of next year's earnings growth rate be used to reap extraordinary profits?
   a. Yes.
   b. No.

The upper right-hand corner of Figure 13.1 shows the percentage of companies that fell into the positive-earnings-surprise cells (where the companies with the worst forecasted earnings changes turned out 12 months later to have had the best actual earnings changes). The lower left-hand corner of Figure 13.1 shows the percentage of companies that fell into the negative-earnings-surprise cells (where the companies with the best forecasted earnings changes turned out 12 months later to have had the worst actual changes). Specifically, 6.9 percent (2.5 + 2.1 + 2.3 = 6.9) of the companies fell in the three positive-earnings-surprise cells in the upper right-hand corner, and 11.2 percent (3.9 + 5.0 + 2.3 = 11.2) of the companies fell into the three negative-earnings-surprise cells in the lower left-hand corner. The presence of such a reasonable number of pleasant and unpleasant surprises is a prerequisite for my hypothesis that

Actual Earnings Changes 12 Months Later

Forecasted Earnings Changes for Next 12 Months		Worst	2	3	4	Best	
	Worst				2.5	2.1	20%
	2					2.3	20%
	3						20%
	4	3.9					20%
	Best	5.0	2.3				20%
		20%	20%	20%	20%	20%	

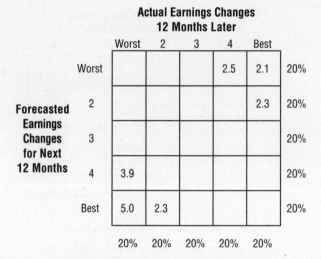

FIGURE 13.1 Percentage of Companies
Source: Hagin Investment Research, Inc.

earnings surprises play an enormous role in explaining the real-world investment performance of value and growth managers.

Figure 13.2—*categorically one of the most important figures in this book*—shows the average returns when the stocks are arrayed by forecasted earnings changes and actual earnings changes 12 months later.

First, notice how earnings disappointments trigger large losses. The portfolios represented by the cell in the lower left-hand corner had returns that were 19.8 percent below those of the market. Conversely, notice how pleasant earnings surprises trigger large gains. The portfolios represented by the cell in the upper right-hand corner had returns that were 15.1 percent above those of the market.

Earlier I documented the concurrent earnings-change/return-change effect, whereby the stocks of companies with successively more (less) favorable year-to-year earnings changes have provided better (worse) year-to-year investment returns. The reason for this (and other) effects appears in Figure 13.2.

Look closely at the leftmost column. This column contains the companies that 12 months after the forecast was made actually had the worst earnings changes. The average return for these stocks was –15.2 percent. Now look at the worst-worst cell in the upper left-

Actual Earnings Changes 12 Months Later

Forecasted Earnings Changes	Worst	2	3	4	Best	Avg.
Worst	–8.6	–0.7	4.1	10.3	15.1	1.4
2	–13.2	–4.0	2.5	10.9	17.7	2.6
3	–18.1	–6.8	0.3	9.0	16.6	1.4
4	–19.6	–10.7	–5.7	4.2	11.8	–2.5
Best	–19.8	–11.0	–6.6	1.0	8.1	–3.3
Avg.	–15.2	–5.3	0.5	7.7	11.6	

FIGURE 13.2 Returns (Percentage)
Negative returns are shaded.
Source: Hagin Investment Research, Inc.

hand corner. Here stocks that were forecasted to have the worst earnings growth—and actually 12 months later had the worst relative earnings growth—had an average return of –8.6 percent.

Notice, however, what happens as you move down the left column. All of the stocks in this column share the misfortune of having their actual earnings changes fall into the worst category. Note, however, that as you move down the column the higher the quintile of forecasted earnings change the worse the return.

Now look closely at the column labeled "2." All companies that fall into this column share the misfortune of having their actual year-end earnings changes fall into the next-to-worst category. The returns of the portfolios represented by the cells are, however, markedly different—depending on their year-earlier earnings forecasts. This general pattern is found in each of the five actual-earnings-change columns.

Without question, an appropriate sign for your desk is: "*The higher the expectation for earnings growth the deeper the disappointment if it is not realized.*"

Look, now, at the performance of the stocks in the top row of Figure 13.2. These are the stocks for which analysts expected the worst earnings changes. The stocks in the portfolios along this row provided an average return of 1.4 percent.

Look carefully at the pattern of the returns in the rows in Figure 13.2. Regardless of the forecasted-earnings-change category, returns increase monotonically as you move from left to right and to higher and higher actual-earnings-change categories.

Next, notice the return that would have accrued to someone who had purchased the stocks in the bottom row of Figure 13.2. These stocks—for which analysts forecasted the best year-to-year earnings changes—had an average return of –3.3 percent. Thus, *one sure way to lose money over the past 25 years would have been to purchase the stocks for which analysts had the highest expectations.*

How could this happen? There are two answers. First, the high-earnings-expectation portfolio (represented by the best forecasted-earnings-change category) contained a sufficient number of earnings-disappointment stocks to torpedo the entire portfolio.

Second, notice how intolerant the market was of any degree of earnings disappointment when one invested in the best forecasted-earnings-change category (in the bottom row). Find the portfolio (cell) in Figure 13.2 with the largest positive or negative return. It is –19.8 percent. It is in the portfolio of stocks where the best forecasted-earnings growth turned out to be in the worst actual-earnings-change category one year later.

Finally, notice the pattern of returns along the right side of Figure 13.2. This pattern of returns—even though much smaller—is almost the opposite of the pattern found with the concurrent earnings-change/return-change effect. Under the concurrent earnings-change/return-change effect, price changes and actual earnings changes move together. Thus, if we could have forecasted earnings changes without any surprises, we could have earned a handsome reward (as is evident from the returns along the bottom of Figure 13.2). But, when we use actual earnings forecasts, the pattern is reversed; the most favorable earnings forecasts lead to negative returns.

Thus, the answer to Question 13.1 is "b"—no, the consensus estimate of next year's earnings growth rate cannot be used to reap extraordinary profits. However, if you knew next year's earnings a simple one-trade-per-year strategy would lead to extraordinary returns. Remarkably, however, substituting consensus earnings forecasts leads to the opposite result.

You have now successfully untangled a puzzle that eludes many investors.

■ Anyone who can accurately forecast changes in next year's earnings can reap extraordinary gains.
■ Analysts can accurately forecast next year's earnings.
■ You cannot use analysts' average forecasts to earn consistently above-average investment returns because "torpedo stocks" (high-expectation stocks that are rocked by earnings disappointments) consistently sink the returns of high-expectation portfolios.

Question 13.2.   Over the past 25 years has the power of the torpedo effect diminished?
a. Yes.
b. No.

Table 13.1 shows the average return over five five-year periods. This table shows that—even in this universe of 800 of the largest, most followed companies measured over one-year holding periods—merely avoiding the approximately 320 stocks in the two best forecasted earnings quintiles would have provided above-average returns.

TABLE 13.1   Universe Relative Returns (Percent)

Forecasted Earnings Change Categories	Five-Year Periods					25-Year Period
	3/77 Through 3/82	3/82 Through 3/87	3/87 Through 3/92	3/92 Through 3/97	3/97 Through 3/02	3/77 Through 3/02
Worst	3.7%	3.0%	0.1%	0.8%	0.1%	1.4%
2	2.3	4.0	1.1	1.8	4.4	2.6
3	–1.2	2.8	1.9	–0.1	3.6	1.4
4	⎡–2.7⎤	–4.0	0.7	⎡–2.4⎤	⎡–4.6⎤	–2.5
Best	–2.5	⎡–6.2⎤	⎡–4.0⎤	–0.4	–3.8	⎡–3.3⎤

☐   Lowest return for holding period.
Source: Hagin Investment Research, Inc.

Although the impact of the torpedo effect ebbs and flows, during the most recent five-year period the negative returns from high-expectation portfolios were close to those of some of the earlier periods. Hence, the answer to Question 13.2 is "b"—the power of the torpedo effect remains strong in the post-bubble market.

Before turning to the next subject, I should emphasize that this 25-year study analyzed the largest, most actively traded sector of the market. *Part of the wonder about these findings is that they are so strong that they appear in such a crude study—analyzing only the most actively traded sector of the market and making only one investment decision a year.*

CHAPTER 14.

Size Effect

Question 14.1. Studying the 800 largest stocks in the I/B/E/S database, we would see that over the course of a year stocks of larger companies (as opposed to smaller companies in that universe) respond to a given level of earnings changes with:
   a. Accentuated price changes.
   b. Dampened price changes.
   c. Virtually the same price changes as the stocks of smaller companies.

This chapter examines the often overlooked and often misunderstood relationship between company size and actual earnings changes. "Size" is defined as equity capitalization—year-end price times the number of common shares outstanding. I use the same analytical framework and the same database with 25 years of history for between 500 and 800 large, actively traded stocks. I should emphasize that the results reported here are for size differences *within* this large-stock universe.

Even though the figure is not shown here, all of the cell frequencies in the 5-by-5 table that contrasts company size and the magnitude of earnings changes are very close to 4.0. Thus, within a universe of the 500 to 800 largest actively traded stocks, there is no relationship between the size of a company and the size of its earnings changes. There is no evidence, for example, as some believe, that the smaller companies in actively traded groups—such as the S&P 500—have most of the larger earnings changes. The patterns of returns within the rows and columns, however, are extremely interesting.

Compare the returns in the columns of Figure 14.1. The companies

Actual Earnings Change
12 Months Later

	Worst	2	3	4	Best	Avg.
Smallest	−20.0	−6.6	2.6	9.9	18.4	0.8
2	−18.2	−5.8	1.1	10.4	13.9	0.4
Size (Equity Capitalization) 3	−14.3	−6.2	−0.2	7.8	9.4	−0.6
4	−12.5	−5.3	0.4	6.4	9.3	0.0
Largest	−11.7	−3.5	−0.6	4.2	4.9	−0.9
Avg.	−15.2	−5.3	0.5	7.7	11.6	

FIGURE 14.1   Returns: Size versus Actual Earnings Change
Source: Hagin Investment Research, Inc.

in the left column share a characteristic. All had the worst earnings changes. As you saw earlier, the stocks in the worst actual-earnings-change category had a return of −15.2 percent. Similarly, the fortunate companies in the right column that had the best actual earnings changes had a return of 11.6 percent. What is critically important, however, is to understand how different-size companies respond to the same earnings changes.

Look, for example, at the leftmost (worst actual-earnings-change) column. Here the negative return of the smallest companies that had the worst earnings changes (−20.0 percent) was almost double that of the largest companies that also had the worst earnings changes (−11.7 percent). Similarly, the positive returns derived from owning the best earnings-change stocks depend a lot on company size. Note in the best actual-earnings-change column that the smallest companies returned more than three times as much (18.4 percent) as large companies (4.9 percent).

From the size perspective, the difference in return between the smallest companies (shown in the top row of Figure 14.1) that had the worst and the best earnings changes was 38.4 percentage points (−20.0 and 18.4 percent). The comparable size spread in the return of the largest companies was almost half—16.6 percentage points (–11.7 and 4.9 percent).

Finally, even though there is no classical size effect (whereby smaller stocks have higher returns) within this large-stock universe, the sensitivity of stock prices to earnings changes increases dramatically as you invest in successively smaller companies. Thus the answer to Question 14.1 is "b"—the stocks of the larger companies within the universe of the largest 500 to 800 companies in the I/B/E/S database respond to a given level of earnings changes with dampened price changes.

Part of the wonder of the extraordinary differences between larger and smaller companies is that the smaller companies in this study were the smaller stocks *within* the largest 800 stocks in the I/B/E/S database.

I have conducted similar investigations that have studied smaller companies. In all cases the conclusion drawn from the larger stocks holds. The same earnings changes consistently trigger accentuated price changes in the small-capitalization stocks. In my view the greater sensitivity of small company returns to the same level of earnings changes reflects the resolution of a greater amount of uncertainty about the earnings of smaller companies.

CHAPTER 15

Price-Earnings Effect

There is much evidence that markets quickly embed all available opinions into stock prices. In such a world it is reasonable to expect that the stocks with the worst forecasted earnings changes for the next 12 months should also have the lowest current price-earnings (P/E) ratios; stocks with the best forecasted earnings changes for the next 12 months should also have the highest current P/E ratios.

If this relationship holds, current price-earnings ratios will contain all of the information that is contained in forecasted earnings changes for the next 12 months. If this is the case, there will be no need to forecast earnings changes—analysts can just look at the current price-earnings ratio.

Question 15.1. What best describes the relationship between current price-earnings ratios (using trailing-12-month earnings) and forecasted earnings changes for the next 12 months?
  a. Very strong—price-earnings ratios contain virtually all of the information in forecasted year-ahead earnings changes.
  b. Strong—price-earnings ratios contain most of the information in forecasted year-ahead earnings changes.
  c. Weak—price-earnings ratios contain little of the information in forecasted year-ahead earnings changes.

Figure 15.1 shows the *ex ante* relationship between current price-earnings ratios and forecasted earnings changes.[1] Here 12.3 percent of the companies fall in the six cells in the lower left-hand corner of the grid. These anomalous companies have among the highest price-earnings ratios (measured relative to the rest of the stocks) and among the worst forecasted earnings changes (also measured relative to the rest of the stocks).

**Forecasted Earnings Changes
for Next 12 months**

		Worst	2	3	4	Best	
	Lowest	**9.8**	**4.6**	2.6	1.8	1.2	20.0
	2	**5.3**	**6.2**	3.7	3.2	1.7	20.0
Current P/E Ratios	3	2.7	**5.0**	**4.9**	**4.5**	2.9	20.0
	4	1.4	3.1	**5.6**	**5.1**	**4.7**	20.0
	Highest	0.8	1.1	3.2	**5.4**	**9.6**	20.0
		20.0	20.0	20.0	20.0	20.0	

FIGURE 15.1   Percentage of Companies: P/E Ratio versus Forecasted
Earnings Changes
Percentages greater than 4% are in boldface type and are shaded.
Source: Hagin Investment Research, Inc.

Similarly, 13.4 percent of companies fall in the six cells in the
upper right-hand corner of the grid. These anomalous companies
have among the lowest price-earnings ratios and the best forecasted
earnings changes.

Taken together, 25.7 percent of the companies do not conform
to the pattern whereby high-P/E stocks also have the best forecasted
earnings changes. Thus the correct answer to Question 15.1 is
"b"—strong relationship—price-earnings ratios contain most of the
information in forecasted year-ahead earnings changes.

*Question 15.2.   Measured over the past 25 years (using the same
universe of large, actively traded stocks), the difference between the
return derived from an investment in the low-P/E quintiles and an
investment in the high-P/E quintiles can be best described as:*
    a. Low-P/E stocks outperformed high-P/E stocks by 15 percent-
         age points per year.
    b. Low-P/E stocks outperformed high-P/E stocks by 10 percent-
         age points per year.

c. Low-P/E stocks outperformed high-P/E stocks by 5 percentage points per year.

d. There was little difference between the return from low-P/E and the return from high-P/E stocks per year.

e. High-P/E stocks outperformed low-P/E stocks by 5 percentage points per year.

f. High-P/E stocks outperformed low-P/E stocks by 10 percentage points per year.

g. High-P/E stocks outperformed low-P/E stocks by 15 percentage points per year.

Figure 15.2 compares the returns that you would have derived from the joint P/E ratio and actual-earnings (12 months later) classification. Notice the highest-P/E portfolios along the bottom row in Figure 15.2. When portfolios in the highest-P/E quintile had the misfortune to have an earnings change (12 months later) in the worst category, the return was –25.8 percent. Moving from left to right along the bottom row you see that the companies in only one of the five highest-P/E categories had positive returns.

Actual Earnings Changes
12 Months Later

		Worst	2	3	4	Best	Avg.
	Lowest	**–10.1**	2.3	8.8	17.4	25.9	4.1
	2	**–11.3**	**–3.1**	3.4	10.8	20.5	2.4
Current P/E Ratios	3	**–16.4**	**–7.8**	**–0.2**	8.5	15.2	–0.4
	4	**–18.2**	**–11.4**	**–3.9**	6.6	12.6	–0.9
	Highest	**–25.8**	**–19.4**	**–7.1**	**–2.3**	3.8	–6.4
	Avg.	–15.2	–5.3	0.5	7.7	11.6	

FIGURE 15.2 Returns (Percentage): P/E Ratios versus Actual Earnings Changes Negative returns are in boldface type and are shaded.
Source: Hagin Investment Research, Inc.

Clearly, high-expectation stocks (over this 25-year period) punished investors with losses in four of the five actual-earnings-change categories.

Conversely, the returns in the top row show that investors in low-P/E stocks had positive returns in four of the five actual-earnings-change categories. The numbers in the average column along the right-hand side of the grid reveal that low-P/E investors had an annual above-benchmark return of 4.1 percent. Conversely, investors in high-P/E stocks lost an average of 6.4 percent per year. The spread between the low-P/E return of 4.1 percent and the high-P/E return of −6.4 percent is 10.5 percent. Hence, the best answer to Question 15.2 is "b"—low-P/E stocks outperformed high-P/E stocks by 10 percentage points per year.

Question 15.3.   Measured over each of the past 25 years (and using the same universe of large, actively traded stocks) in how many of the 25 years did the return of the high-P/E quintile exceed the average return for that year by at least 2.5 percent?
   a. All 25 years.
   b. Between 20 and 24 years.
   c. Between 15 and 20 years.
   d. Between 10 and 15 years.
   e. Between 5 and 10 years.
   f. Fewer than 5 years.

It is often misleading to look only at average returns over long periods. Average returns can mask period-to-period variability that you might find unacceptable.

Table 15.1 shows the return for each of five P/E portfolios over 25 years. The portfolios with the lowest returns are shown in the boxes.

Most investors believe the correct answer to Question 15.3 is "d"—high-P/E stocks had a return that is at least 2.5 percent above the average return between 10 and 15 of the past 25 years.

A careful look at Table 15.1 reveals three surprises. First, the highest-P/E portfolios had universe-relative returns that exceeded the yearly average by at least 2.5 percent in only 2 of the 25 years. (Thus the correct answer is "f"—fewer than 5 years.) The lowest-P/E portfolios had relative returns that exceeded 2.5 percent in 16 of the 25 years.

TABLE 15.1 Relative Returns (Percent)

		Number of Stocks	Price-Earnings Ratio				
Date			Lowest 1	2	3	4	Highest 5
3/77	to	3/78	500	8.6	1.2	−0.4	−0.5	−8.8
3/78	to	3/79	575	5.5	−0.1	−4.4	−3.0	2.1
3/79	to	3/80	720	−3.3	−0.8	−3.8	1.0	6.9
3/80	to	3/81	765	5.3	3.6	−8.5	−5.9	0.5
3/81	to	3/82	765	14.5	10.4	−7.1	−1.9	−15.7
3/82	to	3/83	760	1.5	−3.2	2.6	−6.1	5.2
3/83	to	3/84	750	10.9	4.9	−0.2	−4.3	−11.4
3/84	to	3/85	800	14.0	8.7	1.3	−5.4	−18.6
3/85	to	3/86	800	5.4	13.2	−1.8	−4.2	−12.7
3/86	to	3/87	800	−0.4	−1.4	0.2	0.4	1.2
3/87	to	3/88	800	−4.1	−0.5	1.3	4.2	−0.9
3/88	to	3/89	800	5.5	1.0	2.3	0.2	−9.0
3/89	to	3/90	800	−7.0	0.3	4.2	1.2	1.4
3/90	to	3/91	800	−8.4	−0.6	1.2	7.1	0.5
3/91	to	3/92	800	11.8	2.5	0.9	−5.7	−9.4
3/92	to	3/93	800	12.7	5.1	−2.2	−3.0	−12.6
3/93	to	3/94	800	−0.6	−3.7	1.2	2.9	0.2
3/94	to	3/95	800	−1.6	2.0	−2.7	0.5	1.7
3/95	to	3/96	800	5.2	1.2	0.2	−1.1	−5.5
3/96	to	3/97	800	8.1	−0.5	−1.8	0.9	−6.7
3/97	to	3/98	800	3.8	9.6	6.7	−3.9	−16.2
3/98	to	3/99	800	−4.2	−2.7	0.3	5.7	1.0
3/99	to	3/00	800	8.1	−5.6	−1.4	−3.3	2.2
3/00	to	3/01	800	20.0	17.0	1.4	−2.8	−35.9
3/01	to	3/02	800	4.9	4.5	2.9	−2.4	−10.0
Twenty-Five-Year Average			4.1	2.4	−0.4	−0.9	−6.4

☐ Quintile with lowest return.
Source: Hagin Investment Research, Inc.

TABLE 15.2   Relative Returns

| Price/
Earnings | Five-Year Periods | | | | | 25-Year
Period |
	3/77 Through 3/82	3/82 Through 3/87	3/87 Through 3/92	3/92 Through 3/97	3/97 Through 3/02	3/77 Through 3/02
Lowest	6.3%	6.4%	−1.0%	4.4%	5.9%	4.1%
2	3.1	4.3	0.5	0.6	3.6	2.4
3	−4.8	0.4	2.0	−1.1	1.6	−0.4
4	−1.8	−3.9	1.6	0.1	−0.9	−0.9
Highest	−4.2	−7.9	−3.4	−4.5	−12.0	−6.4

☐ Highest return for holding period.
Source: Hagin Investment Research, Inc.

Second, even though it was a very bumpy ride, the lowest-P/E portfolio had a positive relative return of 4.1 percent per year over this 25-year period. Conversely, the highest-P/E portfolio underperformed the average stock in the universe by 6.4 percent per year.

Finally, notice in Table 15.1 that the low-P/E strategy wins two ways. It avoids losses in the high-P/E stocks and profits from the gains in the low-P/E stocks.

Question 15.4.   Has the power of the P/E effect diminished over time?
 a. Yes.
 b. No.

Table 15.2 shows that the comparative power of the P/E effect in five five-year periods appears to be alive and well—with the exception of the period between 3/87 and 3/92. The most recent five-year period (which includes the post-bubble crash of high-P/E stocks) shows that a strategy of buying the lowest-P/E stocks and avoiding (or shorting) high-P/E stocks was stronger than in any of the other five-year periods.

CHAPTER 16

The Magic of Growth

Question 16.1. *Imagine you have agreed to conduct an experiment with 12 of your friends and colleagues. You ask your subjects to select the portfolio that they expect will earn the highest return over the next year.*

Portfolio A is comprised of the 160 large well-known and actively traded stocks for which Wall Street analysts have forecast the highest *year-over-year earnings growth rates.*

Portfolio B is comprised of the 160 large well-known and actively traded stocks for which Wall Street analysts have forecast the lowest *year-over-year earnings growth rates.*

When your answers are pooled with those of your friends and colleagues, what percentage of the subjects do you believe will have selected Portfolio A?

    a. Almost 100 percent.
    b. More than 90 percent.
    c. Roughly 50 percent.
    d. Fewer than 10 percent.

Investors love growth. Almost 100 percent of typical subjects prefer Portfolio A. Many participants ask: Why would *anyone* prefer Portfolio B? The answer is, of course, price.

In the early 1980s, when I was heading the quantitative-research department at Kidder Peabody & Co., Inc., we ran screens for large clients using the research department's database. These clients—all large institutions spread across the globe—might request a list of companies ranked in the order of our analysts' forecasted five-year growth rates, showing other data such as price-earnings ratios, price-sales ratios, income growth, and so on.

To my surprise (at the time), out of the several hundred screens that we ran only *two* did not begin with some variation of "highest forecasted growth rates." My epiphany: If every investor wants the stocks with the highest forecasted earnings growth rates, *growth must be overpriced*. Later I came to understand that for many participants in financial markets growth is not just a *number*—growth is a *story*.

Buying a stock on the basis of forecasted earnings growth, and nothing else, is like clapping with one hand. The other half of the question—basically, how is the market pricing this growth—is missing. Nonetheless, most investors—both individuals and investment professionals—foolishly start their search by screening for companies with above-average forecasted growth.

Question 16.2.   Price-earnings (P/E) ratios reflect in large part a stock's expected earnings growth. One task of security analysis is to evaluate whether a stock's current P/E ratio is high or low—based on the analyst's assessment of the company's prospects for future earnings growth.

In doing, or interpreting, analysis that seeks to discern incremental value-added growth it is important to remember to include nominal (before inflation) earnings growth funded from:
   a. Investments made from retained earnings.
   b. Investments that a firm makes at rates equal to the firm's current return on equity.
   c. Investments that a firm makes at rates above the firm's current return on equity.
   d. All of the above—all earnings growth increases the value of a company.

A milestone in the history of investing was Salomon Brothers' decision in 1970—the first such decision on Wall Street—to hire Martin Leibowitz as an in-house mathematician. Since then Leibowitz has written many significant articles (*Investing: The Collected Works of Martin L. Leibowitz* numbers a staggering 1,168 pages.) His articles are replete with important insights. One insight that is particularly useful to equity analysts is presented in his 1990 paper (with Stanley Kogelman), "Inside the P/E Ratio: The Franchise Factor."[1]

The crux of Leibowitz's franchise factor is to separate a company's sources of earnings into two distinct components: the current business that generates visible earnings and a franchise value that includes all future activities and opportunities that can provide above-market returns. Leibowitz's extremely useful insight is that *the franchise value is the source of all incremental P/E values.*

In turn, the franchise value itself can be usefully separated into two factors. The first factor is a measure of the size of each opportunity in present-value terms. The second factor—the "franchise factor"—contains all information regarding the returns available from new businesses. The surprising finding is the magnitude of new business required to generate even moderate levels of P/E improvement. In Leibowitz's words,

> Investors generally fail to appreciate the magnitude and type of growth required to support a high P/E multiple . . . for equities, *growth is not enough.* The routine investments that a firm makes at the market rate do not add net value, even though they may contribute to nominal earnings growth. (Investments at below-market returns actually subtract from value.) Incremental value is generated only through investment in exceptional opportunities that promise above-market ROEs [returns on equity]. Only this *exceptional* "high-octane" growth fuels the engine for higher P/E multiples.[2]

Thus the correct answer to Question 16.2 is "c"—only investments at what Leibowitz calls "high-octane" growth can fuel higher P/E multiples.

It is difficult for an enterprise to find repeated investment opportunities that offer returns above those of the company's return on equity. Such opportunities usually require that the firm enjoy some degree of monopoly. *It is important to remember that, by definition, these extraordinary opportunities for P/E growth cannot last.*

CHAPTER 17

Estimate Revisions

Question 17.1.   It is reasonable to expect that revisions in analysts' earnings forecasts can be used to attain above-benchmark returns.
   a. Fact.
   b. Fiction.

The preceding chapters have shown (I hope unambiguously) that today's stock prices reflect an amalgamation of uncertain expectations—including uncertain estimates of future earnings. As more and more time passes, more and more of the uncertainty about coming earnings is resolved. For some companies, earnings expectations reach a level above the initial expectation; for other companies earnings expectations move to a lower level. As time advances, earnings expectations reflect ever more complete information. Investment returns follow the resolution of this uncertainty in either direction.
   One way to think about what I have presented thus far is that I have taken two snapshots. The first snapshot shows what we know today. The second snapshot moves one year ahead and looks at how earnings and stock prices have changed. What happens to stock prices as time unfolds through the year is the fertile ground I now explore.
   Earlier I illustrated my discovery and naming of an extremely important phenomenon—the concurrent earnings-change/return-change effect. Over the course of each of the past 25 years the companies with the worst earnings changes concurrently had the worst investment returns; the companies with the best earnings changes concurrently had the best investment returns.
   The existence of this phenomenon shows (1) that the year-ahead earnings expectations that are embedded in today's stock prices are

wrong,[1] and (2) that over the course of the next 12 months the portfolios of the stocks with the best unfolding actual earnings changes will concurrently provide their owners with the best investment returns. Thus, the correct answer to Question 17.1 is "a"—fact. It is reasonable to study *revisions* in analysts' earnings estimates for clues to understanding this unfolding earnings-change/return-change process.

Recognizing the interest in studying analysts' earnings expectations, the Institutional Brokers Estimate Service (I/B/E/S)—then part of the brokerage firm Lynch, Jones & Ryan—in 1971 began collecting and selling the earnings forecasts of institutional equity analysts. In 1981 Zacks Investment Research began providing another source of analysts' earnings forecasts.

Over the intervening years researchers have tested virtually every permutation and combination of the usefulness of earnings forecasts, unfolding estimate revisions, differences between the prognostications of "star" versus "also-ran" analysts, and measures of "diffusion" between the number of estimates raised and lowered as well as techniques to assign more weight to more recent estimate revisions.

In the old days, I/B/E/S and Zacks Investment Research released their revised data on certain preannounced release dates. This was an era when messengers on motorcycles, motors racing, wearing leather jackets and with white silk scarves blowing in the wind, eagerly awaited the release of the latest tapes. Once passed to the messengers, the tapes were scurried into the night to be analyzed before the market opened the following morning.

Today motorcycle messengers are gone, replaced long ago by banks of multicolored monitors that stream up-to-the-second data to voracious analysts. The clues to the usefulness of these data are found among a long list of research studies.

Question 17.2. The so-called "cockroach theory"[2] holds that once an analyst raises or lowers his or her earnings forecast more such revisions are likely to follow. (As, so the theory goes, "Once you see one cockroach more will follow.")
    This theory is largely:
    a. Fact.
    b. Fiction.

An early study by Eugene Hawkins, Stanley Chamberlin, and Wayne Daniel,[3] using a database that contained earnings estimates for over 2,400 stocks made by more than 70 brokerage firms for each of the 24 quarters from March 1975 through December 1980, found that month-to-month percent changes in consensus estimates could be used to predict changes in stock prices.

In 1984 Edwin Elton, Martin Gruber, and Mustafa Gultekin[4] found that analysts had a tendency to overestimate earnings growth for companies they believed would do well and underestimate earnings growth for companies they believed would do poorly. Later studies by Edwin Elton, Martin Gruber, and Mustafa Gultekin;[5] and D. van Dijk,[6] using larger samples of analysts' expectational data, showed that revisions of earnings forecasts could be used to predict future returns.

In 1985 Robert D. Arnott, chief executive officer at First Quadrant, reported, "Although the market is relatively efficient in discounting current consensus, the startling fact is that it seems to reflect essentially none of the information in recent shifts in consensus!"[7]

Patricia O'Brien has found that analysts' most recent forecasts are more accurate. Thus, when aggregating forecasts, eliminating the most out-of-date forecasts improves the accuracy of the overall forecast.[8]

In 1991 Dan Givoly and Josef Lakonishok[9] found that news of revisions is absorbed slowly, giving rise to the possibility that investors who act upon this type of publicly available information can earn above-benchmark returns. Also in 1991 Scott Stickel,[10] after studying 173,620 revisions for 1,465 companies by 1,869 analysts from 83 brokerage firms, reported that "prices continue to drift in the direction of the revision for about six months after the revision."

In 1998 I participated in an internal study of the estimate-revision effect using 20 years of quarterly data on the 500 largest stocks. The results of this study, summarized in Table 17.1, showed that the estimate-revision effect was very strong from 1977 through 1981. The 120 stocks in the upward-revision portfolio gained 6.4 percent; the 120 stocks in the downward-revision portfolio fell 5.8 percent. The effect decreased somewhat but remained strong from 1982 through 1991. During the five-year period between 1992 and 1996 the effect vanished.

TABLE 17.1   Relative Returns: Earnings Estimate Revisions (Quintiles)

	1	2	3	4	5
5 years (1977 to 1981)	6.4	2.0	−0.6	−2.8	−5.8
10 years (1982 to 1991)	4.5	1.8	0.7	−2.5	−5.0
5 years (1992 to 1996)	0.6	0.1	−0.1	0.2	0.9

Note: Returns are annualized, using quarterly rebalancing.
Source: Morgan Stanley Investment Management.

In 1994 Langdon Wheeler,[11] president of Numeric Investors L.P., tested the usefulness of several estimate-revision measures to predict investment returns within a broad universe of stocks. He found that data on analysts' revisions of consensus earnings estimates were useful predictors of coming changes in stock prices in each of the years he studied. Further, he showed that a more accurate predictor of coming price changes could be created by assembling several measures—such as changes in the consensus estimate and the number of estimates raised or lowered in the last few months—into a combined score.

Finally, Wheeler tested the effectiveness of his score in predicting returns in different market environments and in different market sectors. He found that his score was most effective when used across all economic sectors and when applied to smaller-capitalization stocks.

As you might expect, many other researchers (and practitioners) have mined the historical estimate-revision data in hopes of finding more useful measures of the earnings forecasts that are embedded in the consensus aggregation.

Specifically, researchers have shown that more useful data can be extracted from the following: more recent forecasts (see Patricia O'Brien,[12] Scott Stickel,[13] and Lawrence Brown[14]); forecasts that deviate from the average forecasts (see Haim Mozes and Patricia Williams[15]); company preannouncements (see Sandip Bhagat[16] and Leonard Soffer, Ramu Thiagaragan, and Beverly Walther[17]); forecasts by historically more accurate forecasters (see Parveen Shinka, Lawrence Brown, and Somnath Das[18]); and classifications of analysts as "leaders, followers, or rebels" (see Ronald Kahn and Andrew Rudd[19]).

Martin Herzberg, James Guo, and Lawrence Brown[20] have found that a composite measure incorporating the newness of the forecast, deviation of recent forecasts from the consensus measure, and the better-than-average skill of particular forecasters provides more accurate forecasts.

Today aggregations of many of the aforementioned categories are available through StarMine. Collecting every estimate and recommendation compiled by Thomson Financial I/B/E/S and First Call, StarMine monitors the roughly 5,200 estimates that are published each day. In turn, this service identifies the persons whom it considers the top analysts, tracks estimate revisions by the top analysts, predicts earnings surprises, and ranks stocks by changes in analysts' sentiment.

Several of these researchers have found persuasive evidence that analysts nibble away at forecast revisions. One revision is, indeed, likely to be followed by another. Thus, the answer to Question 17.2 is "a"—fact.

Before turning from the subject of estimate revisions it is useful to contemplate the fate of a perfect forecaster in a world in which portfolio managers devour estimate-revision data. In Richard Bernstein's book *Navigate the Noise: Investing in the New Age of Media and Hype*[21] he spins a wonderful story of a security analyst who is a great forecaster. She makes her full-year forecast on January 1. Over the course of the next 12 months her prognostications materialize exactly as she had forecasted.

Succumbing to the belief that each analyst's forecasts must be up-to-the-minute to be useful—with no interim dribble coming from the analyst of the "up a few cents" or "down a few cents" variety, this great forecaster might actually be dropped from some real-time databases *because she has not updated her earnings estimate within a certain number of months.*

Contrast Bernstein's great forecaster with one of her contemporaries down the hall who is continually revising his forecasts. His phone rings constantly with calls from investors who want to know the reasons for his most recent changes. When he calls the supposedly impossible to reach manager of a large mutual fund with a message like "Tell her I have revised my estimate on Dell," he always gets through.

Question 17.3.   Imagine you are a Wall Street analyst who makes quarterly earnings estimates. You note that 12 other Wall Street analysts routinely make quarterly forecasts of ABC Widget's earnings.

Your firm meticulously tallies the number of telephone calls that you make to and receive from your firm's clients. Your "contact scorecard"—which is reviewed at compensation time—gives many more points to contacts that you make with the firm's largest clients—which, not incidentally, produce the largest percentage of the firm's commissions. (Such "contact scorecard" systems for security analysts are the norm with Wall Street firms.)

Which of the following statements are true?

    a. Your earnings forecasts are less likely to be wrong if they "hide" near the 12-analyst consensus.

    b. You know from experience that your telephone never rings (with clients' calls) when your estimate "hides" near the consensus.

    c. Not yet enjoying "star" status on the Institutional Investor All-Star Analyst Team, you discover that an extremely high or low forecast entices your clients to call—and to accept your calls.

    d. All of the statements are true.

The correct answer is "d"—all of the statements are true.

Question 17.4.   If you are the analyst, what would you do?

    a. Hide near the consensus for fear of being marred with a bad forecast.

    b. Start your telephone ringing.

Many researchers assume the former—that Wall Street analysts operate in fear of making poor forecasts. But in my considerable experience working in Wall Street research departments, I believe *many* analysts "game" the system—placing their estimates where their telephones will start ringing.

Three

Landmark Insights

CHAPTER 18

Nobel Laureate Markowitz

I encourage you to ask your broker, your financial planner, and your investment manager these questions. If any of them cannot give you a satisfactory answer, move on until you find someone who can.

Question 18.1. In 1990 the Royal Swedish Academy of Sciences awarded the Alfred Nobel Memorial Prize in Economic Sciences to Harry Markowitz, Merton Miller, and William Sharpe.

What landmark contribution did Harry Markowitz make in the 1950s?

How should his insight influence your day-to-day investment decisions?

The insight for which Harry Markowitz received the Nobel prize was first published in 1952 in an article entitled "Portfolio Selection"[1] and more extensively in his 1959 book, *Portfolio Selection: Efficient Diversification of Investments.*[2] In his article and book Markowitz showed that under certain conditions an investor's choice of a portfolio can be reduced to balancing two dimensions—the expected return of the portfolio and its risk (measured by its variance).

Thus Markowitz showed us that the risk of an asset that really matters is not the risk of each asset in isolation but the contribution that each asset makes to the risk of the aggregate portfolio. With this insight Markowitz reduced the complicated and multidimensional problem of portfolio construction with respect to a large number of different assets, all with varying properties, to a conceptually simple two-dimensional problem known as "mean-variance" analysis. We all want to hold a portfolio with the highest mean (i.e., average) expected return and the lowest variance (the risk of not realizing the expected return).

When published in 1952 Markowitz's ideas scarcely took the investment profession by storm. As with insights from other researchers, his equation-filled presentation is over the heads of most investors. Without the benefit of Markowitz's insights, dangerous homilies such as "put all of your eggs in one basket, and watch the basket" still prevail.

Even though more than 50 years have passed since the publication of Markowitz's seminal article, some people lump his contributions under the umbrella of "modern" portfolio theory. Personally, I have trouble referring to something that was first articulated more than 50 years ago as "modern." I first studied Markowitz's insights in 1961; I wrote the *Dow Jones–Irwin Guide to Modern Portfolio Theory* in 1979. His insights are profoundly important; they are not, however, "modern" insights. They *are* "portfolio theory."

Markowitz's work has permanently changed the course of investment-related thought. Before Markowitz's article it was more or less taken for granted that the proper way to construct an investment portfolio was just to select the best securities. It was erroneously assumed that this technique would maximize the expected return of the resultant portfolio. Markowitz correctly pointed out, however, that the goal of portfolio management is not solely to maximize the expected rate of return. (If this were the only aim, then rather than diversifying, investors should concentrate all of their assets in those securities with the highest expected returns—regardless of risk.) Markowitz demonstrated instead that the objective of portfolio management is to maximize that dreaded thing from the economics course you took many, many years ago—"expected utility."

Happily, you do not need to know a lot about "utility" to be an astute investor and a knowledgeable fiduciary. The concept of utility is based on the fact that different consumers have different desires and that, as individuals, we derive personal satisfaction in different ways. As a consumer you purchase goods that satisfy your needs or desires. To avoid the complex task of attempting to measure the relative importance of everyone's needs and desires, economists have devised the concept of utility. From the perspective of an economist, purchases are said to provide the consumer with some measure of utility.

Markowitz uses the concept of utility in much the same way. Basically, utility embraces all that an investor wants and all that an investor wants to avoid. If I set the complexities aside, "utility" can be viewed as being synonymous with "satisfaction"—as you the consumer see it. When satisfaction is translated into investment terms, each investor's preferred combination of investments depends on his or her preference for positive returns relative to his or her distaste for risk. In turn, then, the goal of all rational investing can be thought of as maximizing satisfaction (or, in economic jargon, utility).

The trouble with this definition is that it ends up exactly where it starts. We say that investors seek to maximize utility. But what is utility? It is what investors seek to maximize! Of what use, then, is the economist's assumption that investors seek to maximize utility?

The answer is that if all investors are attempting to maximize this thing called utility, *all investors must behave in essentially the same way.* Consistent behavior by investors means that very specific statements can be made about their aggregate behavior. This, in turn, permits accurate descriptions of their future actions.

A means of somehow measuring utility and determining precisely how much utility someone would attain from a given amount of consumption would be very desirable. Unfortunately, no one has ever been able to devise a satisfactory method for measuring utility. This makes it impossible to gauge marginal utility directly—the additional unit of satisfaction the consumer gets for each additional dollar of expenditure.

Happily, the inability to measure marginal utility is not a problem. Although utility cannot be gauged on an absolute scale, it is possible to evaluate it on a relative scale—much as temperature might be gauged without a thermometer. That is, various states of hot and cold can be distinguished even if the absolute differences cannot be determined. Similarly, a consumer without an explicit scale of measurement can still express judgments about relative levels of satisfaction and dissatisfaction. For any individual these relative judgments can be put in the form of indifference curves.

A typical investor's indifference curve (or utility function) is shown in Figure 18.1. Here I have placed risk (measured as the standard deviation of return) on the horizontal axis and expected return on the vertical axis. This labeling of the axes produces a utility function that is upward-sloping to the right.

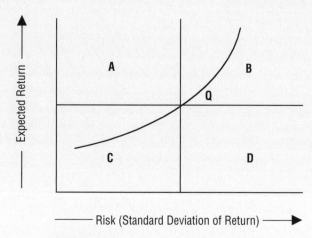

FIGURE 18.1   Investor's Indifference Curve

To provide a point of reference, I have divided the investor's indifference curve in Figure 18.1 into four quadrants—A, B, C, and D.
Moving from the midpoint Q, all investors would prefer any point
in quadrant A—offering a higher expected return and less risk. Conversely, all investors would be less satisfied with any point in quadrant D—with a lower expected return and more risk.

The choice of the points in the other quadrants depends on each
individual's preference for return and distaste for risk. Moving
along the curve in quadrant B, this typical investor is willing to accept additional risk only in exchange for proportionately larger increases in expected return.

Conversely, moving along this curve in quadrant C, the typical
investor is willing to accept lower expected return only in exchange
for proportionately larger declines in risk. Note, however, that moving to different points along the indifference curve neither increases
nor decreases your total level of satisfaction.

Figure 18.2 shows a typical investor's indifference map—a set of
indifference curves that profile an investor's willingness to trade off
changes in risk against changes in expected return. The important
characteristic of an investor's indifference map is that each successive curve moving upward to the left represents a higher level of utility (or, if you prefer, satisfaction).

It should not be presumed that all of the curves on the indifference

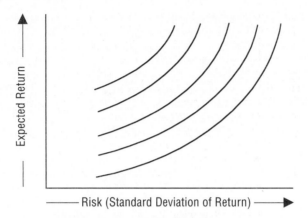

FIGURE 18.2   Investor's Indifference Map

map are possible. Instead, what the indifference map shows is that, depending on the available alternatives, a rational investor would always prefer a higher curve, one with less risk and a greater expected return. Again, given the highest available curve, the investor's personal preferences are such that he or she will be indifferent to any combination of risk or expected return along that particular curve.

Figure 18.3 illustrates two cases of investor indifference. Both investors are risk-averse. The adventuresome investor (A) is willing to trade relatively smaller increases in incremental expected return for a given increment of risk than the "conservative" investor (B).

An inefficient relationship between risk and expected return is illustrated in Figure 18.4. Here expected return is plotted on the

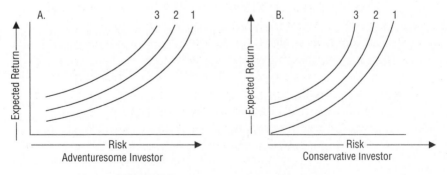

FIGURE 18.3   Typical Cases of Indifference

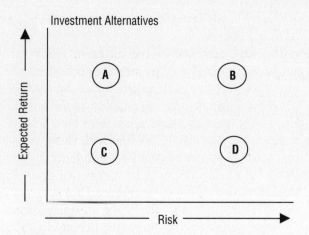

FIGURE 18.4   An Inefficient Set of Investment Alternatives

vertical axis and risk is plotted on the horizontal axis. Which investment in Figure 18.4 best meets the objective of maximum return with minimum risk? Investment alternatives A and B have the same expected return, but B carries more risk. Thus, since investment A would be preferred by any rational, risk-averse investor, B can be eliminated from consideration.

Of alternatives A and C, both have the same risk, but A has a higher expected return. Accordingly, alternative C can be eliminated from consideration. A comparison of the two remaining alternatives, A and D, reveals that A has both a higher expected return and a lower risk than D. Thus, investment A—with the highest expected return and the lowest risk—is the preferred alternative for *any* rational investor.

What would happen if the four investment alternatives that are depicted in Figure 18.4 existed in a competitive real-world marketplace (while maintaining the assumption that everyone has the same estimates of expected return and risk)? Because all investors would prefer investment A to the other alternatives, their demand for investment A would drive up its price. As the price of investment A increased, the expected return per unit of investment would decrease.

Through what the classical eighteenth-century economist Adam Smith[3] referred to as the "invisible hand," prices in competitive markets quickly adjust to the forces of supply and demand. These adjustments in price eliminate any market inefficiencies whereby one investment is so attractively priced that it is preferred to all others.

Thus, even though investors have different risk/return preferences, rational investors will always attempt to find portfolios that provide (1) the maximum rate of return for every level of risk, or, conversely, (2) the minimum level of risk for every possible rate of return. Markets that reflect this goal are said to be efficient. Markets containing investments that are out of line with this goal, such as alternative D in Figure 18.4, are said to be inefficient.

Since inefficiencies are eliminated by competition, the hypothetical investment alternatives depicted in Figure 18.4 would vanish. Instead, as long as everyone used the same estimates for expected return and risk, the inefficient marketplace depicted in Figure 18.4 would, through price changes, become efficient, and the new investment alternatives would array themselves as shown in Figure 18.5. The curve XYZ in Figure 18.5 thus represents the so-called efficient frontier of investment alternatives. That is, the investments on this line offer the highest level of return for this degree of risk or, alternatively, provide the lowest level of risk for this rate of return.

Working from the efficient frontier of investment alternatives depicted in Figure 18.5, suppose it is necessary to select an investment for someone whose investment preferences closely reflect those of a classic conservative investor. Such a person would want to attain the highest available return that is consistent with a minimum

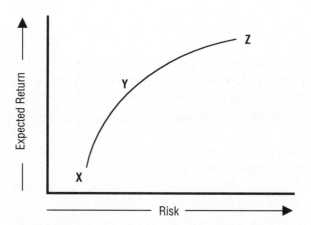

FIGURE 18.5 An Efficient Set of Investment Alternatives

level of risk. Of the three alternatives shown in Figure 18.5, the investment with the lowest risk—the overriding consideration for this person—is investment X.

At the other extreme, suppose that an investment must be selected for a classic speculator. Here, the objective is to select the alternative with the lowest available risk that is consistent with the highest expected return. Of the three hypothetical investments shown in Figure 18.5, the one with the highest expected return—the overriding preference for this person—is investment Z. The middle ground between the two extremes—essentially a balance between risk and expected return—is represented by investment Y.

Figure 18.6 shows the comparative distributions of the likely returns for two hypothetical investments, A and B. Note that both investments have the same average expected returns. The distributions of the expected returns are, however, quite different. Specifically, investment A has more dispersion around the mean than investment B. Thus, investment B emerges as superior because it offers the same expected return but with less variance of estimated returns.

It is important to remember that, from an investor's point of view, the more assurance that you have that the actual results will parallel the expected results, the better the investment. Thus, as we put into operation the maxim that rational, risk-averse investors will always seek investments with a minimum level of risk for a given level of expected return, the statistical variance (or its square root, the standard deviation) of the distribution of possible expected returns is a viable measure of risk.

In summary, Markowitz demonstrated that the two relevant characteristics of a portfolio are its:

1. Expected return.
2. Risk—operationally defined as the dispersion of possible returns around the expected return.

He also demonstrated that rational investors will choose to hold efficient portfolios that:

■ Maximize the expected return for a given degree of risk.
■ Minimize risk for a given level of expected return.

Investment A

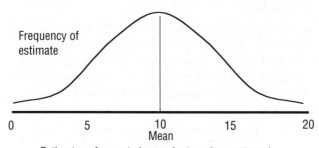

Estimates of expected annual return (percentages)

Investment B

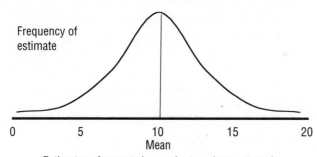

Estimates of expected annual return (percentages)

FIGURE 18.6 Comparative Distributions of Likely Returns

He further demonstrated that the identification of efficient portfolios requires estimates of each security's:

- Expected return.
- Variance of return.
- Covariance of return with every other security under consideration.

The crux of Markowitz's "covariance" insight is elegant yet simple. The hypothetical investment A in Figure 18.7 earns a positive return over time, but its interim valuations fluctuate.

Imagine you could find another investment with the same underlying positive rate of return over time *but* with fluctuations *exactly opposite* to those of investment A. Figure 18.8 shows that if you purchased both investments A and B the interim fluctuations would cancel one another, resulting in a steadily increasing return—without any interim fluctuations.

Figure 18.9 provides a different perspective. Here expected return is on the vertical axis and expected risk is on the horizontal axis. In Figure 18.9 investment X offers lower expected return commensurate with lower expected risk. Investment Y offers higher expected return commensurate with higher expected risk.

Next, suppose that the expected risks and expected returns for investments X and Y fluctuate together in lockstep. If this were true, the expected risks and expected returns for perfectly correlated combinations of X and Y would all fall on a straight line connecting the two investments in Figure 18.9.

Suppose that instead of being perfectly correlated investments X and Y are perfectly uncorrelated. That is, whenever the expected return of X moves up the expected return of Y will move down by a proportionate amount. Whenever the expected return of X moves down Y will move up by a proportionate amount. This is shown in

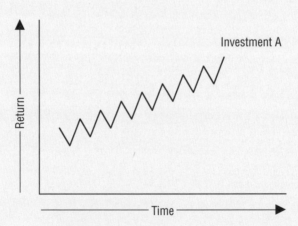

FIGURE 18.7 Hypothetical Investment

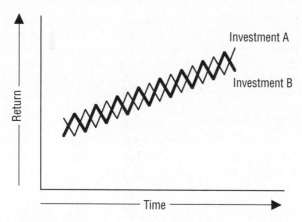

FIGURE 18.8 Hypothetical Risk-Offsetting Investments

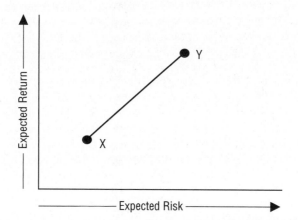

FIGURE 18.9 Two Hypothetical Perfectly Correlated Investments

Figure 18.10. Here because the risks of holding X and Y individually cancel out in an appropriately weighted portfolio that includes investments X and Y, the expected risk can be reduced to zero.

Now the magic. Typical expected risks and expected returns are neither perfectly correlated nor perfectly uncorrelated. Usually they fall somewhere in the middle. When this occurs, portfolios composed of different proportions of investments X and Y plot on the efficient frontier connecting X and Y that is similar to that shown in Figure 18.11.

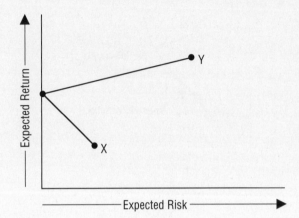

FIGURE 18.10 Two Hypothetical Perfectly Uncorrelated Investments

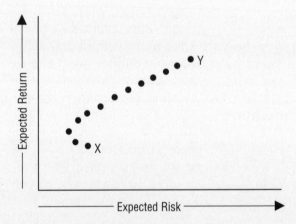

FIGURE 18.11 Hypothetical Efficient Frontier Derived from Investments X and Y

I cannot overemphasize the importance of the insight that comes from the outword bow on the left side of the curve in the efficient frontier. Because not all of the securities in a portfolio move in lock-step, the efficient frontier traces a curve, offering investors higher expected returns and lower risks. Notice here that there is absolutely no reason to hold only investment X. A higher return is available for the same or lower expected risk.

The matching of the available investment alternatives along the efficient frontier with the investor's highest indifference curve in Figure 18.12 is the final step in the investment selection process. Impor-

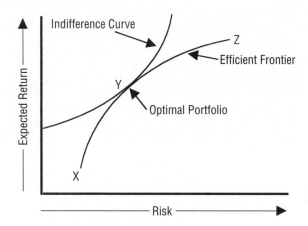

FIGURE 18.12 Optimal Portfolio

tantly, the fact that all investors agree about the optimal combination of risky securities does not mean that all investors will choose the same portfolio. Different sets of indifference curves, representing either more defensive or more aggressive investors, would lead to the selection of different investments from the wide-ranging set of efficient alternatives.

Returning to Question 18.1: Markowitz has shown us the benefits of owning well-diversified portfolios and conversely, the poor combination of expected return and expected risk when you hold only a few stocks.

CHAPTER 19

Nobel Laureate Sharpe

Question 19.1. In 1990 the Royal Swedish Academy of Sciences awarded the Alfred Nobel Memorial Prize in Economic Sciences to Harry Markowitz, Merton Miller, and William Sharpe.

What was Sharpe's landmark contribution?

How does his insight influence your day-to-day investment decisions?

During the 1960s a number of researchers—William Sharpe,[1] John Lintner,[2] Jack Treynor,[3] and Jan Mossin,[4] among whom Sharpe was the leading figure—used Markowitz's portfolio theory as a basis for developing a pricing theory—the capital asset pricing model (CAPM—pronounced "cap-em"). Sharpe's pioneering achievement is contained in his 1964 article, "Capital Asset Prices: A Theory of Market Equilibrium under Conditions of Risk."

Using the framework of the CAPM, all investors—each with his or her own unique preferences for risk—can, by using a combination of a risk-free investment (or borrowing) and the "market portfolio," hold an "optimal" portfolio.

The capital asset pricing model brings together two key concepts—efficient markets and risk premiums. The concept of an efficient capital market indicates that market prices cannot be expected to diverge by much or for long from the consensus view of an equitable rate of return for a given level of risk. The concept of a risk premium indicates that as investors we expect to be paid whenever we expose ourselves to any risk above that of a risk-free investment. The CAPM provides the framework for determining the relationship between risk and return and the amount of the risk premium.

The classic example of a risk-free investment is a short-term obligation of the U.S. government. Since the government can always print money, there is no dollar risk with such an instrument. This is not, of course, a truly risk-free investment. Any investment that returns a fixed number of dollars is subject to the risks inherent in the fluctuations of the future purchasing power of the dollar.

According to the CAPM, investors who select a risk-free investment (such as short-term government securities) can expect to be compensated for the use of their money—nothing more, nothing less. This risk-free compensation can be thought of as the amount the government is willing to pay to "rent" money.

Other investors opt for risky investments, including common stocks. Such investors expect a higher rate of return as compensation for the risk that they assume. The difference between the risk-free rate of return and the total return from a risky investment is called a risk premium.

Theoretically, the market encompasses all securities in proportion to their market value. In practice, value-weighted indexes, such as the NYSE or the S&P Composite indexes, are used as proxies for the market. Given the assumption of an efficient capital market, the pricing of the market portfolio at any point in time accurately reflects an equilibrium relationship between the market's consensus of risk and expected return.

Figure 19.1 shows the relationship between risk and expected return underlying the CAPM. The horizontal axis measures risk (defined as the standard deviation of return). The vertical axis measures expected return. Note that when risk is zero, the expected return is the risk-free rate of return. Note that as you increase your exposure to market risk to 1.0 on the market risk scale (at which point you are fully invested in the market) you earn the entire equity risk premium offered by the market portfolio (M). The difference between the expected risk-free rate of return (R) and the expected return of the market portfolio (M) is the equity risk premium offered by the market portfolio. By assuming that investors can lend or borrow at the risk-free rate it is possible to select combinations of risk-free investments and the market portfolios that plot along line RMZ.

Thus, CAPM provides an explicit statement of the equilibrium expected return on all assets. When the market is in equilibrium, there is no pressure for change. In disequilibrium investors are dissatisfied with either the securities they hold or the prices of those se-

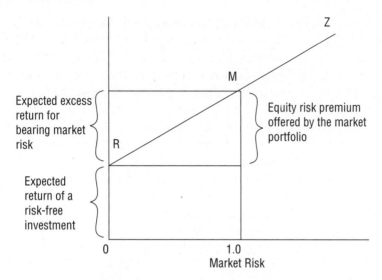

FIGURE 19.1 Risk and Expected Return

curities and as a result there is pressure for change. At any moment, however, the market is in equilibrium, reflecting the combined influence of all investors' wealth, preferences, and predictions. Whenever disequilibrium occurs because of changes in wealth, preferences, or predictions, these changes are translated to the market and equilibrium is restored.

Adding the assumption that every investor can borrow and lend *changes the optimal combinations of risk and expected return.* Figure 19.2 shows the investment alternatives that become available with lending and borrowing. These range from the riskless rate of return, obtained by lending to the Treasury at the riskless rate (point R), through to choosing to be fully invested in the most desirable combination of risky investments (point M)—the market portfolio—to leveraging the market portfolio through borrowing (point Z). Next, the investment that best matches the investor's personal preferences (i.e., the point of tangency between the highest level of investor utility and line RMZ) represents combinations of borrowing and lending and the market portfolio.

Thus, the CAPM provides an explicit statement of the equilibrium expected return for all securities. According to CAPM, the prices of assets will be in equilibrium when the expected return on a

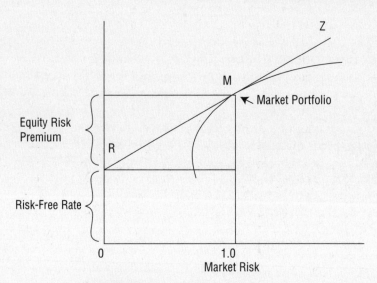

FIGURE 19.2 Investment Alternatives

security is equal to a riskless rate of interest plus a premium that is proportional to the amount of market-related risk.

To state it another way, the expected excess return for a security, or portfolio, will come entirely from the market component of return. This is because in equilibrium a security with zero systematic risk will have the expected return that is available for a riskless asset. Furthermore, in equilibrium the expected excess return from the nonmarket component is always zero.

Returning to Question 19.1, Sharpe extended Markowitz's work in two important dimensions. First, Sharpe broadened the analysis to include riskless assets (such as short-term government securities) and the possibility of borrowing. Second, he developed a simplified model that alleviates the burdensome data collection and computing problems inherent in the Markowitz model.

How should Sharpe's insight influence your day-to-day decisions? The market portfolio is "mean-variance-efficient"—at any instant the market portfolio reflects everyone's best thinking. Thus, there is no other combination of securities, held in these proportions at these prices, that can have a higher mean expected return or a lower variance.

Broad-based index funds approximate the mean and variance of the market portfolio. If you want less risk than is inherent in the market portfolio, you can combine an investment in a broad-based index fund with an investment in Treasury bills; by doing so you acquire an efficient portfolio. If you want more risk than is inherent in the "market portfolio," you can borrow money to buy more of the market portfolio; thus you still own an efficient portfolio.

As an aside, one of my favorite stories about the media and the dissemination of investment news goes back to when Bill Sharpe learned that he would be awarded the Nobel prize. At the time of the announcement we were both attending a Q-Group meeting in Tucson, Arizona. Knowing this was a rare event, representatives of the national press arrived after long flights in their chartered jets, and there was a hastily prepared news conference. Within two or three minutes it was clear what kinds of questions the newscasters wanted Sharpe to answer: What are your favorite stocks? Which stocks do you own in your personal portfolio? Sharpe's reply, that he owned a diversified group of index funds managed by the Teachers Insurance and Annuity Association—College Retirement Equities Fund (TIAA-CREF), was *not* what they wanted to hear.

Dale Berman of the Q-Group, who monitored the press and television for their subsequent stories, was not completely surprised to find that there were no press or television reports of the press conference. Stocks make good stories; index funds do not.

In this context, it is interesting to note that following the announcement of Daniel Kahneman's 2002 Nobel prize, CNBC aired its interview with Kahneman. Proving that some things do not change, CNBC asked: "What investment tip do you have for investors?" Proving further that some things do not change, Kahneman replied, "Buy and hold index funds."[5]

CHAPTER 20

Compensation for Bearing Risks

Few investors and fiduciaries answer the following question correctly. It is not a trick question. To answer the question correctly (and to understand why your answer is correct) you need a keen understanding of one of the most important—and practical—insights about the risks of investing. Good luck.

Question 20.1.   A fundamental fact is that investors expect to be compensated for taking risks. Why else would investors invest?

Investors as a whole are compensated for undertaking the risk of investing in:

   a. The stocks of well-run large and small companies.
   b. The stocks of small, unseasoned, growing companies.
   c. A portfolio composed of all of the stocks (weighted by their size) that constitute a fast-growing industry.
   d. A broad-based index fund composed of all of the stocks (weighted by their size) that make up the market.
   e. All of the above.
   f. "a" and "b."
   g. "c" and "d."

"Excess return" is the return that is expected to be derived from the security (during a specified holding period) less the estimated return from holding a riskless security (such as a short-term government obligation) during the same period.

The "market model" describes the relationship between the excess return on a security and that of the overall market (represented by a single index). This important concept divides a security's excess return into two components: (1) market-related (or systematic) return, and (2) non-market-related (or residual) return.

The underlying "equation" for the market model is:

Since a security's

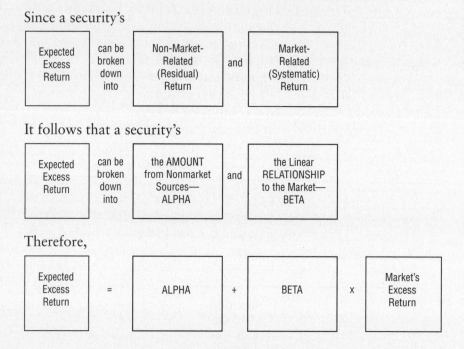

Here excess return is the return derived from a security, or a portfolio of securities, less the return from holding a riskless security (such as T-bills) during the same period.

It is often said that "a rising tide lifts all boats." Alpha has nothing to do with the rise and fall of the market. Alpha is the non-market-related component of a security's excess return. Alpha can be either positive or negative. If it is positive, it is due either to the investor's luck or to his or her skill—rather than to the return of the overall market. If it is negative, it is due either to poor luck or to the investor's lack of skill.

Beta measures the sensitivity of a portfolio, or a particular security, to general market movements. If the beta is 1.0, the portfolio or security mirrors market swings. If the beta is less than 1.0, the portfolio or security is expected to dampen market swings. If the beta is greater than 1.0, the portfolio or security is expected to accentuate market swings.

There are two very important takeaways from this "equation." (If you were in a classroom, reconstructing the foregoing "equation" from memory would most certainly be on the next test.)

The first takeaway is that portfolios and individual securities have alphas—some positive and some negative. The market and index funds do not have an alpha. The second takeaway is that the "equation" appears to mix apples and oranges: Beta is an estimate of a *relationship* to the market's excess return; alpha is an estimate of an *amount*—the expected risk-adjusted return. For this reason an explicit statement of a security's characteristics requires estimates of: (1) alpha, (2) beta, and (3) alpha's variance.

It follows that if a security's excess return can be broken down into two components—alpha (non-market-related) and beta (market-related)—a security's risk can also be divided into the same categories. Thus, the risk associated with an investment outcome can be broken into the systematic part and the residual part. Therefore, the "equation" for a security's risk is:[1]

Total Security Risk	=	Risk of the Residual (Nonmarket) Component	+	Risk of the Systematic (Market) Component

Question 20.1 begins: "A fundamental fact is that investors expect to be compensated for taking risks. Why else would investors invest?" Next, the question asks you to select from a list of choices the risks for which the market compensates investors. The return derived from investing in the market portfolio is *the only return that is earned by suppliers of risk capital.*

Any risks and returns that are left over after accounting for market risk and market return are known by a variety of names, including residual, nonmarket, unsystematic, and, in the words used by practitioners, *stock-selection risk*. Stock-selection risk pinpoints the source of the risk as coming from selecting a portfolio that is different from the market portfolio.

It is impossible for me to overemphasize the importance of understanding the correct answer to Question 20.1. The insight required to answer this question correctly is that the capital markets reward only *undiversifiable risks*. For the market at large, there is no compensation for specific risk (arising from factors that are specific to the company) and extra-market risk (arising from groups of stocks whose movements do not parallel those of the market) because these risks can be completely avoided by merely owning the market portfolio.

What you need to remember about these classifications is that the risk from each investor's stock selections is always offset by other investors' stock selection risk. Looked at another way, the capital-market system cannot, and does not, reward investment selection. The capital-market system rewards only capital-market risk. *Any above-market gains derived solely from astute investment selection are at the expense of the investors who have offsetting selection losses.* Thus the correct answer to Question 20.1 is "d"—a broad-based index fund composed of all of the stocks (weighted by their size) that make up the market.

Much as alpha and beta have taken on very explicit meanings in investment management jargon, *R-squared* defines the proportion of either a security's or a portfolio's total risk that is attributable to market risk.

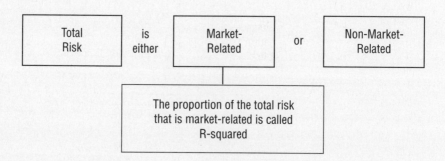

In a portfolio context, R-squared measures the completeness of diversification relative to that of the overall market. At one extreme the market portfolio is completely diversified. Thus, in the market portfolio systematic, or market-related, risk is the only source of uncertainty. Because R-squared is a measure of the proportion of the total risk that is market risk, the R-squared value of the market portfolio is 1.00. To put it another way, a portfolio with an R-squared value of 1.00 will have zero selection risk.[2]

The value of R-squared for a typical stock is about 0.30. This means that around 30 percent of a typical stock's behavior (and, hence, risk) is explained by the behavior of the market. In contrast, the R-squared value of a well-diversified portfolio will typically exceed 0.90. This means that more than 90 percent of a well-diversified portfolio's total price movements can typically be explained by the market's behavior.

The simple decomposition of return (and risk) is:

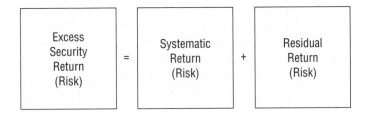

Barra (following Barr Rosenberg's research) goes a step further by decomposing residual risk and return.

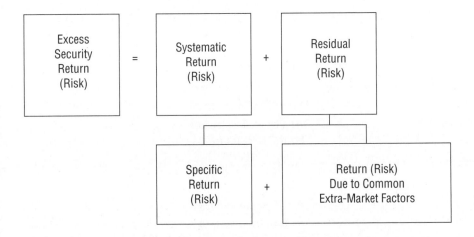

As discussed earlier, systematic risk is the degree to which security returns, or portfolio returns, are related to market moves. The measure of systematic risk is beta. Systematic return, equal to the security beta times the market's excess return (the market's return above the risk-free rate) is the component of return arising from systematic risk. The residual return is merely any remaining return that cannot be explained by the systematic return. The residual risk can, however, be further broken down into specific risk and extra-market risk.

Specific risk is the uncertainty in the return that arises from events that are specific to the company. Specific risk is unrelated to events that have an impact on other companies.

Extra-market covariance is the remaining component of residual risk. It is manifested as a tendency of related assets to move together in a way that is independent of the market as a whole. The term "covariance" refers to the tendency of stock prices to move together, or "covary." The term "extra-market" means that these co-movements are not related to the movements of the market as a whole. Extra-market covariance can be thought of as the middle ground between systematic and specific risk. Systematic risk affects all companies. Specific risk affects only one company. Extra-market covariance affects a homogeneous group of companies, such as those belonging to a certain industry or those with large capitalizations.

For individual stocks specific risk is most important, accounting for about 50 percent of the total risk; the remainder is about equally divided between systematic risk and extra-market covariance. For a well-diversified portfolio, systematic risk is likely to be 80 or 90 percent of the total risk.

For portfolios with concentrations of stocks in certain industry groups or classes of stocks such as interest-sensitive stocks, extra-market covariance is very important. Thus, the construction of prudent, well-reasoned portfolios requires the prediction of all three aspects of risk—systematic, specific, and extra-market. Barra derives estimates of both market returns and extra-market covariances from a single underlying model. Interested readers will find a general explanation of this procedure in Rosenberg and Guy[3] and a detailed explanation in Rosenberg et al.[4]

In 1992 two respected academics, Eugene Fama and Kenneth French,[5] published a landmark article in which they argued that the risk of common-stock investments needs to be characterized not just by the market factor set forth by Sharpe but rather by three factors—a market factor, a size factor, and a value factor. In this and subsequent papers,[6] they argued that three factors best describe the risks and returns of a portfolio—the extra risk of stocks versus a risk-free asset (the market factor), the extra risk of small-capitalization stocks over large-capitalization stocks (the size factor), and the extra risk of value stocks over growth stocks.

Fama and French's belief that the market prices a size factor gives rise to the question: Why are some risks priced? How does the portfolio advice an investor receives from a multifactor world differ from the advice for a single-factor world? Are multifactor models more useful to investors who need to build portfolios? Take the case of recession risk.[7] Most investors hold jobs and are thus sensitive to recessions. If these investors compare two stocks with the same CAPM beta, given their mutual concerns about recession risk, it would be rational for them to accept a lower return from countercyclical stocks and accept a higher return for cyclical stocks. In contrast, an investor with inherited wealth and no job-loss concerns would be willing to accept the recession risk.

If the investors with jobs bid up the price of countercyclical stocks, then recession risk will be priced. At the same time, cyclical stocks would be less in demand by working investors and thus would have lower prices. Thus, as Cochrane notes, investors can "earn a substantial premium for holding dimensions of risk unrelated to market movements."[8]

This view of risk has portfolio implications. The average investor is exposed to and negatively affected by cyclical risk, which is a priced factor. (Risks that do not affect the average investor should not be priced.) Investors with jobs (and thus with labor income) want lower cyclical risk and create a cyclical risk premium, whereas investors without labor income will accept more cyclical risk to capture a premium for a risk that they do not care about. All else equal, an investor who faces lower-than-average recession risk optimally tilts toward greater-than-average exposure to business cycle risk.

In summary, investors should know which priced risks they face and analyze the extent of their exposure. Compared with single-factor models, multifactor models offer a rich context for investors to search for ways to improve portfolio selection.

CHAPTER 21

Daring to Be Different

Question 21.1. Which of the following are ways in which a portfolio can differ from the market?
    Weights invested in (or not invested in):
    a. Broad economic sectors such as technology, energy, or financials.
    b. Industry sectors such as retailing and banks.
    c. Identifiable factors such as P/E and size.
    d. Individual securities.
    e. All of the above.

Question 21.2. To earn significantly above-benchmark returns you must repeatedly:
    a. Discover and exploit investment opportunities that have been missed by other investors due to their incompetence, and/or inattention.[1]
    b. Hold a portfolio that is significantly different from the benchmark portfolio.
    c. Be right! Overweight the sectors, industries, factors, and/or securities that provide above-benchmark returns; underweight the sectors, industries, factors, and/or securities that provide below-benchmark returns.
    d. Be cognizant of, and control for, any tagalong risks (as a decision to increase a portfolio's exposure to dividend yield, unless explicitly controlled for, might simultaneously increase your exposure to nuclear-powered utilities).
    e. Control costs (so that the expenses and fees that you incur implementing your strategy do not eclipse any gains that you derive from your investment acumen).
    f. All of the above.

A portfolio can differ from its benchmark portfolio in many ways. Using Barra's risk indexes (shown in Table 21.1), a portfolio can be tilted toward or away from volatility, momentum, size, size nonlinearity, trading activity, growth, earnings yield, value, earnings variability, leverage, currency sensitivity, and dividend yield.

TABLE 21.1   Risk Indexes

Volatility	**Earnings Yield**
Beta times sigma	Analyst-predicted earnings-to-price ratio
Daily standard deviation	Trailing annual earnings-to-price ratio
High-low price	Historical earnings-to-price ratio
Log of stock price	
Cumulative range	**Value**
Volume beta	Book-to-price ratio
Serial dependence	
Option-implied standard deviation	**Earnings Variability**
	Variability of earnings
Momentum	Variability of cash flows
Relative strength	Extraordinary items in earnings
Historical alpha	Standard deviation of analyst-predicted earnings-to-price ratio
Size	
Log of market capitalization	**Leverage**
	Market leverage
Size Nonlinearity	Book leverage
Cube of log of market capitalization	Debt-to-total-assets ratio
	Senior debt rating
Trading Activity	
Share turnover rate (annual)	**Currency Sensitivity**
Share turnover rate (quarterly)	Exposure to foreign currencies
Share turnover rate (monthly)	
Share turnover rate (five years)	**Dividend Yield**
Indicator for forward split	Predicted dividend yield
Volume to variance	
Growth	
Payout ratio over five years	
Variability in capital structure	
Growth rate of total assets	
Earnings growth rate of five years	
Analyst-predicted earnings growth	
Recent earnings change	

Source: Barra.

At first glance, how difficult could it be to place companies into meaningful descriptive categories? In truth, however, assigning companies to various classification categories is a daunting task. Take, for example, classifying stocks into two style categories: value and growth. Whose definitions of growth and value will prevail?

Practitioners use several ways to group companies into categories. The statistical approaches hold, basically, that if the prices of two stocks move together they belong together. A more pragmatic approach is to begin with a list of groups and themes and plug stocks into the categories that fit the best. The difficulty with this approach lies in determining groups that are widely accepted by investors, applicable across countries and regions, and relatively stable over time. The other approaches classify companies from an economic perspective.

The relatively new Global Industry Classification Standard (GICS) was developed by Morgan Stanley Capital International (MSCI) and Standard & Poor's in the hope that it will be widely accepted as an industry framework for investment research, portfolio management, and asset allocation (see Table 21.2). The enormous drawback of the GICS methodology is that it assigns each company to an industry, a subindustry, and an industry group according to its principal business activity. Since the classification is strictly hierarchical, at each successive level a company can belong to only one group.

Consider the evolution of Sears, Roebuck & Co. Sears began as a catalog seller of virtually everything a consumer (and particularly a rural consumer) might need. The company enjoyed much success following World War II as it established its brand identities—Craftsman tools, Kenmore washers and driers, and DieHard batteries. With Allstate Insurance, Dean Witter Reynolds, and Coldwell Banker, Sears evolved from a retailer into a financial services company. Spinning off Dean Witter in 1993 and Allstate in 1995, Sears drew sales through the "softer side of Sears" and its flagship—hardware, tools, tires, and batteries. Sears launched Sears.com in 1999 as it evolved from "bricks" to "clicks." With the recent acquisition of Lands' End, Sears returned to catalog retailing. To solve this problem Barra uses an industry classification scheme that allows a company to be classified as being in up to six industries.

The importance of security classifications is to use software: *ex post* to allow investors to study the sources of returns and *ex ante* to

TABLE 21.2 Industry Classifications

Energy
Energy

Materials
Materials

Industrials
Capital Goods
Commercial Services and Supplies
Transportation

Consumer Discretionary
Automobiles and Components
Consumer Durables and Apparel
Hotels, Restaurants, and Leisure
Media
Retailing

Consumer Staples
Food and Drug Retailing
Food, Beverages, and Tobacco
Household and Personal Products

Health Care
Health Care Equipment and Services
Pharmaceuticals and Biotechnology

Financials
Banks
Diversified Financials
Insurance
Real Estate

Information Technology
Software and Services
Technology Hardware and Equipment
Semiconductors and Semiconductor Equipment

Telecommunications
Telecommunications Services

Utilities
Utilities

Source: MSCI/Standard & Poor's.

tilt simultaneous portfolios toward desired industries and factors and away from undesired industries and factors, while eliminating tagalong risks.

Question 21.1 offered a list of ways in which a portfolio can differ from the market. The correct answer is "e"—all of the above. A portfolio can differ from the market portfolio by the weights invested in (or not invested in) broad economic sectors such as technology, energy, and financials; industry sectors such as retailing and banks; identifiable factors such as P/E and expected earnings growth; and individual securities.

What should be emphasized is that consistently tilting a portfolio toward, or away from, any economic sector, industry sector, factor such as P/E, or individual companies cannot consistently lead to above-average returns. First and foremost, there is no consistent above-market reward for investing in, say, technology. If there was a persistent above-market reward for owning technology stocks we would all invest more in technology. In turn, the prices of technology would rise and the expected reward would fall. And so the story goes—today's hero is often tomorrow's goat.

The correct answer to Question 21.2 is also "f"—all of the above. To earn significantly above-benchmark returns you must repeatedly discover and exploit investment opportunities that have been missed by other investors due to incompetence and/or inattention; hold a portfolio that is significantly different from the benchmark portfolio; overweight the sectors, industries, factors, and/or securities that provide above-benchmark returns; underweight the sectors, industries, factors, and/or securities that provide below-benchmark returns; be cognizant of, and control for, any tagalong risks; and control costs (so that the expenses and fees that you incur implementing your strategy do not eclipse any gains that you derive from your investment acumen).

Successful active investing is a difficult business. When you dare to be different you must consistently outperform other investors. To put it in a nutshell, to attain above-average returns you must repeatedly capitalize on others' mistakes, know how to be different, be right, and control your trading costs.

CHAPTER 22

Law of Active Management

Question 22.1.   Assume you are on the investment committee of a local hospital. Your committee is interviewing two investment organizations for an "active equity management" assignment.

The first manager, ABC, explains that the firm has been organized around a quest to uncover one or two "winning ideas" a year.

The second manager, XYZ, explains that the firm has been organized around a quest to "know a little bit about a lot of stocks."[1]

Which manager will your committee believe has the more appealing story?
a. ABC.
b. XYZ.

Question 22.2.   Which manager stands the better chance of success?
a. ABC.
b. XYZ.

Two very important constructs—"information ratios" and the "law of active management"—have extremely important implications for how investors organize their research activities, how they design and implement their investment strategies, and how fiduciaries select professional investment managers.

An information ratio defines the opportunities that are available to an active manager. As stated earlier, return is composed of systematic and residual (or unsystematic) returns. By this definition, residual return is uncorrelated with systematic return.

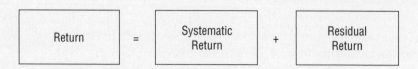

Also, as stated earlier, risk is composed of systematic and residual (or unsystematic) risks.

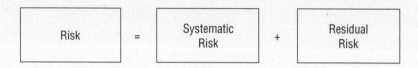

The information ratio is what we want—residual return—divided by what we do not want—volatility of residual return. The larger the information ratio, the larger the possibility of successful active management.

A relatively simple formula called the law of active management gives a very useful approximation of the information ratio.[2] The law is based on two attributes of an investment strategy—breadth and skill. The breadth of a strategy is the number of independent investment decisions you make each year; skill—represented by the information coefficient or (IC)—measures the quality of your investment decisions. The "equation" that brings breadth and skill together into an information ratio is (approximately[3]):

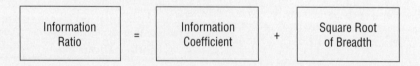

What this "equation" shows is that for you to increase your information ratio from 0.5 to 1.0 you need to either double your skill (the information coefficient), increase your breadth (the number of independent investment decisions) by a factor of four, or do some combination of the two. If your information coefficient is 0.25 and you have four opportunities to "play the game," your information ratio is 0.25 times the square root of four, or 0.5. If you double your skill so that your information ratio is 0.5 and still have four "plays," your information ratio doubles to 1.0. If your information coefficient remains at 0.25 and you increase the original number of plays from 4 to 16, your information ratio doubles to 1.0.

In the words of Grinold and Kahn, the law of active management:

> is designed to give us insight into active management; it isn't an operational tool. Its usefulness is that it quantifies the tradeoffs between increasing the breadth of the strategy—by either covering more stocks or shortening the time horizons of the forecasts—and improving skill.[4]

Imagine you are making an assessment of three strategies for which you want an information ratio of 0.50. Start with a market timer who has independent information about market returns each quarter. The market timer needs an IC of 0.25, because 0.50 equals 0.25 times the square root of four.

As an alternative, consider an investor who follows 100 companies and revises her assessments each quarter. Because she makes 400 bets per year she needs an IC of 0.025, only one-tenth of the market timer's IC, because 0.50 = 0.025 times the square root of 400 (which is 20). "We can see from these examples that strategies with similar information ratios can differ radically in the requirements they place on the investor."[5]

Roughly 8 out of 10 people who are asked to select the more appealing story in Question 22.1 answer "a"—ABC has the more appealing story. The interesting point about Question 22.1 is that the story most people find more appealing is not the approach that stands the better chance of success. The answer to Question 22.2 is "b"—XYZ, an investor with a little information about a lot of securities stands the better chance of success.

CHAPTER 23

Nobel Laureate Nash and Keynes

Question 23.1.   How are the views about investing of the famous economist John Maynard Keynes similar to those of Nobel laureate John Nash?

They both emphasize:

a. That investors are forced to make investment decisions without complete information.

b. It is important to base your decisions on how you expect your competitors to decide—when facing the same decisions, with the same information.

An often quoted view of Keynes is the parallel between selecting winning stocks and selecting the winning contestants in a beauty contest. In Keynes' day, London newspapers found that they could increase their readership by having readers vote in beauty contests. Under the rules of a typical contest, readers were asked to vote for the six most attractive women out of 100 women whose pictures appeared in the newspaper. The newspaper tallied the votes and declared the contestant with the most votes the winner. The enticement for the voters was that if they were sage enough (or lucky enough) to have the winner be one of the six women they voted for on their ballot, they were entered in a newspaper-sponsored lottery that gave them a chance to win valuable prizes.

Keynes reasoned that the best contest strategy was not to vote for the six contestants whom he considered most attractive but, instead, to vote of the six contestants that he believed others would find most attractive. The story goes that Keynes—applying this approach to the stock market—earned several million pounds in his personal account and a tenfold increase in the endowment of King's College, Oxford.

Contrary to what most people assume, Keynes' insight did not stop with his view of the six contestants other voters would find most attractive. His important insight was that if other voters also used Keynes' reasoning, they, too, would vote for the contestants that they thought others would find most attractive. And so on, and so on. Of course, this iterative process goes on forever—which is the real point of Keynes' insight. Beauty contest winners and successful investors must anticipate, in Keynes' words, "what average opinion expects the average opinion to be."[1]

In 1994 the Royal Swedish Academy of Sciences awarded the Bank of Sweden Prize in Economic Sciences in Memory of Alfred Nobel jointly to John Harsanyi, University of California, Berkeley; John Nash, Princeton University; and Reinhard Selten, Rheinische Freiderich-Wilhelms-Universität, Bonn, Germany, for their pioneering analysis of game theory. Whereas probability theory ensued from the study of games of chance, game theory emanates from the study of the strategic interactions in games such as chess or poker, in which players have to think ahead and devise strategies based on the expected countermoves of other players. The relevance of game theory to economists and investors is that the strategic interactions that occur among players in certain games have parallels in many real-world investment situations.

Akiva Goldsman, who wrote the screenplay for the Academy Award–winning film *A Beautiful Mind*—the story of Nash's life—used a clever vignette to describe the epiphany that led to Nash's Nobel prizewinning insight. In the film sequence, four friends are with Nash in a college bar when five attractive women—one of whom is a stellar blonde—enter. As Nash and his friends strategize about how best to approach the blonde, one of Nash's friends remembers the lesson of Adam Smith, the father of modern economics: "In competitive markets individual ambition serves the common good. The best result comes when everyone in the group does what is best for himself." After some reflection Nash exclaims, "Adam Smith needs revision."

Nash's epiphany: If Nash and his four friends all approach the blonde simultaneously—each doing what is best for himself—they will get in each other's way, and they will all be unsuccessful. If, having failed to strike up a conversation with the blonde, Nash and his friends then approach her friends, Nash speculates, "We will all get a cold shoulder because the four other girls will not like being our second choice." However, "if no one goes for the blonde, we do not get in each other's way and we do not insult the other girls. It is the only way we all win." The scene ends with Nash's four friends each dancing with one of the attractive women and Nash rushing past the bewildered blonde—presumably to write more equations on the windows in Princeton's library.

Keynes and Nash understood that many of our decisions must take into account how others will react to our decisions. This led Nash to his Nobel prizewinning articulation of "Nash equilibrium."

Thus the correct answer to Question 23.1 is "b"—both Keynes and Nash emphasize the importance of basing our decisions on how you expect our competitors to decide—when facing the same decisions, with the same information.

Question 23.2. Armed with Keynes' and Nash's insight, imagine you are a member of a group in which each person simultaneously selects a number that is 80 percent of any number between 0 and 100. Next, you and the other members of the group are asked to guess the average of the number submitted by all of the participants. The person—or persons in the case of a tie—with the closest estimate receives a gift of $20.

In the early rounds of play the average number that is selected by the group is:
a. Above 50.
b. 50.
c. 40.
d. 32.
e. 26.
f. Below 26.

Question 23.3. During many rounds of play the average number selected by the group:
a. Increases.
b. Does not change.
c. Decreases.

When asked for the average number that will be selected by a group that is asked to choose a number that is 80 percent of any number between 0 and 100, some people reason that on average the number others select will be 50. Because 40 is 80 percent of 50, they will guess 40. You, now steeped in Keynes' and Nash's need to think ahead, might guess 32, which is 80 percent of 40. Others might anticipate that people will guess 32, and so they would guess 25.6, which is 80 percent of 32. Thus, the correct answer to Question 23.2 is "d"—in the early rounds of the game guesses of the participant's average number tend to hover around 32.

If you continue to play this game, with more and more iterations of this reasoning about others' reasoning, you will all reach the Nash equilibrium response, which is 0. Because everyone wants to choose a number equal to 80 percent of the average, the only way all players can all do this is by choosing 0, the only number equal to 80 percent of itself. At zero everyone wins. The Nash equilibrium results when individuals modify their actions until they can no longer benefit from changing them in light of others' actions.[2] Thus, the correct answer to Question 23.3 is "c"—with more and more iterations, the players' estimates of the average decrease toward zero—where everyone ties and everyone wins $20.

Nash shared his Nobel prize with Reinhard Selten and John Harsanyi. Selten was recognized for his work in refining Nash's equilibrium concept for analyzing dynamic strategic interaction. Harsanyi showed how games in which players have incomplete information can be analyzed. In so doing he provided a theoretical foundation for understanding the economics of information.

Why are Keynes' and Nash's insights extremely important to today's fiduciaries and investors? There is much evidence that today's financial markets are "efficient." Typically, efficient markets are said to be those markets in which everything that is known today is embedded in today's prices. In fact, the notion of stock market efficiency goes much further.

Many investors have a point of view as to whether the Federal Reserve will raise, hold unchanged, or lower short-term interest rates at its next meeting. The consensus of this myriad of viewpoints as to what the Federal Reserve may or may not do is not what is priced! The consensus view of what the Federal Reserve may or may not do and how you believe other investors will react (or will not) to the news and, in turn, how other investors believe you and millions of other investors will (or will not) react—all occurring in a matter of seconds—is what is priced.

Question 23.4.   Which of the following are zero-sum games?
   a. Coin tossing.
   b. Roulette.
   c. Blackjack.
   d. Active investment management.
   e. All of the above.

A zero-sum game is one in which the gains some players enjoy are exactly offset by the losses suffered by other players. Coin tossing, where each player has exactly a 50–50 chance of winning (or losing) on each successive toss, is a zero-sum game. Roulette and blackjack are zero-sum games because even though the house has an advantage in each play, what players lose, the house wins. Active investment management is a zero-sum game because all positive excess returns (that is, the returns above the market's return) are offset by negative excess returns. Thus the correct answer to Question 23.4 is "e"—all of the above.

Question 23.5.   You are invited to a luncheon at which a well-known finance professor is speaking about the stock market. In the course of her presentation she says, "If active managers and their clients realized that they were playing a 'negative-alpha' game, the proportion of actively managed portfolios versus fully indexed portfolios would shift further toward indexed portfolios." A negative-alpha stock market is one in which:
   a. All active managers compete with each other in a "game" in which—after commissions and management fees—fewer than half of the players can earn above-average returns.
   b. Fewer than half of all active managers can outsmart (or be luckier than) their active and passive competitors.
   c. Both of the above.

Alpha measures an active investor's risk-adjusted skill. For the market as a whole, alpha is zero because an investor's skill (or good luck) is offset by other investors' misfortune (or bad luck) in earning a negative alpha. However, because every buy or sell transaction results in costs that lower active investors' returns—and lower the returns of the other active investors with whom they trade—the average excess return earned by all active investors is negative.

It is important not to forget that—for all investors who comprise the market—there is no compensation for: owning or not owning individual securities; overweighting or underweighting broad economic sectors (such as technology or consumer goods); overweighting or underweighting certain industries (such as software or retailing); or security characteristics (such as P/E or dividend yield). Just half of the securities that compose the market will be above average—and half below average. The above-market return to you if you invest in all securities, all economic sectors, all industries, and all imaginable factors is zero—less expenses and fees for active management. Thus, the answer to Question 23.5 is "c"—both of the above. Because they incur trading costs, all active investors compete with each other in a "game" in which fewer than half of the players can earn above-average returns. Fewer than half of all active investors can outsmart (or be luckier than) their competitors.

It is important to remember that the moment you move away from the market portfolio you are playing a negative-alpha game.

In the game of investing it is very easy to be a consistent winner (defined as an investor who *consistently* attains above-average returns). To be certain to be a winner all an investor has to do is own index funds that have very low expense ratios.

Index funds buy and sell stocks only when the index they are tracking changes, when new shareholders add investments that need to be deployed, or when shareholders redeem (sell) their shares. Thus, index-fund investors avoid the insidious drain on returns caused by the commissions and bid-ask spreads that active investors and the fiduciaries who hire them effectively *lose* each time a security is bought or sold. Moreover, investors in index funds *avoid* the fees that portfolio managers charge investors for active management.

Question 23.6. Charles Ellis, prolific author, founding partner of Greenwich Associates, and past chairman of the Association for Investment Management and Research, in a landmark book described professional investment management as a "loser's game."[3]

What is a "loser's game"?

a. Amateur investors are all "losers."

b. Professional investors are all "losers."

c. People who employ professional investors are "losers."

d. In aggregate, professional investors are so talented, so numerous, and so dedicated to their work that as a group they make it difficult for any of their brethren to distinguish themselves, particularly in the long run.

e. The harder investors try to produce above-average investment returns, the more they trade; the more they trade, the more likely they are to end up with below-average long-term returns.

f. "a" and "b."

g. "d" and "e."

Ellis makes an important distinction between a "winner's game" and a "loser's game." In a winner's game the outcome is determined by the actions of the winner. Points are won. In a loser's game the outcome is determined by the actions of the loser. Points are lost.

Ellis attributes his insight to the noted scientist Simon Ramo—the "R" in TRW. Ramo has published a dozen books on subjects ranging from technology to one of his favorite pastimes, tennis. Approaching tennis as a scientist might, he *studied* the game. This study led to his insight that tennis is really two games—the game that is played by tennis professionals and a few gifted amateurs and the game that is played by the rest of us.

After making extensive tabulations Ramo determined that in tennis games between expert players most outcomes are determined by the actions of the winner. The person with the most service aces, brilliant passing shots, and agile net plays wins. Games are decided by who wins the most points. It is a winner's game.

Ramo also discovered that most of us who are amateur tennis players, trying to emulate the extraordinary skill of the professionals, make repeated unforced errors. Tennis games between amateurs are decided by who loses fewer points. It is a loser's game.

Ellis saw the parallel between tennis and investing. His insight is that "because so many talented, informed, experienced, and diligent professionals are working so hard at institutional investing they make it unrealistic for any one manager to outperform other professionals"[4]—particularly in the long run.

As pointed out by Mark Kritzman in an earlier version of this manuscript, even when the average return earned by all active investors is less than zero there are situations in which both parties to a transaction can increase their utility or their risk-adjusted returns. For example, two investors from different countries with global portfolios could both benefit by trading currencies with each other to hedge the embedded currency risk of their respective portfolios.

Such cases aside, the correct answer to Question 23.6 is "g"— both "d" and "e." In aggregate, professional investors are so talented, so numerous, and so dedicated to their work that as a group they make it difficult for any of their brethren to distinguish themselves, particularly in the long run. And the harder investors try to produce above-average investment returns, the more they trade; the more they trade, the more likely they are to end up with below-average long-term returns.

I remember having lunch with a well-known mutual fund manager in New York in the mid-1980s when he leaned forward and asked in a low tone if I had heard of Charles Ellis' "loser's game." Following a short discussion of Ellis' thesis, the fund manager whispered, "This guy Ellis is dangerous." Somewhat startled, I asked, "Why is he dangerous?" My luncheon companion slowly looked to his left and then slowly to his right for anyone who might overhear his answer. Leaning forward, he whispered, "Because he's right."

When contemplating the riches that lie in wait for tomorrow's winners it is useful to remember that—whether by omission or commission—the only way to beat the market, after adjusting for market risk, is to discover and exploit other investors' mistakes.[5]

CHAPTER 24

Nobel Laureates Kahneman and Smith

Question 24.1. In 2002 the Bank of Sweden Prize in Economic Sciences in Memory of Alfred Nobel was awarded to Daniel Kahneman (currently at Princeton University) and Vernon Smith (currently at George Mason University).

What were some of Kahneman's landmark contributions?

How do his insights influence your day-to-day investment decisions?

As testimony to the breadth of research directed at our better understanding of the behavior of financial markets, Nobel laureate Daniel Kahneman is not an economist. Currently he is a professor of psychology at Princeton University. The Nobel committee praised Kahneman for "having integrated insights from psychological research into economic science, especially concerning human judgment and decision-making under uncertainty."[1]

Working with another psychologist, Amos Tversky, who died in 1996, Kahneman pioneered the field of behavioral economics. Classical economic theories assume that people are always rational decision makers. Kahneman and Tversky devised experiments that showed that we repeatedly make judgmental errors that can be predicted and categorized. Their 1979 paper on "prospect theory" is one of the most widely cited papers in economics.

In contrast to the evolution of modern finance that began in earnest in the 1960s, the field of behavioral economics is relatively new. Even though experimental psychologists and decision theorists have a long history of studying how decision makers behave when faced with difficult decisions, it was not until the early 1980s that research papers written by Kahneman and Tversky began to pique the interest of economists and financial researchers. An important catalyst, who worked with Kahneman and Tversky at Stanford University in the late 1970s (and who became a champion of their cause) is Richard Thaler.

To put it in a nutshell, behavioral economists believe that there are predictable differences between how certain elements of economic theory say people should behave and how people actually behave. An important description of how investors—and consumers at large—behave is captured by the value function shown in Figure 24.1. Here, the vertical scale measures value. Value in this context can be thought of as measuring how people feel about realizing the gains or losses that are shown on the horizontal scale.

Notice the shape of the line in the upper right quadrant that describes the relationship between positive value (which can be thought of as pleasure) and gains. Moving from the center—which represents the "reference price"—the line starts out on a moderately steep trajectory and gradually flattens as it moves upward toward value. This shape (said to be concave for gains) depicts a very realistic world in which an investor would perceive the gain from $10 to $20 to be greater than the difference between $110 and $120.

Now compare the line in the upper-right quadrant with the line in the lower-left quadrant. Notice that the line falls away from the reference price at a much steeper rate—illustrating that the pain we feel from losses is more than the pleasure that we derive from a gain of the same amount.

Suppose, for instance, an investor buys stock at $50 per share

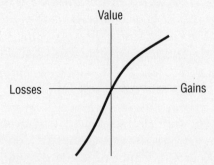

FIGURE 24.1   A Hypothetical Value Function

and it jumps to $70. In this situation, Kahneman and Tversky found, investors are inclined to sell the stock for a profit. They also found, however, that if an investor buys a stock at $90 per share and it falls to $70 investors are less inclined to sell it. (Terrance Odean and Brad Barber document this behavior in Chapter 25.)

Question 24.2.[2] You have been given $1,000. Now you must select either A or B:

Choice	*Additional Payment*	*Chance of Payment*
A	$1,000	50%
B	$500	100%

Notice that the expected return after the windfall $1,000, followed by either choice A or choice B, is the same. Over many repetitions, choice A has an expected additional payment of 50 percent of $1,000, or $500. However, on a single choice the outcome will be an additional payment of either $0 or $1,000. Choice B has a certain payoff of $500.
What is your choice between A and B?

Question 24.3. *You have been given $2,000. Now you must select either C or D (both choices, C and D, involve losses).*

Choice	*Amount of Loss*	*Chance of Loss*
C	–$1,000	50%
D	–$500	100%

Notice here that the expected return after the windfall of $2,000, followed by either choice C or choice D, is the same. Choice C offers a 50 percent chance of losing $1,000 (which has an expected loss of $500); choice D offers a certain loss of $500 from the windfall $2,000.
What is your choice between C and D?

Returning to Question 24.2, if you are like most investors, when faced with choice A (a 50 percent chance of doubling the $1,000 windfall and a 50 percent chance of losing the entire $1,000 windfall) versus choice B (the certainty of adding $500 to your $1,000 windfall), you select choice B—opting for the sure thing instead of the gamble. You are risk averse.

In Question 24.3, if you are like most investors, when you are faced with choice C (a 50 percent chance of losing $1,000 of the $2,000 and a 50 percent chance of losing nothing) versus choice D (the certainty of losing $500 of the $2,000 windfall), *you choose choice C—the gamble!* Now you are no longer risk averse. Now you are a gambler.

These questions illustrate something that every investor and fiduciary should know: You, private and professional investors, and fiduciaries who supervise investors will behave very differently when facing gains than when facing losses.

Question 24.4.[3] Imagine that you have paid a nonrefundable $200 for dinner for two at a highly rated local gourmet restaurant. (If you are accustomed to paying more, or less, than $200 for a dinner for two, please substitute an amount that would be a lot for you to pay.) A few days later you are invited for dinner on the same evening at a friend's house where there will be a guest from Australia whom you would very much like to meet. What do you do?
   a. Have dinner with your friends.
   b. Have dinner at the restaurant.

Most people who are faced with this choice are unable to ignore the sunk cost—they choose to have dinner at the restaurant. Their reasoning goes something like this: $200 is a lot to pay for a dinner. The concept of mental accounting helps us understand why people have so much trouble ignoring sunk costs.

Question 24.5. You enjoy playing blackjack in Atlantic City once or twice a year. You know that in the long run playing blackjack is a losing proposition; however, you enjoy the swings that occur during an evening's play. While walking along the boardwalk on your way to your favorite casino you find a $100 bill.
   Will this "lucky $100" alter your gambling behavior?
   If so, how does your good fortune change your behavior?

Question 24.6. Suppose that, instead of the good fortune of finding $100, you have $100 stolen from your wallet while you are taking a swim.

Will this loss alter your gambling behavior?
If so, how does this misfortune change your behavior?

Students of decision theory and economics are taught to focus on incremental costs. In reality, historical gains or losses influence our behavior in very predictable ways. Under some circumstances prior gains increase your willingness to gamble; prior losses can decrease your willingness to take risks. In response to Question 24.5, most people gamble more freely having found $100. In response to Question 24.6, most people gamble more conservatively after having had $100 stolen from them.

The relevant theory tells us that you and I—as rational consumers—make decisions on the basis of the relevant choices in *front* of us. Behavioral economists demonstrate that you and I make decisions using what is both behind and in front of us.

Readers who have ever played a casino game like blackjack may have firsthand experience as to how gamblers change their betting strategies when they are playing with the house's money. That is, when gamblers are ahead they tend to become more reckless. (After all, they reason, it's not their money.)

These questions illustrate that you, other investors, and the fiduciaries who supervise professional investors are likely to make quite different choices when you are looking at a sunk cost in comparison to when you are playing with the house's money.

Question 24.7. Assume that you enjoy drinking excellent wine and serving it to your friends. You do not have a large wine collection, but you have from time to time purchased a case of wine in the $20-to-$30-per-bottle price range. You have never paid more than $40 for a bottle of wine.

Your wine merchant calls with the news that Wine Spectator *has a very favorable article on the wine you purchased four years earlier for $20 a bottle. The wine merchant is eager to buy your entire case for $100 per bottle.*

Do you sell?

When I studied economics I was taught that "opportunity costs" are the same as "out-of-pocket costs." Economists use the construct that the amount of time or money spent to acquire or do something has a mirror image: the forgone opportunities, or opportunity costs, that were sacrificed to acquire whatever you acquired or do what you did. If as a student you read Paul Samuelson's classic text, *Economics*,[4] you may remember his example of Robinson Crusoe, who pays no money to anyone. Nonetheless, Crusoe realizes that the "cost" of the time he spent picking strawberries is the same as the "cost" of the time he sacrificed by not spending the same time and effort picking raspberries. Your cost of acquiring something else or doing something else is called your opportunity cost.

To put it in a nutshell, behavioral economists have shown us that the mirror-image equality of out-of-pocket costs and opportunity costs is an illusion. It turns out that we (you, I, investors, and fiduciaries) view out-of-pocket costs as losses. And because we do not like losses we overweight the importance of out-of-pocket costs. On the flip side, we underweight (compared with a rational economist) opportunity costs.

Returning to Question 24.7, most people would *not* sell their wine (barring special circumstances such as unexpected medical bills). Posit a world in which out-of-pocket costs are viewed as *losses* and opportunity costs are viewed as *gains*. In such a world we disdain successively larger losses and are unwilling to take increased risks in the quest for successively larger gains. Behavioral economists call this effect—whereby goods that are included in an individual's property take on an added value—the "endowment effect."

Behavioral economists have repeatedly demonstrated that choices made by consumers depend on an objective comparison of the choices that confront them and on the way the choices are *framed*.

Richard Thaler[5] has set forth four principles of framing, each of which leaves us happier. These principles are aptly illustrated by the following four pairs of scenarios. In each case two events occur in Mr. A's life and one event occurs in Mr. B's life. You are asked to judge whether Mr. A or Mr. B is happier. If you think the two scenarios are emotionally equivalent, check "c"—no difference. In all cases the events are intended to be financially equivalent.

Question 24.8. Mr. A was given tickets to two lotteries. He won $50 in one lottery and $25 in the other. Mr. B was given a ticket to a single, larger lottery. He won $75.

Who was happier?
a. Mr. A.
b. Mr. B.
c. No difference.

Here most people believe Mr. A would be happier. The framing principle illustrated here is that people are generally happier with "segregated gains." This is why people wrap each Christmas gift separately (instead of putting each unwrapped gift in one large box).

Question 24.9.   Mr. A received a letter from the IRS saying that he had made a minor mistake on his tax return and owed $100. He received a similar letter the same day from his state tax authority saying he owed $50. There were no other repercussions from either mistake. Mr. B received a letter from the IRS saying that he made a minor mistake on his tax return and owed $150. There were no other repercussions from his mistake.
Who was more upset?
a. Mr. A.
b. Mr. B.
c. No difference.

Here most people believe Mr. A would be more upset. The framing principle at work here is that people are generally happier when they "integrate losses."

Question 24.10.   Mr. A bought his first lottery ticket and won $100. Also, in a freakish accident, he damaged the rug in his apartment and had to pay the landlord $80. Mr. B bought his first lottery ticket and won $20.
Who was happier?
a. Mr. A.
b. Mr. B.
c. No difference.

Here most people believe Mr. A would be happier. The framing principle illustrated here is that people are happier when "losses are canceled against larger gains."

Question 24.11. Mr. A's car was damaged in a parking lot. He had to spend $200 to repair the damage. The same day the car was damaged he won $25 in the office football pool. Mr. B's car was damaged in a parking lot. He had to spend $175 to repair the damage.

Who was more upset?

a. Mr. A.

b. Mr. B.

c. No difference.

Here most people believe Mr. B would be more upset. The framing principle at work here is what Thaler has referred to as the tendency to "segregate the 'silver' linings."

Thaler's four principles reveal: We are happier when we: (1) segregate gains, (2) integrate losses, (3) cancel losses against larger gains, and (4) segregate silver linings.

The Nobel committee is not alone in recognizing the importance of behavioral economics. In April 2001 the American Economic Association awarded its prestigious John Bates Clark medal for leading economists under 40 years of age to Matthew Rabin, a University of California at Berkeley economist who has developed mathematical models explaining why people do irrational things such as procrastinate. In September 2001 the MacArthur Foundation awarded one of its annual $500,000 "genius" awards[6] to Sendhil Mullainathan, a Massachusetts Institute of Technology behavioral economist who has studied how traits like willpower and a sense of self-interest affect economic behavior.

In 2002, Vernon Smith (currently at George Mason University) shared the Bank of Sweden Prize in Economic Sciences in Memory of Alfred Nobel with Daniel Kahneman. The following question and its surprising answer—based on Vernon Smith's discoveries—provide a valuable insight into how financial markets work.

Question 24.12.[7] You are monitoring an experiment whereby participants are endowed with a combination of dividend-paying securities and cash. Participants with more securities are given less cash and vice versa so that the endowments of the participants are equal. Participants are not told anything about the endowments of the other participants. The dividend-paying securities pay 24 cents for 15 consecutive periods.

Participants are free to trade their securities with other participants.

The securities start out being worth $3.60 (because they will pay a 24-cent dividend at the end of each of the 15 periods). At the end of each period the securities are worth successively less ($3.36, $3.12, etc.) until they are worth nothing at the end of the 15th period.

Which of the following best describes the pattern of prices at which the securities will trade over the 15 periods?

  a. The trade prices cluster near the dollar value of the securities—starting at $3.60 and falling by 24 cents over each of the successive periods.
  b. Skeptical traders keep the trade prices slightly below their dollar value throughout most of the 15 periods.
  c. The trade prices start out above their dollar value and crash to below their market value.
  d. The trade prices start out below their dollar value, rise to a bubble significantly above their dollar value, and subsequently crash to a price below their market value.

Nobel laureate Vernon Smith, with colleagues Gerry Suchanek and Arlington Williams[8] has devised and tested many experiments along the lines of the one described in Question 24.12. This very simple security—for which we know the dollar value over each of the 15 periods—typically begins trading below its dollar value of $3.60. In subsequent periods trading prices move quickly above $3.60 as a bubble takes shape. Next, the bubble bursts and a crash ensues. These prices are superimposed on the underlying values of the security as shown in Figure 24.2.

In dissecting the formation of bubbles—and the subsequent crashes—Gunduz Caginalp, David Porter, and Vernon Smith[9] uncovered two contributing factors: price momentum and available cash. In virtually every experiment, they found that the price at the end of the first period is well below the expected value of the dividends. As the price moves up toward the underlying value of the security it appears that momentum followers observe the rising prices and, as long as they have enough cash, rush to get on the bandwagon. In turn, the next round of price momentum feeds on itself carrying the price further upward and into a bubble. Next, as the

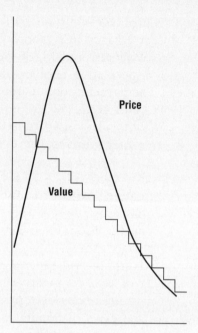

FIGURE 24.2   Bubble and Crash

remaining dividends become fewer and fewer, the value of the underlying security shrinks. This diminution of the underlying value
of the security (much as the underlying earning power of companies slows in recessions), coupled with the slowing of upward momentum, causes the shares to turn into "hot potatoes" that no one
wants to hold and the crash ensues.

The correct answer to Question 24.12 is "d"—the trade prices
start out below their dollar value, rise to a bubble significantly
above their dollar value, and subsequently crash to a price below
their market value.

*Question 24.13.   To buffer such sudden collapses in real-world
markets, regulators of some markets have instituted so-called "circuit breakers" that put a temporary floor under precipitous declines.
Is the imposition of circuit breakers consistent with Smith's research?*
   a. Yes.
   b. No.

Not surprisingly, regulators have imposed circuit breakers without having first tested their efficacy in a laboratory. Ronald King, Vernon Smith, Arlington Williams, and Mark van Boening[10] have studied several aspects of speculative bubbles—including the efficacy of circuit breakers. Their conclusion: "Circuit breakers generally made bubbles worse and certainly did not eliminate them. Apparently, the false sense of security imposed by the downside limits of the circuit breakers *causes bubbles to grow even faster* [emphasis added]."[11]

Thus the correct answer to Question 24.13 is "no"—the imposition of circuit breakers is not consistent with Smith's research.

In summary, Vernon Smith was awarded the Nobel prize for his pioneering work in experimental economics. Economics has traditionally looked to theories to explain observed real-world outcomes. Smith championed laboratory experiments as a way to increase our understanding of how competitive markets—with the behavioral quirks of their participants—set prices. His work on stock markets found repeated cases of booms and busts that were brought on because of the way investors behave.

CHAPTER 25

What Guides Investors

Question 25.1. Investors tend to:
   a. Lack confidence.
   b. Be overconfident.

Question 25.2. Investors who stay on top of their portfolios and do not hesitate to dump bad stocks in favor of good ones enjoy higher investment returns.
   a. Fact.
   b. Fiction.

Question 25.3. Male investors trade more frequently than female investors.
   a. Fact.
   b. Fiction.

Question 25.4. If you routinely drive an automobile, do you consider yourself an above-average driver?
   a. Yes.
   b. No.

There is persuasive evidence that investors are overconfident about their knowledge, their abilities, and their assessments of the returns that they will derive from their investments.[1] Thus it is not a surprise that, after accounting for trading costs, Brad Barber and Terrance Odean[2] show that individual investors, buoyed by overconfidence, consistently underperform their relevant benchmarks. Moreover, they document that the *individuals who trade the most have, by far, the worst returns.*

On the question of gender differences, broad-based research finds that men tend to be more confident than women[3]—particularly in financial matters.[4] To determine if this higher level of confidence in men causes differences in investment returns, Barber and Odean studied more than two million trades for which they knew the gender of the person who opened the brokerage account. Noting that married couples may influence each other's investment decisions, Barber and Odean also studied trading differences between married men and women and single men and women.

To many people's surprise, Barber and Odean found that women turn their portfolios over approximately 53 percent per year; men turn their portfolios over approximately 77 percent per year. Because of the costs associated with turnover, both men and women consistently lose money when compared with the returns they would have derived from merely holding their beginning-year portfolios for the entire year.

In their study of the differences between accounts of single men and single women—in comparison with the accounts of married men and married women—Barber and Odean found that differences in turnover are larger between single women and men than between married women and men. Again they found meaningful differences between the returns earned by women and those earned by men. They could not trace the higher returns earned by women to either superior market timing or superior security selection. Instead, they found that *trading* lowers returns for both men and women. Because men (and particularly single men) trade more than women, men earn measurably lower returns.

Recognizing that differences in portfolio turnover and investment returns between men and women may appear because gender is a proxy for other demographic characteristics, Barber and Odean studied returns categorized by age, marital status, the presence of children in a household, and income. Of these variables they found that only age was significant. As you would expect, turnover declines as we grow older (and, it appears, wiser).

Using four different measures of risk (portfolio volatility, individual stock volatility, beta, and size) Barber and Odean found that both women and men tilt their investments toward stocks of smaller, more volatile firms. Here again they found meaningful gender differences: Women hold less risky stocks than men. Again, as you would expect, Barber and Odean also found that young and single persons invest in smaller, more volatile stocks; those with higher incomes assume more risk.

Thus, the answer to Question 25.1 is "b"—investors tend to be overconfident. This overconfidence extends to their knowledge, their abilities, and their return expectations. The answer to Question 25.2 is "b"—investors who do not hesitate to sell the stocks they believe are bad and buy ones they believe are good increases their trading, and this trading lowers returns for both men and women. The answer to Question 25.3 is "a"—men trade more than women. They also are more overconfident than women and lower their returns more than women because they trade more—not because their security selections are worse.

If your answer to Question 25.4 was "yes" you are not alone. An astounding 90 percent of automobile drivers consider themselves to be above-average drivers.

Question 25.5.   Which of the following is true regarding the stock purchases of individual and professional investors?
   a. The assertion that the stocks purchased by individual and professional investors differ in some measurable way is a popular fiction.
   b. Individual investors, with knowledge of a relatively small number of companies, tend to invest in companies that are in the news.
   c. Professional investors cast a wider net and tend to purchase stocks from a larger pool than the stocks that are in the news.
   d. Both "b" and "c" are true.

Studying investors who use discount as well as full-service brokers and professional money managers, Barber and Odean found that "individual investors are more likely to be buyers of attention-grabbing stocks than are institutional investors."[5] Barber and Odean believe that this finding results from differences in how amateur and professional investors find purchase candidates. Professional investors typically use a variety of search techniques that throw a wide net in their process of ferreting out purchase candidates. Individual investors, in contrast, are more likely to be net buyers of stocks on "high-attention" days. (Barber and Odean define high-attention days as days when particular stocks experience abnormally high trading volume, days that follow extreme price moves, and days on which stocks are in the news.)

Question 25.6.   Is there any difference between the subsequent returns of stocks that individual investors buy and of the stocks they sell?
   a. There is no difference—the average is the average.
   b. The stocks that individual investors buy typically perform better than the stocks they sell.
   c. The stocks that individual investors sell typically perform better than the stocks they purchase.

In another study Odean[6] discovered something that is truly remarkable. On average, *the securities individual investors buy subsequently underperform those they sell*. When Odean controlled for liquidity demands, tax-loss selling, rebalancing, and changes in risk aversion, he found that the return differences between individual investors' purchases and sales were even worse.

Question 25.7.   Looking at the brokerage accounts of more than 65,000 households at a large discount broker, what is the average number of stocks held in each account?
   a. Between 1 and 5.
   b. Between 5 and 10.
   c. Between 10 and 15.
   d. Between 15 and 20.
   e. More than 20.

In spite of the undeniable advantages derived from holding large, well-diversified portfolios, investors with accounts at a large discount brokerage firm hold, on average, only *four* stocks. With this level of concentration these investors are unknowingly—and unnecessarily—subjecting themselves to an extraordinary amount of idiosyncratic risk.

Question 25.8.   Individual (taxable) investors who hold a portfolio with both "winner" and "loser" stocks are more likely to sell their:
   a. Winners.
   b. Losers.
   c. No difference.

Hersh Shefrin and Meir Statman[7] labeled preferences of investors for selling their winners and holding on to their losers the "disposition effect." Odean[8] verified the presence of this effect in the trading records of 10,000 accounts at a large (undisclosed) discount broker.

Remarkably, taxable investors have a proclivity to sell their best performing stocks (and, in so doing, create taxable gains) and, at the same time, hold their worst performing stocks (and, in so doing, forgo the realization of offsetting taxable losses).

Dissecting Returns

CHAPTER 26

Luck or Skill?

Question 26.1.   Imagine a stock market in which two-thirds of the investors actively throw darts at a suitably designed dartboard to select the number of stocks that they hold in their portfolios, the length of time that they hold each stock, and the specific stocks that they buy and sell. The remaining one-third passively hold a low-cost index fund made up of the stocks that are on the active investors' dartboard.

In such a market which of the following statements would be true?
a. Given that two-thirds of the investors incur transaction costs, their average return (properly weighted by the size of their holdings) will be below that of a buy-and-hold index.
b. Some of the investors who throw darts will earn above-average returns.
c. All of the dart-throwing investors who earned above-average returns did so because of luck—not skill.
d. All of the above.

There are three fundamental truths of investing. All three are frequently forgotten. The first, discussed earlier, is that for active equity investors as a group (whether they select their investments by throwing darts or use elaborate schemes in the quest to outperform their active brethren), the average return *must* be below that of passive investors who merely hold a broad-based sample of the same stocks. The second fundamental truth is that some percentage of active managers (usually fewer than half) will earn above-average returns.

The third fundamental truth is that some percentage of the investors who have earned above-average returns (100 percent in the case of the dart throwers in Question 26.1) will have done so for the wrong reason—namely, because of luck instead of skill. Thus the correct answer to Question 26.1 is "d"—all of the above.

John Paulos, in his entertaining book, *A Mathematician Plays the Stock Market*,[1] tells the story of a teacher who asks her class if anyone can name two pronouns. When no one volunteers, the teacher calls on Tommy, who says, "Who, me?" It is always nice to be right—even if it is for the wrong reason.

Question 26.2. Suppose an investment manager whom you are considering hiring to manage an all-stock portfolio has outperformed her peer group by 2.5 percent per year over each of the past four years. Her actual annual returns were 5.5, 8.0, 5.0, and –7.5 percent. (For readers who are reaching for their calculators: the average return of the manager (in decimal format) is 0.0275; the average return of the peer group is 0.0025; the standard deviation of the manager's return is 0.06; and the square root of the number of years of the manager's history is 2.0.)

How many years of 2.5 percent above-peer-group returns are required to conclude with 95 percent confidence that this investment manager's returns were the result of skill?

a. Four years.
b. Eight years.
c. Sixteen years.
d. More than sixteen years.

Question 26.3. What changes in historical measures of a manager's return would increase your confidence that the manager's above-peer-group investment record was derived from skill?

a. Higher returns relative to the peer group's returns.
b. Less variability in the manager's returns.
c. More years of above-peer-group returns.
d. All of the above.

Question 26.4. Using your intuition (which will work here), when working with short histories of investment returns do you expect the comparison framework to be:

a. More tightly clustered than a normal distribution?
b. About the same as a normal distribution?
c. More spread out than a normal distribution?

Understanding the answers to Questions 26.2 through 26.4 is high on the "must know" list for every investor and every fiduciary that hires and fires professional investment managers.

There is an old anecdote, "If you place an infinite number of monkeys in front of an infinite number of typewriters, one of them will type the full text of *King Lear*." Similarly, there is some probability that beating the average manager by 2.5 percent per year over four years could happen by pure chance. Thus, as difficult as it is, we need to be cautious about immediately inferring that this investment manager has skill (just as we would probably not bestow the name "Shakespeare" on the monkey that, by pure chance, typed *King Lear*).

What we need in a situation such as this is a way to estimate the likelihood that what we observe (in this case, an investment manager who has outperformed the average manager by 2.5 percent per year for four years) has not occurred by chance. Intuitively we know that our confidence in saying that someone has attained a certain level of return through skill depends on the distribution of the peer group's returns.

If, on the one hand, the returns of the managers that compose the peer group vary so widely that, on average, two-thirds of the manager's returns fall within a range from plus 10 to minus 10 percentage points of the average manager, we would not be very confident that someone whose return was above the mean by 2.5 percent did so by skill. On the other hand, suppose the peer group's returns are so tightly clustered around the mean that, on average, two-thirds of the returns of all managers fall within a range from plus 1 to minus 1 percentage points of the average return. In this case we would certainly have more confidence that a manager who beat the average manager in the peer group by 2.5 percent per year over four years did so through skill. Happily, statistical tests allow us to quantify these generalizations.

Many statistical tests assume that data are normally distributed.[2] One of the most important features of a normal bell-shaped distribution is that it is completely described by its mean and standard deviation. In brief, standard deviations measure variations around an average. In a normally distributed sample approximately 68 percent of the values are within plus or minus one standard deviation from the mean, approximately 95 percent of the values are within plus or minus two standard deviations from the mean, and more than 99 percent of the values are within plus or minus three standard deviations from the mean.

Let's look at the example: A manager's peer group's average (mean) rate of return is 15 percent, and the standard deviation around this average is plus and minus 10 percent. In this example roughly 95 percent of the peer group's returns will fall within a two standard deviation band from minus 5 percent [15 – (2 × 10)] to plus 35 percent [15 + (2 × 10)].

How can we use means and standard deviations to gauge our confidence in our hypothetical manager's skill? Consider for the moment a broad-based universe of managers' returns with a normal distribution of returns. The return of a manager selected from this universe is not likely to have exactly the same return as the average return of the universe itself. (Remember with the coin-toss illustrations in Chapter 5, a small number of repetitions will often produce sequences that vary widely from the results we expect from a large number of repetitions.)

We can, however, determine the range of managers' returns that we expect to encompass a sample return drawn randomly from the overall universe. As noted earlier, 95 percent of normally distributed observations fall within a range from plus two to minus two standard deviations from the observations' mean. Thus, there is only a 5 percent chance that the manager's return drawn randomly from a normally distributed universe of managers' returns will fall outside a band defined by plus two and minus two standard deviations from the universe's mean. These confidence intervals are extremely important because they allow us to quantify our confidence that a manager's returns are in fact significantly different from the mean return of the manager's peers.

Let's simplify our problem to the case of an investment manager whose return for *one year* was 2.5 percent above the mean return of similar managers. In this example we need to determine where the manager's return lies in relation to the returns within a given confidence interval. If the manager's 2.5 percent above-peer-group return lies *within* the confidence interval we can conclude that the manager's return could easily have been the result of chance. If the manager's return lies *outside* this confidence interval we can conclude that the manager's 2.5 percent above-peer-group return is likely the result of skill.

In our simplified case, in which we know the standard deviation of the return of the peer group, we can "standardize" our manager's mean return (which in this illustration is only one measurement) by calculating a z-score. Here the "standardization" converts the manager's investment return from "percentages" to "standard deviation units"—the horizontal unit of measurement under a normal bell-shaped curve. This can be done (using the following "equation") by subtracting term 2, the average return of the peer group, from term 1, the average return of the manager, and dividing the result by term 3, the standard deviation of the returns of the peer group, divided by term 4, the square root of the number of time periods used to calculate the average return of the manager and the peer group. (More about the intuition behind these steps in a moment.)

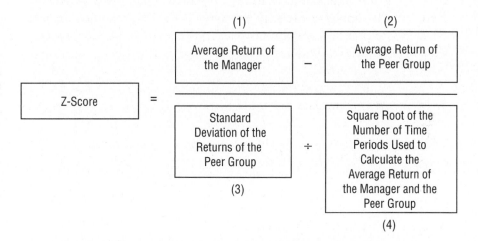

Assume that the average annual return from the investment manager's peer group is zero, the standard deviation of the returns in the peer group is 6 percent, and the investment manager's return is 2.5 percent. Plugging these numbers into the equation, we obtain a standardized z-score of 0.42. This tells us that when the manager's 2.5 percent above-peer-group return is converted into standard deviation units, it lies 0.42 standard deviations above the mean.

$$0.42 = \frac{2.5 - 0}{6 \div 1}$$

Since 0.42 is well within the range of plus to minus two standard deviations (that contain 95 percent of the observations around the mean of zero) we can say—with 95 percent confidence—that the manager's one-year return is not meaningfully different from the one-year returns of her peers.

Tables 26.1 through 26.3 (using decimal notation such as 0.06 for 6 percent) show how sensitive z-scores are to changes in the underlying variables. Happily, this is one of the cases in finance where we are well served by relying on our intuition.

Line 2 in each of the tables is the base case from Question 26.2 in which our hypothetical manager's return is 2.5 percent above that of her peer group. Lines 1 and 3 in Table 26.1 illustrate how the z-score changes as the volatility (measured here by the standard deviation) of the peer group's return changes. Intuitively, as the returns of all managers become less volatile (line 1, column d) the 2.5

TABLE 26.1 Z-Score's Sensitivity to the Standard Deviation of the Peer Group

	(a) Z-Score	(b) Manager's Average Return	(c) Peer Group's Mean Return	(d) Standard Deviation of Peer Group's Return
(1)	0.50	0.025	0.00	0.05
(2)	0.42	0.025	0.00	0.06
(3)	0.36	0.025	0.00	0.07

TABLE 26.2 Z-Score's Sensitivity to the Manager's Average Return

	(a) Z-Score	(b) Manager's Average Return	(c) Population Mean	(d) Standard Deviation of Peer Group's Return
(1)	0.33	0.020	0.00	0.06
(2)	0.42	0.025	0.00	0.06
(3)	0.50	0.030	0.00	0.06

TABLE 26.3 Z-Score's Sensitivity to Both the Standard Deviation of the Peer Group and the Manager's Average Return

	(a) Z-Score	(b) Manager's Average Return	(c) Population Mean	(d) Standard Deviation of Peer Group's Return
(1)	0.33	0.020	0.00	0.06
(2)	0.36	0.025	0.00	0.07
(3)	0.38	0.030	0.00	0.08

percent by which our hypothetical manager's return is above that of the average manager becomes more likely to be the result of skill. The converse is also true. Line 3, column d shows that when the standard deviation of the peer group's return is increased, the z-score falls.

Table 26.2 illustrates how changes in the manager's return change the z-score. As we should expect, an increase in a manager's average return in column b increases the z-score, which, in turn, makes it more likely that the manager's above-peer-group return did not occur by chance.

Table 26.3 shows the z-score's sensitivity to both the standard deviation of the peer group's returns and the manager's average return. In these examples, more volatile peer-group returns have an offsetting effect on the increases in the manager's average return.

Our problem becomes slightly more complicated when we (more realistically) measure our hypothetical manager over more than one year. Technically, instead of determining the probability of one observation, we need to compare the means of two distributions—the mean of the peer group's returns and the mean of our hypothetical manager's returns.

Two issues complicate matters further. First, we do not know the standard deviation of the peer group's returns. We must estimate this measure (which, of course, adds another element of variability) from the standard deviation of the manager's return. Second, we usually need to make inferences from a relatively small sample size (only four years in the case of our hypothetical manager).

These are the same problems that W. S. Gosset, a chemist at the Guinness Breweries, faced around the turn of the century. If we think of the dreary working conditions portrayed so well by Charles Dickens (around the mid-1800s), it is easy to picture Gosset's working conditions. Gosset was asked to make inferences about the quality of various brews. But Gosset had two problems.

First, quite understandably, the Guinness Breweries were unwilling to supply Gosset with a large number of samples of different brews. This limitation on sample size spurred Gosset to an important discovery. He found that when working with small samples, errors were introduced unless the underlying normal distribution was replaced with a distribution that had more variability and a higher probability of large deviations. (Remember from Tables 26.1 through 26.3 that as the variability of the returns of the peer group increases, larger and larger above-average investment returns are required to provide confidence that the manager's returns are not likely to have occurred by chance.)

Having discovered something of great importance to the scientific community, Gosset faced a second problem: Guinness Breweries prohibited Gosset from using his name to publish the results of his on-the-job discovery. Undaunted, and believing in the importance of his discovery, Gosset published his findings anonymously under the pen name "Student." Statisticians have ever since been introduced to "Student's t" or, as it has come to be known, the "t-test." The t-test is especially important for financial researchers who—working with short histories of annual returns—share Gosset's problem of being forced to work with small samples.

The ingredients of a t-test are quite intuitive. First, we expect to have more confidence in statistics derived from large samples than in statistics derived from small samples. We do not expect, however, that an increase in sample size of 10 will have the same effect on our confidence when the sample increases from 10 to 20 as when it increases from 20 to 30. This is why the "square root" appears in the equations. The square root of 4 is 2, of 9 is 3, and of 16 is 4.

The "equation" to calculate "t" (customized to measure the significance of an investment manager's return) is:

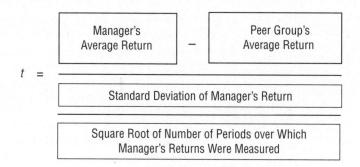

$$t = \cfrac{\boxed{\text{Manager's Average Return}} \quad - \quad \boxed{\text{Peer Group's Average Return}}}{\cfrac{\boxed{\text{Standard Deviation of Manager's Return}}}{\boxed{\begin{array}{c}\text{Square Root of Number of Periods over Which}\\ \text{Manager's Returns Were Measured}\end{array}}}}$$

Notice that the t-score calculation uses the standard deviation of the manager's return to estimate the standard deviation of the peer group's return. Conceptually, if we calculated the return above or below the peer group's mean return for a four-year random sample and repeated the experiment 1,000 times, we would expect 95 percent of these returns to be within the 95 percent confidence interval. As we saw earlier with coin-tossing examples, even though the confidence interval will bob around for each sample, 95 percent of the intervals so formed will capture the true mean of the population.

Let's return to our hypothetical example. The average return of our hypothetical manager (in decimal format) is 0.0275; the average return of the peer group is 0.0025. The standard deviation of the manager's return is 0.06. The square root of the number of years of the manager's history is 2.0. Plugging these values into the foregoing "equation" we have:

$$t = \frac{0.0275 - 0.0025}{\dfrac{0.06}{2}}, \text{ or } 0.83$$

A useful rule of thumb is that a t-statistic must be at least 2.0 to be significant. To be more specific, the t-distribution (following Gosset's insight) depends on the sample size. By consulting a table of t-statistics for various sample sizes,[3] we find that with a sample size of four we need a t-statistic of at least 2.35 to conclude that there is only a 5 percent chance that beating the market by 2.5 percent per year for four years was an accident. Because the t-distribution becomes less spread out as we increase the sample size, the t-statistic required for statistical significance decreases as sample size increases.

When the sample size reaches 30, the t-distribution is very close to the normal distribution.

The data in row 1 of Table 26.4 show the t-statistic for the manager who has outperformed peer groups by 2.5 percent for four years. The calculated t-score in column e is 0.83. The required t-score in column f—to be 95 percent confident that the results did not occur by chance—is 2.35!

Notice in row 2 that if the manager had outperformed the benchmark for nine years the calculated t-score is 1.25—still well below the required t-score, which for nine years of history has fallen to 1.86. The successive rows in Table 26.4 show that given our assumptions, we cannot conclude—with 95 percent confidence—that our manager's average annual return truly exceeds that of her peer group until she outperforms the average return of the peer group by 2.5 percent for more than 16 years. At this point, the required t-score and the calculated t-score are approximately equal. To be precise, the calculated t-score does not exceed the required t-score until the 18th year, when the calculated t-score is 1.74 and the required t-score is 1.74. Thus the correct answer to Question 26.2 is "d"—using a conservative assumption that the standard deviation of the manager's return is only 6 percent, 18 years of returns that are 2.5 percent above the benchmark are required before we can conclude (with 95 percent confidence) that the manager attained her record with skill.

TABLE 26.4   Years of Above-Peer Returns Required to Show Manager Skill

	(a) Number of Years of Manager's Performance History	(b) Manager's Average Annual Above-Peer-Group Return	(c) Standard Deviation of Peer Group's Return	(d) Square Root of Number of Years of Manager's Performance History	(e) Calculated t-Score	(f) Required t-Score
(1)	4	0.025	0.06	2	0.83	2.35
(2)	9	0.025	0.06	3	1.25	1.86
(3)	16	0.025	0.06	4	1.67	1.75
(4)	25	0.025	0.06	5	2.08	1.71
(5)	36	0.025	0.06	6	2.50	1.69

It should be noted that this is what statisticians call a "two-tail" test. This means that a manager who has four consecutive years of below-benchmark returns of –2.5 percent (and the other parameters are the same) can use this analysis to say that you will not know that he lacks the necessary skill to outperform the market for another 14 years.

The equation for calculating t-statistics contains the three things that intuitively increase or decrease our confidence that a manager's investment return was derived from skill: (1) the larger the manager's return the greater the confidence, (2) the smaller the standard deviation of the manager's return the greater the confidence, and (3) the more years of historical returns for the managers the greater the confidence. Hence the correct answer for Question 26.3 is "d"—all of the above.

The correct answer for Question 26.4 is "c"—when working with small samples the descriptive distributions need to be more spread out than normal. It is this intuition that led Gosset to his discovery of t-tests. The t-distribution creates higher and higher hurdle rates for smaller and smaller samples. Its exact form is a function of the sample size: The smaller the sample the more spread out the distribution becomes.

The foregoing example of a manager who has outperformed her peer group by 2.5 percent per year for four years is extremely important. It illustrates the difference between a level of above-benchmark returns that are acceptable to most fiduciaries and investment practitioners (beating the stock market by an average of 2.5 percent for four years) and the significantly higher and objective standards to which the academic community holds its research.

CHAPTER 27

Measuring Investment Returns

Question 27.1.   The widely used Association for Investment Management and Research Performance Presentation Standards (AIMR-PPS) require managers to provide their clients with "total time-weighted geometrically linked" returns. Here "total" means that all income that is accrued in the period must be included in the calculation. What does "geometrically linked" mean?
   a. Geometrically linked returns weight recent returns more heavily than distant historical returns.
   b. Geometrically linked returns compound period-to-period returns.
   c. Geometrically linked returns smooth out period-to-period fluctuations so that we can measure the true underlying trend of a portfolio's return.

Question 27.2.   Table 27.1 shows the average returns earned by two hypothetical investment managers over five periods. If you invested $100 with each manager at the beginning of the first period, how much would you have at the end of the last period?
   a. Manager A $114; Manager B $107.
   b. Manager A $193; Manager B $140.
   c. Manager A $141; Manager B $140.

The AIMR-PPS have standardized the way investment managers compile and present performance data. Being able to use readily available software to calculate your own performance correctly and being able to understand performance data supplied to you by professional investors are important steps toward successful investing.

TABLE 27.1 Two Hypothetical Return Patterns

Period	Manager A	Manager B
1	20%	7%
2	40	7
3	20	7
4	(50)	7
5	40	7
Average return (arithmetic)	14%	7%

Source: Hagin Investment Research, Inc.

Table 27.1 shows that on the basis of *arithmetic* averages Manager A had a five-period average return of 14 percent (+ 20 + 40 + 20 − 50 + 40)/5 = 14), and Manager B had a five-period average return of 7 percent per year. ("Period" is used for the time interval so that the results can be generalized to any length of time—days, months, or years.)

Did Manager A really provide twice the return of Manager B? Table 27.2, which compares the accumulated wealth of the portfolios of the two managers by *geometrically* linking (or compounding) the period-to-period returns, provides a very different picture of their average returns. (The correct answer to Question 27.1 is "b"—geometrically linked returns compound period-to-period returns.)

Notice in Table 27.2 that, in this illustration, even though the average arithmetic returns of the two managers were very different, when geometric linking is used the two managers end with almost identical accumulated wealth. The correct answer to Question 27.2 is "c"—Manager A $141 and Manager B $140. The average annual geometric return for both managers was 7 percent per period. As illustrated in Tables 27.1 and 27.2, failure to link returns geometrically (as now required by the AIMR-PPS) can be very misleading.

Question 27.3. Returning to the AIMR's Performance Presentation Standards, what do "time-weighted" returns measure?
   a. The growth of the market value of a portfolio.
   b. The performance of the portfolio's manager—regardless of flows of investments in and out of the portfolio.

TABLE 27.2 Comparisons of Accumulated Wealth

| | Manager A | | Manager B | |
| | Return | Accumulated Wealth (Geometrically Linked) | Return | Accumulated Wealth (Geometrically Linked) |
Period				
0		$100		$100
1	20%	120	7%	107
2	40	168	7	114
3	20	202	7	123
4	(50)	101	7	131
5	40	141	7	140
Average return (geometric)	7%		7%	

Source: Hagin Investment Research, Inc.

There are two ways to measure rates of return on investments. One is called a "dollar-weighted" return; the other is called a "time-weighted" return. The important distinction is that dollar-weighted returns measure the performance of a portfolio; time-weighted returns measure the performance of a portfolio manager.

When evaluating investment managers it is important to remember that managers have no control over the timing of their clients' additions to, or withdrawals from, their accounts. Calculating time-weighted investment returns eliminates the effects of any client-initiated additions or withdrawals that are beyond the control of investment managers. The result is an accurate and unbiased measure of investment performance that is the same with or without periodic additions or withdrawals.

(You will be happy to know that it is not necessary that you learn how to calculate time-weighted returns. It is necessary, however, to understand how to interpret these returns when they are provided.)

Much of the confusion surrounding the meaning of "return" stems from the practice of using different terms to describe the same calculation. Technically, a dollar-weighted return is a constant rate, analogous to an interest rate, which explains the present value of the monies flowing into and out of a portfolio as well as the change in the market value of a portfolio from one time to another. This "rate" is also called the "internal rate of return" and the "discounted rate of return."

Conceptually, a time-weighted return is computed by dividing the interval under study into subintervals and by computing the rate of return of each subinterval. The boundaries of the subintervals are the dates of cash flows into and out of the portfolio. The time-weighted return is the average of the returns for these subintervals, with each return having a weighting proportional to the length of time between deposits or withdrawals. (Hence the label "time-weighted" return.) Thus the correct answer to Question 27.3 is "b"—time-weighted returns measure the performance of portfolio managers regardless of the flows of investments in and out of the portfolio.

Question 27.4. You have hired two investment managers whom you designate as Managers C and D. As shown in Table 27.3, at the beginning of the first period you invest $100 with each manager. At the beginning of the third period you withdraw $50 from each manager and at the beginning of the fifth period you invest an additional $250 with each manager.

Notice, in Table 27.3, that at the end of the sixth period both managers have exactly the same terminal wealth of $330. The only differences between the two managers depicted in Table 27.3 are the interim values. (Again, the time intervals are called "periods" to

TABLE 27.3 Two Hypothetical Performance Histories

		Manager C	Manager D
Period	Additions (or Withdrawals) Made by Client at Beginning of Period	Market Value of Portfolio at End of Period	Market Value of Portfolio at End of Period
1	$100	$106	$110
2	—	110	130
3	(50)	50	90
4	—	40	120
5	250	320	360
6	—	330	330

Source: Hagin Investment Research, Inc.

make the example as general as possible. It may be useful to think of these periods as months or quarters.)

Which manager had the better time-weighted returns?

a. Manager C and Manager D had identical returns.

b. Manager C had significantly better returns.

c. Manager D had significantly better returns.

Even though you invested and withdrew exactly the same amounts at the same times and both managers ended with exactly the same amount, Manager C and Manager D did not have identical time-weighted returns. Moreover, the investments under the control of one of the managers declined significantly in value. The investments under the control of the other manager appreciated significantly in value. Understanding how such extraordinary differences can occur and being able to detect them are essential steps on the road to successful personal investing and successfully carrying out your fiduciary responsibility.

The end-of-period values per unit in the rightmost columns of Tables 27.4 and 27.5 on page 186 show the time-weighted returns for each manager. Notice the huge difference between the returns of the two managers. Specifically, the time-weighted returns show that the monies under Manager C's control *declined* to 83 percent of their initial value while the monies under Manager D's control *appreciated* to 174 percent of their initial value. These enormous differences are not readily apparent when you look only at the beginning and ending values and the interim additions and withdrawals. Thus, the correct answer to Question 27.4 is "c"—Manager D had significantly better returns.

How can this happen? In this carefully constructed example, through the end of period 4 each manager had smaller amounts to invest in comparison with the $250 deposit at the beginning of period 5. Table 27.6 shows the period-to-period percent changes in each manager's value per unit. Notice here that Manager C had the better performance when more dollars were available for investment. Manager D, in contrast, had the better performance when fewer dollars were under management. The amount of capital available for investment, however, is beyond the control of a manager.

The point of this illustration is that from a performance-

TABLE 27.4 Comparative Time-Weighted Return Calculations—Manager C

| | Beginning of Period | | | End of Period | | |
Period	Net Additions (Withdrawal) (1)	Value per Unit (2)	Change in Units (3 = ¹/₂)	Portfolio Value (4)	Number of Units (5)	Value per Unit (6 = ⁴/₅)
0						$1.00
1	$100.00	$1.00	$100.00	$106.00	$100.00	1.06
2		1.06	0.00	110.00	100.00	1.10
3	(50.00)	1.10	(45.45)	50.00	54.55	0.92
4		0.92	0.00	40.00	54.55	0.73
5	250.00	0.73	340.91	320.00	395.45	0.81
6		0.81	0.00	330.00	395.45	0.83

Source: Hagin Investment Research, Inc.

TABLE 27.5 Comparative Time-Weighted Return Calculations—Manager D

| | Beginning of Period | | | End of Period | | |
Period	Net Additions (Withdrawal) (1)	Value per Unit (2)	Change in Units (3 = ¹/₂)	Portfolio Value (4)	Number of Units (5)	Value per Unit (6 = ⁴/₅)
0						$1.00
1	$100.00	$1.00	$100.00	$110.00	$100.00	1.10
2		1.10	0.00	130.00	100.00	1.30
3	(50.00)	1.30	(38.46)	90.00	61.54	1.46
4		1.46	0.00	120.00	61.54	1.95
5	250.00	1.95	128.21	360.00	189.74	1.90
6		1.90	0.00	330.00	189.74	1.74

Source: Hagin Investment Research, Inc.

measurement perspective, interim tabulations of how much a
portfolio manager or a mutual fund has under management are irrelevant, just as the knowledge that the beginning and ending
market values of Managers C and D were the same is irrelevant.
What is relevant is if each manager started with one dollar, and
there were no interim deposits or withdrawals, how much each
manager's dollar is worth today.

TABLE 27.6 Percent Changes in Value per Unit

	Manager C		Manager D	
Period	Value per Unit	Percent Change	Value Per Unit	Percent Change
0	$1.00		$1.00	
1	1.06	6.0	1.10	10.0
2	1.10	3.8	1.30	18.2
3	0.92	−16.4	1.46	12.3
4	0.73	−20.6	1.95	33.6
5	0.81	11.0	1.90	−2.6
6	0.83	2.4	1.74	−8.4

Source: Hagin Investment Research, Inc.

Happily, because investors (in the performance sense) do not care about flows of money into or out of mutual funds, the daily net asset values (NAVs) are time-weighted measures of return. Hence, the percent changes in mutual fund NAVs that are provided to all investors in mutual funds are accurate measures of the return provided by mutual fund managers.

Because of the increasing interest and use of alternative asset classes by fiduciaries, the next few questions[1] deal with important performance-measurement issues that often arise.

Question 27.5. When comparing an infrequently priced invest-ment with a more frequently priced benchmark, the return of the in-frequently priced investment is:
  a. Understated.
  b. Unchanged.
  c. Overstated.

Question 27.6. When comparing an infrequently priced invest-ment with a more frequently priced benchmark, estimates of the volatility (standard deviation) of the infrequently priced invest-ment are:
  a. Understated.
  b. Unchanged.
  c. Overstated.

Question 27.7. When comparing an infrequently priced investment with a more frequently priced benchmark, estimates of the correlation *between the investment and the benchmark are:*
a. Understated.
b. Unchanged.
c. Overstated.

Question 27.8. When comparing an infrequently priced investment with a more frequently priced benchmark, estimates of beta *are:*
a. Understated.
b. Unchanged.
c. Overstated.

Question 27.9. When comparing an infrequently priced investment with a more frequently priced benchmark, estimates of alpha *(the excess return of the portfolio) are:*
a. Understated.
b. Unchanged.
c. Overstated.

Strange things can happen when you compare an infrequently priced investment with a more frequently priced benchmark. In his address to the 2003 Annual Conference of the Association for Investment Management and Research, Nobel laureate Robert Merton cautioned that the standard tools for measuring investment performance and risk do not work for infrequently priced asset classes.

Merton offered the following example: Imagine a low-cost S&P 500 index fund that tracks the S&P 500 perfectly. If we price the index fund each week and compare it with the S&P 500 index each week, the return and volatility of the fund and the index will be identical, the correlation will be 1.0, the beta will be exactly 1.0, and the alpha will be exactly 0.0.

Now imagine a second portfolio that Merton called "S&P 500 Private." The only difference between the S&P 500 index fund and S&P Private is that the S&P Private is priced every other week. This means that when we compare the return of S&P Private with the S&P 500 index each week the price of S&P Private is "stale" on alternate weeks. As a result, the weekly price of the portfolio does not move in lockstep with the weekly price of the benchmark (because every other week the price of S&P Private does not change).

Well, what does change? The average returns of the S&P 500 index fund change and the S&P Private fund do not change. They start out together and end together—making the correct answer to Question 27.5 "b"—unchanged. And even though the return of S&P Private does not move at all every other week, its volatility does not change significantly. Thus the correct answer to Question 27.6 is "b"—unchanged.

The correlation of the two funds, however, changes dramatically. Using return histories from 1995 through 1999 (a period during which the market was up about 24 percent), Merton found the correlation of S&P Private with the benchmark fell from 1.0 to about 0.5. Thus the correct answer to Question 27.7 is "a"—as a result of less frequent pricing the correlation is understated. And because the volatility (measured by the standard deviation) does not change a lot, the beta goes from 1.0 for the more frequently priced fund to 0.5 for the less frequently priced S&P Private. Thus the correct answer to Question 27.8 is "a"—beta is understated.

This means that in any period when the excess return of the market is positive the illusory smaller beta produces a larger alpha. Thus the correct answer to Question 27.9 is "c"—the alpha is overstated.

In Merton's test from 1995 through 1999 he found that the alpha of the S&P Private portfolio went from 0.0 to an enormous 9.9. In this example the calculations that show that S&P Private is a better diversifier (has a lower correlation) and is a better performer (has an enormous alpha) are both an illusion—merely because S&P Private is priced less frequently than the benchmark with which it is compared.

CHAPTER 28

Anatomy of the S&P 500

Question 28.1. The popular S&P 500 index is a capitalization-weighted index of:
  a. The 500 largest actively traded U.S. stocks.
  b. The 500 U.S. stocks that Standard & Poor's (S&P) believes accurately reflect the large-capitalization U.S. equity market.

Many people erroneously assume that the S&P 500 is composed of the 500 largest U.S. stocks. Quite to the contrary, whether or not a stock is included in the index is decided solely by Standard & Poor's. Its criteria for inclusion in the index are that the stocks are of U.S. companies that maintain S&P's desired sector balance, have adequate liquidity, sell at a "reasonable" price (S&P shuns low-priced stocks), have market capitalizations of $3 billion or more, have financial viability (usually measured as four consecutive quarters of positive earnings), and have at least 50 percent of their outstanding stock publicly traded.

S&P drops companies from its indexes when, in its view, a company "substantially violates one or more of the addition criteria."[1] The companies that find their way to the "drop list" also include those that are involved in mergers, are being acquired, or have been significantly restructured so as to no longer meet S&P's inclusion criteria. S&P states that when making changes to its indexes it seeks to avoid "unnecessary and excessive turnover in index membership."

Thus the correct answer to Question 28.1 is "b"—the 500 U.S. stocks that S&P believes accurately reflect the large-capitalization U.S. equity market.

Question 28.2. You are a member of the committee that supervises the investments of your alma mater's endowment. In preparation for

*the semiannual meeting with your investment managers, your com-
mittee's staff has prepared a report showing that the portfolio manager at XYZ Investment Management significantly lagged the S&P
500 during the year just ended. Checking the investment guidelines,
you confirm that the manager's assignment is to outperform the
S&P 500.*

*When asked at the meeting about the below S&P 500 returns,
the manager tells your committee that the problem is not with
XYZ's returns. The problem, the manager asserts, is "with the S&P
500." Elaborating, the manager explains that "the stocks that compose the S&P 500 have changed significantly since XYZ took on the
assignment to "outperform the S&P 500." The manager—noting
that XYZ would have had to include five percentage points of Microsoft in your portfolio "just to own a neutral position vis-à-vis the
S&P"—offers a "recalculated" S&P 500. XYZ's conclusion: "Measured against the S&P 500 as it was composed when XYZ was
hired, our returns are fine." What is your response?*

    a. XYZ's assertion is preposterous. The S&P 500 is a rock-solid
       benchmark against which most endowments and pension
       plans measure their large-capitalization domestic equity
       managers. You terminate XYZ on the spot.

    b. Knowing that the composition of the S&P 500 can drift as
       the valuations in certain sectors (such as technology) change,
       you find XYZ's assertion over-the-top. You terminate XYZ.

    c. You have an epiphany: The "market" (especially as repre-
       sented by the S&P 500) is a moving target! You reason that
       an excellent way to track the market—through all of its
       transformations—is to own index funds. You thank XYZ for
       its insight.

It is important to remember that, over time, the characteristics
of the market change—sometimes significantly. In turn, the indexes
we use to describe the market change—sometimes significantly. The
changing characteristics of widely used indexes, such as the S&P
500, have important implications for both performance and valuation benchmarks.

Specifically, the composition of the S&P 500 can change in three
ways: (1) the stocks that compose the indexes can be changed by
S&P; (2) the capitalization (number of outstanding shares times the

price per share) weightings of each of the stocks that compose the index can change; and (3) the returns of each of the companies can change. (Note that price changes alter both the capitalization weighting and the return calculation.)

For example, as the 1995–1999 "new paradigm" bubble grew larger, the S&P 500—once tilted toward large cyclical stocks—became increasingly dominated by technology companies. As the bubble burst, the "new paradigm" S&P 500 shifted abruptly away from growth toward value sectors.

For example, in 1998, following a record-breaking three consecutive years of higher than 20 percent returns, the S&P 500 rose another 28.5 percent. Microsoft became the largest-capitalization stock in the S&P 500; Intel and Cisco Systems moved into the "10 largest" category. (Five years earlier Microsoft was not even one of the 10 largest companies in the index.) Thus, in 1998, in the calculation of capitalization-weighted indexes such as the S&P 500, which already weighted the returns of larger stocks proportionately higher, the largest-capitalization stocks also significantly outperformed their smaller brethren. As a result, in 1998 five stocks—through a combination of their weightings from their size and their extraordinary returns—contributed 25 percent of the performance of the S&P 500 index; 15 stocks accounted for half of the performance, and the largest 100 stocks accounted for 85 percent of the index's return. The remaining 400 stocks accounted for only 15 percent of the index's return.

The S&P 500 closed 1999 up 21 percent—marking the fifth consecutive year of greater than 20 percent returns. Never before had the S&P 500 index achieved five consecutive years of returns greater than 20 percent. During the five-year run from 1995 through 1999 the S&P 500 gained a staggering 250 percent.

Reflecting how lopsided the valuations of the stocks in the S&P 500 had become, at the end of 1999 technology constituted 30 percent of the index's capitalization. (The next largest group was finance, which accounted for 13 percent of the S&P 500's capitalization.) After climbing an astounding 72 percent in 1998, in 1999 the technology sector returned 75 percent and accounted for roughly 70 percent of the S&P 500's performance. Seven stocks, led by Microsoft, contributed 50 percent of the performance of the index. As the "new era" believers continued to pour money into their favorite stocks, all but four of the top 15 contributors were technology stocks. As the year closed, Microsoft was up over 68 percent and ended the year with an index weighting of close to 5 percent. In 1999 Microsoft alone accounted for over 10 percentage points of the S&P 500's 21 percent return. In 1999 only 50.5 percent of the stocks in the index had a positive return; the other 49.5 percent lost money. Without technology the S&P 500's return would have been only 7.5 percent.

As 2000 began it looked for a while like more of the same. During the first quarter, two technology companies, Intel and Cisco, accounted for all of the S&P 500's gain. When the dust settled at year-end, the S&P 500 index was down 9.1 percent—its worst year's performance in 17 years. The world had changed. As the bubble burst, the largest 100 stocks—down 16.5 percent for the year—pulled the index into negative territory. All other size categories posted positive returns of 14 percent of higher! Technology—where you "had to be" in the "new era"—was the worst-performing sector in 2000, down 41 percent. Technology's weighting in the S&P 500—which peaked at 35 percent on March 8—shrank to 21 percent. By year-end, technology's trailing-P/E multiple—which had reached 79 in March—had more than halved to 33. Microsoft—the biggest detractor—accounted for one-third of the index's negative performance.

The rest of the S&P 500 was a different story. Even though the S&P 500 index declined 11.8 percent, 62 percent of the S&P 500 stocks outperformed the index; 55 percent achieved a positive return. An equal-weighted S&P 500 index was slightly ahead of the S&P 500 capitalization-weighted index with a total return of 0.9 percent for 2001.

In 2002 the S&P 500 index declined 22.1 percent—registering the worst year's performance since 1974. As the technology rout continued, nearly 60 percent of the stocks that compose the S&P 500 index had better-than-index returns. The equal-weighted S&P 500 index—even though it outperformed the capitalization-weighted index for a third straight year—fell 16.8 percent, registering its first negative absolute return since 1990.

Table 28.1 shows the contribution of size categories to the S&P 500 total returns from 1988 through 2002. In 1988, for example,

TABLE 28.1   Contribution of Size Categories to S&P 500 Total Returns 1988–2002

Years	Contribution (Percent)					Total Return (Percent)
	Largest 100	Next 100	Next 100	Next 100	Smallest 100	
1988	56	20	11	10	3	16.7
1989	66	19	9	4	2	31.3
1990	7	–30	–43	–24	–12	–3.2
1991	64	17	11	6	2	30.6
1992	35	28	20	11	6	7.8
1993	50	18	16	12	4	10.1
1994	85	–19	20	9	6	1.4
1995	68	16	10	4	2	37.5
1996	70	15	8	4	2	23.2
1997	70	15	9	4	2	33.3
1998	85	11	3	1	0	28.5
1999	90	3	5	1	1	21.0
2000	–126	9	10	6	1	–9.1
2001	–85	–21	0	3	3	–11.8
2002	–77	–13	–6	–3	–2	–22.1

Note: Total contribution may not equal 100 because of rounding.
Source: Jay Lasus, Morgan Stanley Equity Research, January 9, 2003.

the 100 largest-capitalization stocks in the S&P 500 index contributed 56 percent of the total return for the year. The next category contributed 20 percent, and so forth through the smallest category. (The contributions of the percentages in the five size categories may not total 100 percent because of rounding.)

The year 2000 shows that the 100 largest stocks in the index contributed a negative 126 percent return. This occurred because in 2000 the return of the 100 largest stocks was a negative 11.5 percent. The four other size categories all had small positive returns that offset somewhat the negative 11.5 percent, so that the full index fell only 9.1 percent.

Table 28.1 reveals something very important. Notice 1989 and 1991—two years during which the S&P 500 was up more than 30 percent. During these two years the largest category contributed 66 and 64 percent, respectively.

During 1995, the first year of the 1995–1999 bubble, the contributions of each of the S&P 500's size categories were more balanced. Yet by 1999—the last year of the bubble—90 percent of the return came from the largest-capitalization sector. When the bubble burst in 2000, it is not surprising that the largest-capitalization stocks in the index led the collapse.

Table 28.2 shows the changing character of the 10 stocks in the S&P 500 that have contributed the most to the index's return over the past six years. Only a handful of the top 10 contributors in one year made it to the top 10 list in the following year. In 1998 there were four, and in 1999 and 2000 there were two.

Thus, the correct answer to Question 28.2 is "c." The S&P 500 is not a rock-solid benchmark; its composition drifts. Even though you may disagree with thanking XYZ for its insight, the composition of the S&P 500 can change significantly; it is a moving target.

Question 28.3.   The S&P 500—even though it is an index of only 500 stocks—is a reasonably good proxy for all domestic stocks.

    a. Fact.
    b. Fiction.

The S&P 500 is the most benchmarked index in the United States. Nearly a trillion dollars in assets are directly linked to the index's changes. It is even one of the factors used to compute the Conference Board's index of leading economic indicators.

David M. Blitzer and Srikant Dash have studied how well the returns of the S&P 500 parallel those of the broader U.S. equity market. Comparing the S&P 500 to all stocks traded on the American Stock Exchange, the New York Stock Exchange, and the Nasdaq National Market, they concluded that the S&P 500 moved "in lockstep with the broader market."[2] They also found that the S&P 500 tracks the large-capitalization segment of the broader U.S. market through market cycles without favoring value or growth. Hence the correct answer to Question 28.3 is "a"—it is a fact the S&P 500 is a reasonably good proxy for all domestic stocks.

It is important to remember that the underlying theory of indexing

TABLE 28.2 Top 10 Contributors to S&P 500 Index

Contribution Rank	1997 Company	Rank in Index at Beginning of Year	1998 Company	Rank in Index at Beginning of Year
1	General Electric	1	Microsoft Corp.	3
2	Travelers Group	44	Wal-Mart Stores	14
3	Microsoft Corp.	5	General Electric	1
4	Pfizer, Inc.	14	Lucent Technologies	32
5	Bristol-Myers Squibb	13	Cisco Systems	29
6	Wal-Mart Stores	16	Intel Corp.	7
7	Lilly (Eli)	28	IBM	10
8	Procter & Gamble	10	Dell Computer Corp.	66
9	Coca-Cola Co.	2	Pfizer, Inc.	12
10	AT&T Corp.	11	Merck & Co.	5

Contribution Rank	1999 Company	Rank in Index at Beginning of Year	2000 Company	Rank in Index at Beginning of Year
1	Oracle Corp.	25	Microsoft Corp.	1
2	Northern Telecom	36	Lucent Technologies	7
3	Sun Microsystems	38	MCI WorldCom	17
4	Cisco Systems	14	AT&T Corp.	13
5	EMC Corp.	24	Cisco Systems	3
6	Motorola, Inc.	30	Yahoo Inc.	29
7	Microsoft Corp.	4	America Online	10
8	Texas Instruments	35	Dell Computer Corp.	23
9	Morgan Stanley	27	Intel Corp.	4
10	Amgen Inc.	66	Wal-Mart Stores	6

Contribution Rank	2001 Company	Rank in Index at Beginning of Year	2002 Company	Rank in Index at Beginning of Year
1	Cisco Systems	4	General Electric	1
2	EMC Corp.	16	Intel Corp.	7
3	Oracle Corp.	11	AOL Time Warner	8
4	Merck & Co.	9	Tyco Intl.	17
5	General Electric	1	Microsoft Corp.	11
6	Nortel Networks	23	IBM	2
7	Enron Corp.	47	Citigroup, Inc.	4
8	Sun Microsystems	27	Home Depot, Inc.	6
9	American Intl. Group	8	American Intl. Group	28
10	Qwest Comm. Intl.	43	Pfizer, Inc.	17

Source: Standard & Poor's, Factset, and Morgan Stanley Research.

is based on owning all of the stocks in the market. The Standard & Poor's 500 index—with roughly 75 percent of the market's capitalization—is not the market. Stocks with medium and small market capitalizations (and, typically, higher volatility) are excluded. A preferred standard would be the Wilshire 500 Equity Index of all publicly held stocks in the United States. This said, the S&P 500 index remains the principal measurement standard used by most mutual funds and pension accounts.

CHAPTER 29

Returns Earned by Investors

A very important insight comes from comparing the returns earned from investments with the returns earned by investors. The *annualized* return (the standard metric for reporting investment returns) earned from an investment assumes that the investment is held for an entire year. The annualized return that is earned by investors can be very different *when investors do not hold investments for an entire year.*

Imagine that an investor invests in a mutual fund on January 31, redeems the shares six months later, and earns a 10 percent six-month return. Now imagine another investor who purchases shares of the same fund on September 1 and by the end of the year has lost 5 percent of the initial investment. In this example, the annualized return earned by the mutual fund is very different from the average annualized return that is earned by the two investors.

Dalbar, Inc., a Boston-based consulting firm, has studied how the returns earned by investors differ from returns earned on investments. Using monthly data on mutual fund transactions (purchases, redemptions, and exchanges) all the way back to 1984, Dalbar has estimated the average annual returns earned by investors in equity, fixed-income, and money-market mutual funds.[1]

Question 29.1. As a point of reference, from the inception of Dalbar's data (17 years ago) the average annual (nominal—not in-flation-adjusted) return earned from buying and holding the S&P 500 index was 16.3 percent. What does Dalbar estimate was the

*comparable average annual return earned by the investors in those
equity mutual funds during this period?*
  a. Greater than the 16.3 percent return earned from a buy-and-
     hold S&P 500 index strategy.
  b. Between 15 percent and 16.3 percent.
  c. Between 10 percent and 15 percent.
  d. Below 10 percent.

Over the 17-year period ended December 31, 2000, a buy-and-
hold strategy in the S&P 500 index returned 16.3 percent; during
the same period, Dalbar estimates, the return earned by investors in
equity mutual funds was only 5.3 percent!

*Question 29.2. Over the same 17-year period the Ibbotson Long-
Term Government Bond Index returned 11.8 percent. What was the
average annual return earned by investors in bond mutual funds
over the same 17-year period?*
  a. Greater than the 11.8 percent return earned from a buy-and-
     hold Ibbotson Long-Term Government Bond Index strategy.
  b. Between 10 percent and 11.8 percent.
  c. Between 8 percent and 10 percent.
  d. Below 8 percent.

Over the 17-year period a buy-and-hold strategy for the Ibbotson Long-Term Government Bond Index returned 11.8 percent;
during the same period Dalbar estimates investors in bond mutual
funds earned a paltry 6.1 percent.

*Question 29.3. According to Dalbar, what was the average holding
period (measured in years) for investors in equity and fixed-income
mutual funds in 1984—the first year of the Dalbar database?*
  a. More than eight years.
  b. Between six and eight years.
  c. Between four and six years.
  d. Fewer than four years.

The average holding period for investors in equity and fixed-
income mutual funds in 1984—the first year in the Dalbar database—
was 3.4 years for equity and 3.0 years for fixed-income funds. In the

intervening period between 1984 and 2000 the investment industry has spent many millions of dollars inundating investors—particularly those invested in 401(k)-type programs—with messages such as "don't time the market" and "stay the course."

Question 29.4.   How did the average holding period for equity and fixed-income investors in mutual funds change from 1984 to 2000?
  a. Increase.
  b. Decrease.

In spite of the campaigns to extend the length of the average holding period for investors in equity and fixed-income mutual funds, the average holding period shrank from 3.4 years in 1984 to 2.6 years in 2000.

A significant problem with Dalbar's research is that it has not disclosed either the assumptions underlying the research or precisely how it calculated the estimates. The reason for secrecy is ostensibly that Dalbar sells its studies and does not want someone cloning its study and offering an equivalent analysis at a lower price.

Laurence Siegel, a well-respected and extremely thorough researcher at the Ford Foundation, recently studied the same question. Using fund returns and flows data supplied by Charles Trzincka of Indiana University, Siegel, with programming assistance from Tim Aurthur, concluded that "the Dalbar report got the direction right but overstated the magnitude of the investor's shortfall."[2] In a nutshell, Siegel calculates the shortfalls to be roughly half those reported by Dalbar.

This means that using Siegel's methodology, Dalbar's answers to Questions 29.1 and 29.2 can be roughly doubled—still huge differences versus buy-and-hold equity strategies.

CHAPTER 30

Market Timing versus Asset Allocation

Question 30.1. Is the following definition of "market timing" correct? Market timing involves shifting investments between risky and risk-free asset classes.

    a. Correct.

    b. Incorrect.

Question 30.2. Is the following definition of "strategic asset allocation" correct? Strategic asset allocation involves setting the benchmark, or normal, percentages—and the minimum and maximum percentages—of the asset to be invested in strategic asset-allocation categories such as domestic stocks, investment-grade domestic bonds, foreign stocks, and so forth.

    a. Correct.

    b. Incorrect.

Question 30.3. Is the following definition of "tactical asset allocation" correct? Tactical asset allocation involves shifting the percentages of assets invested in different strategic asset-allocation categories in an attempt to invest more in the asset classes that are expected to be the better performing asset classes and less in the asset classes that are expected to be the poorly performing asset classes.

    a. Correct.

    b. Incorrect.

Even though consistent syntax is not a strong point among academic researchers and investment professionals, "market timing" usually refers to shifts between risky and risk-free assets. An example of market timing would be to move between an investment in a risky asset class (such as an S&P 500 index fund) and a risk-free asset class (such as a short-term U.S. Treasury bill). Thus the correct answer to Question 30.1 is "a"—correct.

Market timers use their forecasts of changes in the market's direction to switch their investments back and forth between being "in the market" or "out of the market." If they expect the market to fall, they shift their investments into risk-free assets (typically U.S. Treasury bills). If they expect the market to rise, they shift their investments into risky assets (such as stocks).

If market timers do this successfully, they can reduce the volatility of their returns and, at the same time, outpace the returns earned from a static buy-and-hold strategy. The substantial risk that market timers face, however, is that they open themselves to the significant risk of being caught holding cash in an advancing market or of being caught holding stock in a declining market.

"Asset allocation" usually refers to shifts between risky assets. Typically, asset allocation strategies have a strategic part and a tactical part. The strategic part specifies the proportions of different asset classes that together compose an investor's benchmark, normal, portfolio. If this normal portfolio is properly designed and if it is held for a sufficiently long period of time, it is very likely that the investor will attain his or her long-term investment goals. The tactical part of an asset allocation strategy, which has some similarity to market timing, involves making opportunistic shifts above or below the strategic, or normal, percentages.

Imagine an asset allocation strategy that has a strategic, or normal, allocation of 60 percent to domestic stocks and 40 percent to domestic fixed-income securities. An example of a tactical shift would be to reduce the allocation to domestic stocks from 60 percent to 40 percent and to increase the allocation to domestic bonds from 40 percent to 60 percent. This is an example of a tactical change in asset allocation—shifting assets from one asset class and into another in anticipation of being overweighted in the subsequently better-performing asset class, and being underweighted in the subsequently poorer-performing asset class.

Thus, the correct answers to both Questions 30.2 and 30.3 are "a"—correct.

CHAPTER 31

Market Timing:
Risk versus Reward

One of the keys to successful investing is to understand the nature and magnitude of the risks that you take as you endeavor to earn above-index investment returns. In this chapter, following a process first introduced by Robert "Tad" Jeffrey[1] in a landmark article in 1984, I examine the amount of skill that is required for you to benefit from market timing (switching between a risky asset class, such as stocks, and a risk-free asset class, such as U.S. Treasury bills).

Question 31.1.   Over the 112 quarters[2] between the end of 1974 and the end of December 2002, the real (inflation-adjusted) annualized return from an investment in U.S. Treasury bills was:
   a. Between minus 2 percent and minus 1 percent.
   b. Between minus 1 percent and zero percent.
   c. Between zero percent and 1 percent.
   d. Between 1 percent and 2 percent.
   e. Between 2 percent and 3 percent.

Question 31.2.   Over the 112 quarters between the end of 1974 and the end of December 2002, the real (inflation-adjusted) annualized return from the S&P 500 was:
   a. Greater than 20 percent.
   b. Between 10 percent and 20 percent.
   c. Between 5 percent and 10 percent.
   d. Between zero percent and 5 percent.

Question 31.3.   When you shift investments out of stocks and into U.S. Treasury bills in anticipation of a broad-based decline in stock prices, the risk/reward ratio is tilted:
a. Strongly in your favor.
b. Moderately in your favor.
c. Moderately against you.
d. Strongly against you.

Intuitively, when you shift out of stocks and into interest-bearing cash, you are shifting out of an investment that, in the long run, will provide significantly higher returns than cash equivalents. This trade-off is quantified in Figure 31.1. Here the line labeled "T-Bills" shows the wealth that you would have accumulated, in real (inflation-adjusted) terms, if you had invested $1.00 in U.S. Treasury bills at the end of 1974 and held that investment for the next 112 calendar quarters (until December 31, 2002). Using this all U.S. Treasury bill strategy you would have had a terminal real wealth of $1.67. This is equivalent to an average annual real rate of return of 1.9 percent. Hence the answer to Question 31.1 is "d"—between 1 and 2 percent.

Notice that these data are plotted on a logarithmic scale. If we

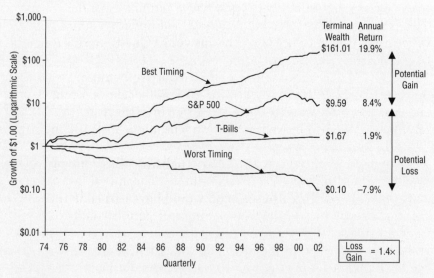

FIGURE 31.1   Comparative Wealth Indexes for Best-Worst Market Timing Study

did not use the logarithmic scale and just plotted changing wealth, when we reached higher rates of return the line would move dramatically upward as it moved to the right side. Such a nonlogarithmic scale would give the illusion that your investment results were getting better and better over time.

It is important to understand the use of logarithms. Imagine that you earned 10 percent a year for each of 10 years. At the end of the first year your wealth would grow by 10 percent and you would have 1.10 times your initial investment. At the end of the ninth year your wealth would have more than doubled to $2.36.[3] When the tenth year is added the $2.36 earns a 10 percent return and grows to $2.59. The increase in wealth between the ninth and tenth years is 23 cents. If we compare the 10 cents earned during the first year with the 23 cents earned in the tenth year, it would appear that you grew smarter and smarter, or luckier and luckier, by making ever-increasing amounts of money—even though you earned a constant 10 percent in each period.

The line labeled "S&P 500" in Figure 31.1 shows the wealth you would have accumulated, in real (inflation-adjusted) terms, if you had invested $1.00 in the Standard & Poor's 500 index on December 31, 1974, and held the investment (including the reinvestment of dividends) until December 31, 2002. Plotting the data on a logarithmic scale, we see that you would have had a terminal wealth of $9.59. This is equivalent to an average annual real (inflation-adjusted) rate of return of 8.4 percent. Hence the answer to Question 31.2 is "c"— between 5 and 10 percent.

Figure 31.1 is very seductive. It is seductive because we cannot help but notice the periods when the S&P 500 declines. Being inherent optimists, we want to know what our investment results would have been if we had moved our investment in the S&P 500 index to Treasury bills *before each of these declines*.

The top line in Figure 31.1 that is labeled "Best Timing" was calculated assuming *perfect* market timing. This line shows the real (inflation-adjusted) wealth that you would have earned if at the beginning of each quarter in this 112-quarter period you had shifted your assets to the soon-to-be-best-performing asset class—specifically, if you invested in the S&P 500 index whenever the return of the S&P 500 index was poised to outperform Treasury bills in the following quarter and invested in Treasury bills whenever Treasury bills were poised to outperform the S&P 500 index in the following quarter.

Note in Figure 31.1 that if you had been a perfect market timer, your $1.00 investment would have appreciated to $161.01 in inflation-adjusted dollars. This is equivalent to an average annual real rate of return of 19.9 percent.

Note that the vertical distances on the logarithmic scale correctly show that the average annual real rate of return increases by 6.5 percentage points (from 1.9 to 8.4) as we move from the "buy-and-hold Treasury bill" strategy to the "buy-and-hold S&P 500 index" strategy and increases by 11.5 percentage points (from 8.4 to 19.9) as we move from the "buy-and-hold S&P 500 index" strategy to the "perfect market timing" strategy.

Now, let's examine the other side of the coin. How would you have fared if you had been a terrible market timer? That is, if at the beginning of every quarter you invested in the asset class that performed worst in the next period. If the market went up, you were in Treasury bills. If the market went down, you were fully invested in the S&P 500. Figure 31.1 shows that your try at market timing turned your initial dollar into 10 cents. This is a real annualized *loss* of 7.9 percent per year.

Thus, if you were a buy-and-hold investor in the S&P 500, your return would have been 8.4 percent per year. If you were a perfect market timer, your return would have been 19.9 percent per year. However, if your normal strategy is to be fully invested in the S&P 500, the instant you move off the S&P 500 line in Figure 31.1 you incur an ugly risk/reward trade-off.

If your market timing goes against you, your potential shortfall versus a "buy-and-hold S&P 500 index" strategy is 16.3 percent per year (from +8.4 to –7.9). If your market timing works, your potential gain versus a "buy-and-hold S&P 500 index" strategy is 11.5 percent per year.

Thus, your *potential loss* from moving away from a strategy of being fully invested in the S&P 500 over this period was 1.4 times larger than your potential gain. Thus the answer to Question 31.3 is "d"—when you shift investments out of stocks and into U.S. Treasury bills in anticipation of a broad-based decline in stock prices, the risk/reward ratio is tilted strongly against you.

What, then, is your biggest risk of market timing? It is being in cash and missing the relatively brief episodes during which equity markets earned all of the above-T-bill return.

Figure 31.2 highlights the 12 best quarters over this 112-quarter period. (It will be clear in a moment why I picked 12 quarters.) Readers who are old enough may remember that the Dow Jones Industrial Average reached 1,000 for the first time in November 1972. Then came the emergence of the Organization of Petroleum Exporting Countries (OPEC) and rising energy prices as we entered 1973. In an agonizing 22-month fall the Dow plummeted to 577 by December 1974.

What was the mood in October 1973? It was terrible. Front-page newspaper stories included descriptions of instances during which people were shot while crowding in line for gasoline in California. The *Harvard Business Review* published an article on how corporations could deal with the suicide of executive officers.

It was, by almost any measure, not a great time in the United States; spirits were very low. Few people were saying "here come two great quarters"; yet the market had two back-to-back quarters (the first half of 1974) that today rank among the 12 best during the past 28 years.

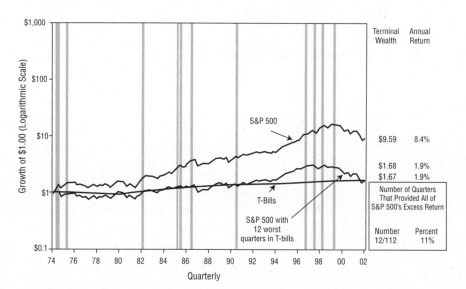

FIGURE 31.2 Result of Removing 12 Best Quarters from S&P 500's Return *Source:* Hagin Investment Research, Inc.

Question 31.4. Of the 112 quarters between the end of 1974 and the end of December 2002, how many quarters explain all of the difference in real returns between the "buy-and-hold S&P 500 index" strategy ($9.59) and the "buy-and-hold-Treasury bill" strategy ($1.67)?
  a. More than 80 percent.
  b. Between 60 percent and 80 percent.
  c. Between 40 percent and 60 percent.
  d. Between 20 percent and 40 percent.
  e. Fewer than 20 percent.

Figure 31.2 shows what your real return would have been if you missed the "12-best" out of the last 112 quarters. Here the line labeled "S&P 500 with 12-worst quarters in T-bills" shows that your initial investment of $1.00 at the end of 1973 would be worth $1.67 at the end of 2002 if you had invested in the S&P 500 index during 100 quarters and had invested in Treasury bills during the 12 quarters during which the S&P 500 delivered its best comparative returns.

Look carefully at Figure 31.2. Notice that between the vertical bars the shapes of the lines that represent the "S&P 500" and the "S&P 500 with 12-worst quarters in T-bills" are identical. This is as they should be. Both lines show the real wealth derived from a buy-and-hold investment in the S&P 500 index.

There are three very important takeaways from this analysis. The first is that if you missed the 12 best quarters you would have earned a return that would have been almost the same as what you would have earned from investing in Treasury bills during each of the 112 quarters.

The second, even more important, takeaway is that *all of the S&P 500's return above that of Treasury bills came in only 11 percent (12/112) of the quarters.* (Thus the correct answer to Question 31.4 is "e"—fewer than 20 percent.)

The third takeaway is that investment returns are not, never have been, and never will be smooth. Returns in equity and fixed-income markets come in spurts that are, by definition, unexpected.

CHAPTER 32

Know the Odds
Before You Play the Game

Question 32.1.   Imagine you have joined the investment committee that supervises the investments of the endowment at a local hospital. XYZ, one of your investment managers, is an aggressive "market timer." At the last day of each quarter XYZ invests all of the monies under its control in either an S&P 500 index fund or cash equivalents in an endeavor to be invested in the better-performing asset class during the coming quarter.

What percentage of XYZ's quarterly allocations need to be correct for you to be assured that the return from its market-timing strategy outpaces that of a simple S&P 500 index fund?

a. 50 percent.

b. 67 percent.

c. 86 percent.

d. 100 percent.

Question 32.2.   Another manager of a portion of the hospital's endowment has an active-equity mandate. As you look at the manager's history you discover that the cash position of this portfolio seems to average around 15 percent. It has been as high as 30 percent and as low as 5 percent.

When you ask the chair of the investment committee, you learn that the firm has a normal cash policy of around 15 percent. It reduces cash to around 5 percent when it is particularly optimistic; it builds cash to around 30 percent when it is particularly pessimistic. Possibly seeing surprise on your face, the chair of the investment committee adds, "This is quite standard in the industry."

a. This is an ideal situation for the hospital's endowment. In effect, you are getting two services in one. You have a manager

who is not only managing a stock portfolio but is also providing a stock-cash asset allocation service.

b. Being foolish with up to 30 percent of the hospital's money is
still being foolish.

The football-shaped diagram in Figure 32.1[1] reveals several insights into the uphill battle facing market timers. The lower left-hand
corner shows the result of perfect failure (being invested in the
worst-performing stock/T-bill asset class during each of the 112
quarters). Over this time period $1.00 would have shrunk in real (in-
flation-adjusted) terms to $0.13 (shown here on a logarithmic scale).
The top right-hand corner shows the result of perfect market timing
(being in the best-performing asset class during each of the 112 quarters). Here $1.00 would have grown, in real terms, to $161.

To construct the "football" in Figure 32.1, beginning in the upper right-hand corner, I rank the 112 best quarterly returns from
highest to lowest.[2] Next, I replace the best quarter's return with the
return of that quarter's opposite asset class. The highest quarterly

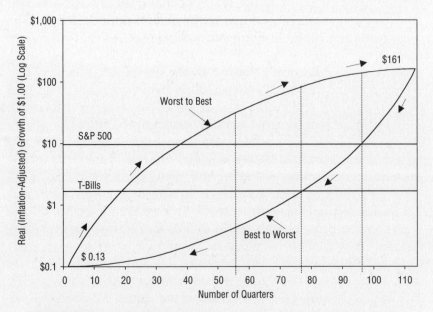

FIGURE 32.1   Real Growth of $1 versus the Number of Quarters in the
Best-Performing Asset Class
Source: Hagin Investment Research, Inc.

return (out of the 112 possible quarters) came from the S&P 500 index in the first calendar quarter of 1975. During that quarter the real quarterly return from the S&P was 21.1 percent; the real quarterly return from Treasury bills was –0.3 percent.

I continue this process of replacing the next-best return with the return of the opposite asset class one quarter at a time until I have switched the returns of all 112 quarters. This process produces the "best to worst" curve along the bottom of the football-shaped curve. (Notice how the slope of the bottom curve falls quickly from $161 as the returns of the quarters that contributed the most to the perfect wealth index of $161 are the first to be replaced.) Finally, after successively replacing each next-best return with the return of the other asset class I reach the "this is as bad as it can get" wealth index of $0.13 at the bottom left corner of the football-shaped curve. Here each of the 112 quarterly returns is the quarter's worst-performing asset class.

Next I rank the 112 worst quarterly returns from most worst to least worst. Next I replace the return of the worst-performing quarter (of the 112 quarters) with the return of that quarter's opposite asset class. I continue this process quarter by quarter until the list contains only the returns of the 112 best-performing asset classes. This process traces the points along the "worst to best" curve along the top of the football-shaped diagram. (Notice how the slope of the top curve rises quickly from $0.13 as the returns of the worst-performing quarters are the first to be replaced.)

The curves that form the top and bottom of the "football" are extremely important. They define the boundary _within which all possible combinations of market-timing selections must fall._ As an extension of the earlier coin-tossing examples, how many different ways can 112 quarterly "stock or cash" decisions be arranged? Substituting "S" (for stocks) in the place of heads, and "C" (for cash) in the place of tails, the toss for the first quarter results in S or C. The toss for the second quarter has two possible outcomes, SC and CS; three tosses produce eight possible outcomes, four produced 16, and so forth. Using the same calculation, 112 choices between either stocks or cash produce 2^{112}, or _5 followed by 33 zeros_, possible sequences. All of these possible sequences fall within the boundaries of the "football." Moreover, as with the amount of air in a football, more of the possible sequences will be concentrated in the middle of the football.

The two horizontal lines show the inflation-adjusted amounts that you would have made from investing $1.00 in 30-day Treasury bills or the S&P 500 stocks, respectively. The first of the several important takeaways comes from comparing the areas within the "football" that are above and below the real wealth derived from owning the S&P 500.

Look particularly at the vertical dotted line above 56 quarters on the horizontal axis. If you have no skill whatsoever in selecting next quarter's best-performing asset class, on average you will select the better-performing asset class (S&P 500 or T-bills) about half the time, or in 56 out of the 112 quarters. Here you see that roughly one-quarter of the length of the vertical dotted line that is within the football is above the horizontal line indicating the real wealth that you would have earned from a simple buy-and-hold S&P 500 strategy. Even without taking the higher density of possible sequences in the middle of the football into account, if your stock/cash decision is right half the time, you have roughly a one-in-four chance of having a return that is above that of a buy-and-hold S&P 500 strategy.

Similarly, if you are right half the time, you have approximately a two-in-four chance that your terminal wealth will be below the S&P 500 but above T-bills, and a one-in-four chance that it will be below T-bills.

Now look at the vertical dotted line above 76 quarters. This line describes an investor who can forecast the best asset class in the coming quarter two out of three times (76 correct quarters out of 112 quarters makes your accuracy rate 67 percent). Unfortunately, the poor soul whose market timing is correct two out of three times has only a 50–50 chance of having a terminal wealth that is above that of an S&P 500 index fund.

Returning to Question 32.1—what percentage of the 112 quarterly stock-cash allocations must be correct for you to be assured that XYZ's returns will outpace those of a simple S&P 500 index fund?—the answer lies in Figure 32.1 on the vertical line above 96 perfect quarters. Here all results are above that of an S&P 500 index fund. Thus, in order for you to be assured that your manager's market-timing strategy will beat the S&P 500 index fund, the manager must make the correct market-timing decision prior to 96 of the 112 quarters (or 86 percent). Hence, the answer to Question 32.1 is "c"—86 percent.

CHAPTER 33

Ten Best Days

Question 33.1. Over the 10-year period ended June 30, 2002, there were 2,521 trading days. If you had been fully invested in the S&P 500 index over this 10-year period, your annualized rate of return would have been 11.4 percent; $1.00 would have grown to $2.95. Suppose, however, you missed the 10 best days—not the 10 best days every year, merely the 10 best days out of 2,521. What is the recalculated annual rate of return?

    a. Between 10 percent and 11.2 percent.
    b. Between 9 percent and 10 percent.
    c. Between 8 percent and 9 percent.
    d. Between 7 percent and 8 percent.
    e. Below 7 percent.

The answer is that if you missed the 10 best days for the S&P 500 index spread over the past 10 years your annualized return would have fallen from 11.4 to 6.7 percent! Thus the correct answer to Question 33.1 is "e"—below 7 percent.

It is difficult to believe that removing only 10 of 2,521 days spread over a 10-year period (that is, only four-tenths of 1 percent of the total number of days), can so change the 10-year annualized rate of return. Amazing, but true!

Question 33.2. Does this phenomenon continue if we remove progressively more of the best-performing days?

    a. By far most of the detrimental punch comes from removing the 10 best days.
    b. The destruction of return remains strong as we remove increasing numbers (20, 30, and 40) of the best days.

Question 33.3.   What is the 10-year annualized rate of return for the S&P 500 if we remove the 40 best-performing days?
   a. Between 5 percent and 6.7 percent.
   b. Between 3 percent and 5 percent.
   c. Between 1 percent and 3 percent.
   d. Between –1 percent and 1 percent.
   e. Below –1 percent.

The correct answer to Question 33.2 is "b"—the destruction remains strong as we remove increasing numbers of the best days. The correct answer to Question 33.3 is "e"—below –1 percent.

Specifically, if you remove the 40 best-performing days from the 2,521 trading days that composed the past 10 years, the average annualized rate of return falls from 11.4 percent to –2.0 percent!

It should be mentioned that this process works similarly in reverse. If you could successfully remove the 10 *worst* days, the annualized annual return would have increased from 11.4 percent to 17.3 percent. Removing the 40 worst days would increase the annualized return to 27.4 percent. Without question, if you successfully remove the worst-performing days, weeks, or months, you could handsomely outperform the returns that you would derive from a buy-and-hold strategy. You should not forget, however, that the playing field is not level. The odds of winning the market-timing game are against you.

Question 33.4.   Which of the following statements are true? Which are false?
   a. Returns derived from investments in stock and bond markets never have been, and never will be, smooth.
       True _____   False _____
   b. Long-term returns that are earned from different asset classes are concentrated in a few days, weeks, or months.
       True_____   False_____
   c. The potential risk of "going to cash" far eclipses the potential reward.
       True_____   False_____
   d. The biggest risk for a long-term investor is not staying the course.
       True _____   False _____

TABLE 33.1   Reasons Not to Invest

1934	Depression	1969	Money tightens—markets fall
1935	Spanish civil war	1970	Vietnam war spreads
1936	Economy still struggling	1971	Wage-price freeze
1937	Recession	1972	Largest U.S. trade deficit ever
1938	War clouds gather	1973	Energy crisis
1939	War in Europe	1974	Steepest market drop in 40 years
1940	France falls	1975	Clouded economic prospects
1941	Pearl Harbor	1976	Economic recovery slows
1942	Wartime price controls	1977	Market slumps
1943	Industry mobilizes	1978	Interest rates rise
1944	Consumer goods shortages	1979	Oil prices skyrocket
1945	Postwar recession predicted	1980	Interest rates at all-time high
1946	Dow tops 200—market too high	1981	Steep recession begins
1947	Cold War begins	1982	Worst recession in 40 years
1948	Berlin blockade	1983	Market hits new highs
1949	Russia explodes A-bomb	1984	Record federal deficits
1950	Korean War	1985	Economic growth slows
1951	Excess profits tax	1986	Dow nears 2,000
1952	U.S. seizes steel mills	1987	Record-setting market decline
1953	Russia explodes H-bomb	1988	Election year
1954	Dow tops 300—market too high	1989	October "mini-crash"
1955	Eisenhower illness	1990	Persian Gulf crisis
1956	Suez crisis	1991	Dow hits 3,000—market too high
1957	Russia launches Sputnik	1992	Clinton elected President
1958	Recession	1993	Tax and budget uncertainties
1959	Castro seizes power in Cuba	1994	Worst bond market since 1927
1960	Russia downs U-2 plane	1995	Dow tops 4,000—market too high
1961	Berlin Wall erected	1996	Greenspan's "irrational
1962	Cuban missile crisis		exuberance"
1963	Kennedy assassinated	1997	Liquidity crisis
1964	Gulf of Tonkin	1998	Emerging markets crisis
1965	Civil rights marches	1999	Technology bubble created
1966	Vietnam war escalates	2000	Dot-com bubble burst
1967	Newark race riots	2001	September 11th
1968	USS Pueblo seized	2002	Lowest interest rates in 40 years

Sources: 1838 Investment Advisors, LLC, and Ned Davis Research.

The correct answer to Question 33.4a is "true"—the returns derived from investments in stock and bond markets never have been, and never will be, smooth. The correct answer to Question 33.4b is "true"—the long-term returns that are earned from different asset classes are concentrated in a few days, weeks, or months. The correct answer to Question 33.4c is "true"—the risk of "going to cash" far eclipses the potential reward. The correct answer to Question 33.4d is "true"—the biggest risk for a long-term investor is not staying the course.

Table 33.1 shows that there are *always* reasons not to invest.

Putting the Pieces Together

Trading Costs

Much can go wrong between the time a portfolio manager decides to buy or sell a stock and the time the requested purchases or sales are completed.

It is reasonable to expect that in certain situations, in addition to the cost of commissions, seller-initiated trades will push stock prices lower—adding a "market-impact cost" to the seller's transaction. Conversely, it is reasonable to expect that in certain situations buyer-initiated trades will push stock prices higher—adding a "market-impact cost" to the buyer's transaction.

Along with market-impact costs, there are two insidious costs incurred by trade initiators—the costs of trading delays and the costs of missed trades. Trading delays occur when there are no readily available counterparties willing to take on the other side of entire transactions. In this case traders frequently (at the behest of the portfolio managers for whom they trade) break large trades into smaller pieces that are, in turn, dribbled into the market. If the market moves against the trade during the dribble period, the cost of the trading delay can be significant.

The costs of missed trades occur when a portfolio manager's buy or sell decisions cannot be completed before the price moves away. In the case of purchases, a momentum manager may decide to buy a million shares of stock "as long as the price is below $30." (As I will demonstrate later in this chapter, a million-share trade is not abnormally large.) If such managers cannot buy the 1 million shares "below $30," the cost of the missed trade lowers the portfolio manager's expected value added. In the case of sales, there may be fear that other traders will "smell the blood in the water" if the million-share trade is announced or if the dribbling alerts sharks. Here, too, the cost of the missed trade lowers the manager's expected value added.

Question 34.1. *What is the approximate average cost of commissions paid by large institutional investors? (The alternatives are shown as percents. Here 0.04 is four one-hundredths of 1 percent, or four basis points.)*
    a. 0.04 percent per order.
    b. 0.10 percent per order.
    c. 0.15 percent per order.
    d. 0.20 percent per order.
    e. 0.25 percent per order.

Question 34.2. *What is the approximate market-impact cost paid by large institutional trade initiators (averaged over all trades)?*
    a. 0.20 percent per order.
    b. 0.25 percent per order.
    c. 0.30 percent per order.
    d. 0.35 percent per order.
    e. 0.40 percent per order.

Question 34.3. *What is the approximate cost of trading delays paid by large institutional trade initiators (averaged over all trades)?*
    a. 0.40 percent per order.
    b. 0.50 percent per order.
    c. 0.60 percent per order.
    d. 0.70 percent per order.
    e. 0.80 percent per order.

Question 34.4. *What is the approximate cost of missed trades paid by large institutional trade initiators (averaged over all trades)?*
    a. 0.10 percent per order.
    b. 0.12 percent per order.
    c. 0.14 percent per order.
    d. 0.16 percent per order.
    e. 0.20 percent per order.

Question 34.5. *Which of the following situations increase the cost of market impact?*
  a. When the number of shares in the buyer- or seller-initiated transaction is large relative to the stock's average daily trading volume.
  b. When the dollar amount of the buyer- or seller-initiated transaction is large.
  c. When the market and sectors within the market are moving in the opposite direction from the buyer- or seller-initiated transaction (that is, down for sellers; up for buyers).
  d. All of the above.

To attain perspective, suppose that the total cost of commissions, market impact, trading delays, and missed trades is 1 percent per buy or sell transaction. If your average holding period is one year, two percentage points of your skill are lost—just to cover your trading costs.

Wayne Wagner, chairman of the Plexus Group, Inc. (a JP Morgan Investor Services company), presented an interesting research paper at the spring 2003 meeting of the Q-Group (a useful shorthand for the Institute for Quantitative Research in Finance) entitled "The Nature of Institutional Order Flow: The Hurdles to Superior Performance."[1]

Using data from the Plexus Group, Wagner studied data on 93 large institutional managers containing 867,321 orders during the primarily up market from the fourth quarter of 2001 and through the end of the first quarter of 2002 and 431,539 orders during the primarily down market in the second quarter of 2002.

Using these data Wagner estimated that the average costs per order were:

Commissions	0.16 percent per order
Market impact	0.31 percent per order
Trading delays	0.71 percent per order
Missed trades	0.12 percent per order
Total	1.30 percent per order

Thus, the closest correct answer to Question 34.1 (the average cost of commission) is "c"—"0.15 percent per order"; the closest correct answer to Question 34.2 (the average cost of market impact) is "c"—"0.30 percent per order"; the closest correct answer to Question 34.3 (the average cost of trading delays) is "d"—"0.70 percent per order"; and the correct answer to Question 34.4 (the average estimated cost of missed trades) is "b"—"0.12 percent per order."

This means that the average round-trip (sell-buy) cost of trading for large investment management organizations is on the order of 2.6 percent per trade. Wagner's research also provides us with a fascinating look inside these data. In Table 34.1 the trades are classified into equal-dollar quintiles. That is, the number of trades times the number of shares times the prices per share were the same in each of the five quintiles. Notice in the bottom row of the table that roughly 1,000 buy or sell trades, each with slightly more than 2 million shares, representing between $75 million and $80 million, accounted for the same dollar amount of trading as each of the other quintiles. At the small-order end of the market, represented by the first row of the table, 444,000 buy and 356,000 sell orders of roughly 2,000 shares, representing between $50,000 and $60,000, were required to produce the same dollar amount of orders as for the other quintiles.

Table 34.2 summarizes Wagner's findings of the median cost of market impact per trade, ranging from the smallest trades to the largest trades in the generally rising market through the first quarter

TABLE 34.1   Equal-Dollar Quintiles

Trade Size Quintile	Number of Trades (thousands)		Median Number of Shares (thousands)		Median Dollars (millions)		Median Average Daily Volume	
	Buy	Sell	Buy	Sell	Buy	Sell	Buy	Sell
1 (small)	444	356	2	2	0.05	0.06	0.4	0.3
2	23	19	154	176	4.82	5.79	10.8	11.1
3	8	7	393	430	13.74	15.61	18.3	18.2
4	4	3	851	923	31.86	35.24	28.1	30.8
5 (large)	1	1	2,014	2,105	75.62	80.91	52.6	53.8

Source: Plexus Group, Inc. (a JPMorgan Investor Services company).

TABLE 34.2 Median Cost of Market Impact per Trade (Percent)

Trade Size	Generally Rising Market 4Q2001–1Q2002		Generally Falling Market 2Q2002	
	Buy	Sell	Buy	Sell
1	0.1	0.1	0.1	0.1
2	0.5	0.4	0.2	0.4
3	0.6	0.5	0.3	0.6
4	0.8	0.7	0.3	1.0
5	0.9	1.3	0.2	1.6

Source: Plexus Group, Inc. (a JPMorgan Investor Services company).

of 2002 and the generally declining market that began in the second quarter of 2002.

The median cost of market impact in Table 34.2 provides us with several important insights into the relationship between trade size and the enormous cost of market impact when trading positions with a median trade size around $80 million. Remember that during the bubble mania that prevailed during Wagner's "rising market" the market leadership was concentrated in technology-related companies. In such a market it is still surprising to see the cost of market impact paid on seller-initiated trades of the then out-of-favor stocks. Managers who initiated buy orders during this two-market period (technology-related companies and all the rest) paid an average market-impact cost of 0.9 percent.

The median cost of market impact that was paid by the initiators of buy and sell trades during the collapse of the bubble in the first quarter of 2002 is evidence of the staggering costs of market impact as panicked sellers all rush to the same exit. Large sell orders in this generally declining market suffered a median market impact cost of 1.6 percent. By comparison, the contrarian investors who initiated large buy orders experienced only a moderate adverse impact on prices of 0.2 percent.

In the answer to Question 34.5, the situations in which the cost of market impact is highest are:

■ When the number of shares in the buyer- or seller-initiated transaction is large relative to the stock's average daily trading volume.

■ When the dollar amount of the buyer- or seller-initiated transaction is large.

■ When the market and sectors within the market are moving down for seller-initiated transactions and up for buyer-initiated transactions.

Hence the answer to Question 34.5 is "d"—all of the above.

Question 34.6. Is there some good news about the large market-impact costs paid by initiators of large buy or sell transactions?
  a. Yes.
  b. No.

For every buyer there must be a seller; for every seller there must be a buyer. Providers of liquidity to people who are eager to buy or sell *earn the market impact*. Hence the answer to Question 34.6 is "a"—yes.

CHAPTER 35

Mutual Funds

Question 35.1. *The mutual fund return histories that appear in your favorite magazine contain reliable aggregations of historical returns.*

   a. Fact.
   b. Fiction.

Most publications report annual-return histories of mutual funds that have been in operation throughout the preceding one, three, or five years *and are currently open for business.* You should be suspicious of these return histories because over the years many of the poorest-performing funds have been closed, causing the average-return summaries to be overstated.

Mark Carhart,[1] while on the faculty of the University of Southern California (currently he is at Goldman Sachs Asset Management), studied biases in the aggregation of mutual fund returns when higher-risk and poorer-performing mutual funds go out of business. Basically, the conclusions drawn from Carhart's research are that the results of mutual fund studies showing average historical returns, measuring performance persistence (the degree to which above-average performers remain above-average performers), and estimating relationships between returns and fund attributes can be meaningfully misstated as poorer-performing funds fall by the wayside.

The reason mutual fund histories frequently overstate returns and performance persistence is that the purveyors of such histories (such as Morningstar, Inc., and Lipper, Inc.) have designed their databases to assist their users in selecting mutual funds. For this reason these databases contain only the histories of mutual funds that are currently open for business.

Suppose the published annual return of the large-growth mutual fund category is 12.0 percent. Using available databases you can look at the returns of each of the funds in this category that are currently open for business and select your favorites for investment.

Suppose, however, that a fund with a terrible year-to-date investment record closed for business during the fourth quarter. Because you can no longer invest in this fund, its history does not appear in the database. But, because the closed fund—and its brethren—have been dropped from the database, the true return of this mutual fund category is lower than the reported return that includes only last year's survivors. This "survivor bias" causes many published mutual fund return aggregations to overstate historical investment returns.

During 2002, for example, 373 funds were liquidated—2.7 percent of the funds in Morningstar's universe. In addition, a record high of 733 funds or share classes, 5.3 percent of the Morningstar universe, were merged into other funds. Simultaneously the number of mutual fund launches fell to a 10-year low. Only 702 funds or share classes opened in 2002, down 49 percent from 2001 and down 60 percent from 2000. Of the 356 technology funds Morningstar tracks, 17 percent went out of business in 2002. International equity funds were hit hard as well, with 12 percent of foreign stock funds eliminated. Of these, 34 were dissolved and 76 were merged into other funds.[2]

Using Standard & Poor's classifications excluding sector funds, 14.8 percent of the actively managed domestic equity funds liquidated or merged in the three-year period 2000 to 2002, including 6.6 percent during 2002. Also, 11 percent of actively managed funds changed their names in 2002 as fund "managements attempted to respond to the downturn by repositioning their offering."[3]

A useful way to think about return aggregations that do not correct for the funds that disappear and the funds that have been added is to append to the description "returns for all funds that were in business continuously throughout the period."

The correct answer to Question 35.1 is "b"—fiction; mutual fund histories that appear in the popular press do *not* contain reliable aggregations of historical returns.

Carhart has shown that turnover has a negative impact on mutual fund returns.[4] James Dow and Gary Gordon have a decidedly cynical view of mutual fund trading. Baffled by the fact that mutual fund managers continue to trade aggressively even though they know such trading reduces their returns, Dow and Gordon speculate that some mutual fund managers may actively trade and thereby knowingly reduce their funds' expected returns simply to create the illusion that they are providing a valuable service.[5]

My, I believe more realistic, view is that much as 90 percent of us believe we are above-average drivers, most mutual fund managers believe they can produce above-average returns—despite being aware that active management must, on average, provide below-average returns. Thus, they are motivated to trade by overconfidence, not cynicism. It is true, by definition, that at the end of the day (or month, or quarter, or year, or any interval you might select) half of the mutual fund managers will have below-average mutual fund returns. Thus, with 20–20 hindsight half of the mutual fund manager brethren will *always* turn out to have been overconfident.

Conclusion: Individual and professional investors are overconfident; overconfident investors trade too much; the more investors trade, the more costs they incur; the more costs they incur, the lower their returns.

Question 35.2.   Morningstar, Inc., ranks mutual funds with one to five stars. We can infer from the widespread use of four- and five-star rankings in mutual fund advertising that the managers of these funds—as well their ad agencies—believe that investors use these star rankings to guide their mutual fund investments.

Do the monies that flow into mutual funds following the release of Morningstar's four- and five-star ratings support the belief that the top-rated funds receive a disproportionately large portion of new investments?

   a. Yes.

   b. No.

Question 35.3.   Is it a good thing or a bad thing to own shares of a mutual fund that receives large inflows of new investment dollars?

   a. Good thing.

   b. Bad thing.

Question 35.4.   Do the mutual fund rating services sold by Morningstar, Inc., and Value Line, Inc., discern better-performing funds?
  a. Yes.
  b. No.

There is much evidence that investors favor the purchase of better-performing mutual funds and funds that are favored by the various mutual fund rating services. Thus the correct answer to Question 35.2 is "a"—yes, monies that flow into mutual funds following the release of Morningstar's four- and five-star ratings support the belief that the top-rated funds receive a disproportionately large portion of new investments.

Imagine that you are the investment manager of a large mutual fund. After your fund receives a Morningstar five-star rating, investors flock to your fund in a rush to get in on the action. When the dust settles you find that the size of your fund has doubled. Your problem: You need to invest these new monies—while maintaining both your investment style and the flexibility to sell your entire investment in each company whenever you choose to do so without swamping the market and driving the price significantly lower. Without question, mutual funds can be destroyed by their own success. Thus the correct answer to Question 35.3 is "b"—it is a bad thing to own shares of a mutual fund that receives large inflows of new investment dollars.

Matthew Morey, currently at Pace University in New York, has conducted an extensive study in which he "rates the mutual fund raters."[6] Working with a database that eliminates the problem of survivor bias, Morey reported that the Morningstar and Value Line "systems show little ability to predict winning funds."[7] Thus the correct answer to Question 35.4 is "b"—no, the mutual fund rating services do not appear to be able to discern better-performing funds.

CHAPTER 36

Advantages of . . .

Question 36.1. *Because fewer Wall Street analysts scrutinize small-capitalization stocks, actively managed mutual funds are more likely to outperform the relevant indexes when they invest in relatively "less efficient" small-capitalization stocks.*
   a. Fact.
   b. Fiction.

Earlier you were reminded to approach each investment decision with the expectation that—over whatever time interval you choose—half of the securities that compose whatever universe you select (properly weighted by the market value of each security) will earn above-average returns, and half will earn below-average returns. Given this fact, it is puzzling that so many people believe that mutual funds investing in small-capitalization stocks can somehow defy the fact that "average is average." For this to be true there would have to be something wrong with how small-capitalization managers measure their returns and/or the benchmarks against which small-cap managers choose to measure their returns.

An article entitled "Does Active Management Work for Small-Cap Stocks?" by David Blitzer and Srikant Dash reports, "Measurement techniques and benchmark selection significantly affect any evaluation of active management performance in small-cap stocks."[1]

Blitzer and Dash studied all funds classified as SmallCap Domestic Equity in the Standard & Poor's Funds database from the beginning of 1998 to the end of 2002 (after deducting management expenses and correcting for survivorship bias). To ensure apples-to-apples comparisons, they measured each fund's returns against the returns of the benchmark for its particular *style* and *size* category using the S&P SmallCap 600 and the Russell 2000 and each fund's "style box."

Next, they calculated both asset-weighted and equal-weighted returns. Average returns for a fund group are often calculated using only equal weighting. When returns are equally weighted the returns of a $10 billion fund affect the average in the same manner as the returns of a $10 million fund. A more accurate representation of how investors fared in a particular period can be ascertained by calculating weighted-average returns, with each fund's returns weighted by net assets.

Blitzer and Dash found that during the five-year market cycle from 1998 through 2002, contrary to conventional wisdom, *a majority of active small-cap managers underperformed their S&P benchmarks*. Exploring the impact of survivorship bias, they discovered that, if one takes only the surviving small-capitalization funds, performance results are skewed upward by an astounding 5 percent to 9 percent. Since most active versus passive comparisons are calculated using only surviving funds, Blitzer and Dash showed, quite convincingly, that the active management returns reported by small-capitalization mutual funds are significantly overstated.

Not surprisingly, Blitzer and Dash also found that the performance of active small-cap managers is greatly affected by their chosen benchmarks. They concluded, "It is incumbent upon fiduciaries and investors to select appropriate measurement techniques and benchmarks when evaluating active-manager performance."[2] Their closing reference to William Sharpe should be emblazoned on a refrigerator magnet: "The simple universal arithmetic of active management—the average after-cost return from active management must be lower than the average return from passive management—holds for small caps as for large caps."[3]

Question 36.2. Actively managed mutual funds perform better in bear markets.
   a. Fact.
   b. Fiction.

Again, approach each investment decision with the expectation that—over whatever time interval you choose—half of the securities that compose whatever universe you select (properly weighted by the market value of each security) will earn above-average returns, and half will earn below-average returns.

Another puzzling misconception is that actively managed mutual funds can somehow perform better than their comparative indexes during bear markets.

After correcting for survivor bias and subtracting fees, Blitzer and Dash's[4] retrospective looks at 2000 through 2002—the worst three-year bear market since 1941—shows that only 46 percent of large-cap funds, 23 percent of mid-cap funds, and 28 percent of small-cap funds outperformed the S&P 500, S&P MidCap 400, and S&P SmallCap 600 indexes, respectively.

Question 36.3.   G. Brinson, R. Hood, and G. Beebower, in their classic paper "The Determinants of Portfolio Performance,"[5] showed that _____ of the variation in the returns realized by large U.S. corporate pension funds was due to "asset mix."
   a. More than 90 percent.
   b. Between 70 percent and 90 percent.
   c. Between 50 percent and 70 percent.
   d. Between 30 percent and 50 percent.
   e. Between 10 percent and 30 percent.
   f. Less than 10 percent.

Question 36.4.   Mark Kritzman and Sebastian Page[6] in a recent research paper have shown that if an investment manager, in fact, has skill in selecting among asset categories or among individual stocks, which has the greater potential for adding incremental return?
   a. Asset categories.
   b. Individual stocks.

The long-held conventional wisdom in the investment management industry is that asset allocation is the most important investment decision. The widely read paper by Brinson, Hood, and Beebower showed that *94 percent of the variations in returns of large U.S. corporate pension funds was explained by variation in returns due to asset allocation.* Hence, the correct answer to Question 36.3 is "a"—more than 90 percent.

It is extremely important to note that Brinson, Hood, and

Beebower looked back *ex post* at the end of each year and concluded that asset allocation had been the most important factor.

Mark Kritzman and Sebastian Page are asking (and answering) a very different question: If you are a skillful forecaster, what factor, *ex ante*, has the greatest potential for delivering above-benchmark returns? In their very interesting study Kritzman and Page used simulation techniques to gauge the natural dispersion of returns associated with asset allocation and security selection. In their first set of simulations they generated thousands of random portfolios that differed only by asset mix. In another set of simulations they generated thousands of random portfolios, all of which had the same asset mix but differed by security composition. To many persons' surprise they found that security selection had a far greater potential than asset allocation to add to or detract from performance.

Properly understood, Kritzman and Page's results do not contradict the Brinson, Hood, and Beebower results. The Brinson, Hood, and Beebower study describes what investors do. It says nothing about what investors should or should not do. Kritzman and Page's research reveals what skillful investors should emphasize and what unlucky investors should avoid.

CHAPTER 37

Style Persistence

Question 37.1.   Imagine that you are on a committee that is in the process of interviewing prospective investment managers for the endowment of a local charity. Manager A's presentation to your committee emphasized that her investment returns had exceeded those of the S&P 500 index over the preceding three years. Manager B's presentation revealed that he had underperformed the S&P 500 index over the preceding three years.

Both managers emphasized that they will never change their stripes. That is, they will continue to use the same investment "style" (such as investing in low price/sales stocks drawn from a large-capitalization universe or investing only in low price/earnings-to-growth stocks drawn from a middle-capitalization universe) over the next three years that they employed in the prior three years. It is not surprising that everyone else on the committee favors hiring Manager A. What do you tell the other members of the committee?

a. No one can ever accuse your committee of wrongdoing if you hire a manager with a solid three-year record. Your recommendation: Hire Manager A.

b. Managers that adhere to a rigid style (as both of these managers assert) with above-index returns over three years are likely to deliver below-index returns over the next three years. Your recommendation: Hire Manager B.

c. Managers that adhere to a rigid style (as both of these managers assert) with below-index returns over three years are likely to deliver above-index returns over the next three years. Your recommendation: Hire Manager B.

d. Both "b" and "c" are correct.

Question 37.1 is very difficult. How can fiduciaries in the prudent exercise of their responsibilities overlook Manager A, who has three years of above-index returns? Also, there is the issue of whether Manager B's firm can survive the outflow of investors' funds that inevitably follows three years with below-index returns.

Statistically, however, there is no doubt: The odds are against investors or fiduciaries who hire yesterday's winners—especially when yesterday's winners pledge to continue doing exactly what they have been doing.[1] Richard Bernstein at Merrill Lynch provides us with a definitive answer to Question 37.1. Using the 40 stock selection strategies tracked by his research team at Merrill Lynch since 1987, Bernstein calculated the probability that a strategy that performed better (or worse) than the S&P 500 index in one three-year period will perform better (or worse) than the index over the following three years.

Bernstein's results are shown in Table 37.1. The top row, labeled "superior performance during the first three years," shows what subsequently happened to strategies that provided above-index returns during the first three years. Here you see that, of the investment managers whose strategies provided above-index returns for three consecutive years, only 47 percent of these strategies also delivered above-index returns over the next three-year period. Roughly the results that you would expect from a coin toss selection strategy.

Similarly, the second column of the first row shows that only slightly more than half (53 percent) of the strategies that excelled in the first three-year period had below-index returns in the subsequent

TABLE 37.1 Probability of a Strategy's Sustained Performance

	Superior Performance during the Second Three Years	Underperformance during the Second Three Years
Superior Performance during the First Three Years	47%	53%
Underperformance during the First Three Years	62%	38%

Based on data from 1987 to 1999.
Source: Merrill Lynch Quantitative Strategy (also appears in Richard Bernstein, *Navigate the Noise*, John Wiley & Sons, New York, 2001).

three-year period. These results also show that the odds of the strategies that made yesterday's winners repeating is roughly a coin toss.

The bottom row, labeled "underperformance during the first three years," shows the results that would have been obtained by contrarian investors. In the first column of the bottom row you see that 62 percent of the strategies that delivered *below-index* returns for the first three-year period delivered *above-index* returns over the next three years—the highest odds "on the table."

Finally, Bernstein shows that if you selected an investment manager who used a strategy that had *underperformed* the market indexes over the preceding three years your odds of having a below-index result over the next three years were only 38 percent—the lowest odds on the table.

Hence, the answer to Question 37.1 is choice "d"—managers that adhere to a rigid style (as both of these managers assert) with above-index returns over three years are likely to deliver below-index returns over the next three years; managers that adhere to a rigid style (again as both of these managers assert) with below-index returns over three years were likely to deliver above-index returns over the next three years.

CHAPTER 38

Asset Allocation

Question 38.1. Rank the returns, measured since 1926, that an investor would have derived from investments in each of the following asset classes (from highest to lowest).
   a. Small-capitalization stocks.
   b. S&P 500 stocks.
   c. Long-term Treasury bonds.
   d. 30-day Treasury bills.

Question 38.2. Rank the volatility (standard deviation of annual return), measured since 1926, that an investor would have experienced from investments in each of the following asset classes (from highest to lowest).
   a. Small-capitalization stocks.
   b. S&P 500 stocks.
   c. Long-term Treasury bonds.
   d. 30-day Treasury bills.

Table 38.1 shows the returns and the standard deviations of returns for each of the four asset classes for three time periods (1927–1964, 1965–2002, and the entire period 1927–2002). Over each of the time periods the returns and the volatilities of the four asset classes ranked from the highest to the lowest were small-capitalization stocks, S&P 500 stocks, long-term government bonds, and 30-day Treasury bills. Thus the answers to Questions 38.1 and 38.2 are "a, b, c, and d."

Question 38.3. Over the 38 one-year periods from 1965 through 2002, in how many years did the S&P 500 rank as the best asset

TABLE 38.1 Returns and Standard Deviations for Four Asset Classes

	Small-Capitalization Stocks	S&P 500 Stocks	Long-Term Government Bonds	30-Day Treasury Bills
	1927–1964 (38 Years)			
Returns (%)	10.3	9.9	3.0	1.3
Standard deviation	40.0	23.8	5.1	1.3
	1965–2002 (38 Years)			
Returns (%)	13.1	10.0	7.9	6.2
Standard deviation	25.5	17.1	11.7	2.6
	1927–2002 (76 Years)			
Returns (%)	12.3	10.2	5.4	3.8
Standard deviation	33.4	20.6	9.4	3.2

Source: Hagin Investment Research, Inc.

class in terms of performance when compared with the returns of small-capitalization stocks, long-term government bonds, and 30-day Treasury bills?

    a. More than 30 years.
    b. Between 25 and 30 years.
    c. Between 20 and 25 years.
    d. Between 15 and 20 years.
    e. Between 10 and 15 years.
    f. Fewer than 10 years.

Ranking right up there with Reno, Nevada, being west of Los Angeles and Rome, Italy being on a latitude nearest that of Boston, is the number of times in the years since 1965 that the S&P 500 has turned in the best relative annual return (relative to the annual returns of small-capitalization stocks, long-term government bonds, and 30-day Treasury bills). Most professional investors believe the correct answer is "between 20 and 25 years."

Table 38.2 shows the investment returns derived from the best- and worst-performing asset classes from 1927 thorugh 2002. Since 1965 the S&P 500 has ranked as the best-performing asset class in only 7 of the 38 years.

Question 38.4.   Over the 38 one-year periods from 1965 through 2002, in how many years did the small-capitalization stocks rank as the worst asset class in terms of performance when compared with the returns of S&P 500 stocks, long-term government bonds, and 30-day Treasury bills?
   a. More than 30 years.
   b. Between 25 and 30 years.
   c. Between 20 and 25 years.
   d. Between 15 and 20 years.
   e. Between 10 and 15 years.
   f. Fewer than 10 years.

Well, here is another chance to win a bar bet. Most professional investors believe that small-capitalization stocks—being clearly the most volatile of the four primary domestic asset classes—rank in the worst comparative-return category between 20 and 25 years. The correct answer is that in the past 38 years small-capitalization stocks ranked in the worst category in only 7 of the 38 years.

Thus, the correct answer to Question 38.4 is "f"—fewer than 10 years. To save you the trouble of counting the "bests" in Table 38.2, small-capitalization stocks ranked in the best category in 17 of the past 38 years.

Of course, being in the best or worst category is far from the whole story. A year-by-year comparison of the total returns derived from the best and worst asset classes appears in Tables 38.3 and 38.4.

TABLE 38.2 Best and Worst Total Return Comparisons

Year	Small-Cap Stocks	S&P 500 Stocks	Long-Term Gov't Bonds	30-Day Treasury Bills	Year	Small-Cap Stocks	S&P 500 Stocks	Long-Term Gov't Bonds	30-Day Treasury Bills
1927		Best		Worst	1965	Best		Worst	
1928		Best	Worst		1966		Worst		Best
1929	Worst			Best	1967	Best		Worst	
1930	Worst		Best		1968	Best		Worst	
1931	Worst			Best	1969	Worst			Best
1932		Worst	Best		1970	Worst		Best	
1933	Best		Worst		1971	Best			Worst
1934	Best	Worst			1972		Best		Worst
1935		Best		Worst	1973	Worst			Best
1936	Best			Worst	1974		Worst		Best
1937	Worst		Best		1975	Best			Worst
1938	Best			Worst	1976	Best			Worst
1939		Worst	Best		1977	Best	Worst		
1940		Worst	Best		1978	Best		Worst	
1941		Worst	Best		1979	Best		Worst	
1942	Best			Worst	1980	Best		Worst	
1943	Best			Worst	1981		Worst		Best
1944	Best			Worst	1982			Best	Worst
1945	Best			Worst	1983	Best		Worst	
1946	Worst			Best	1984	Worst		Best	
1947		Best	Worst		1985		Best		Worst
1948	Worst	Best			1986		Best		Worst
1949	Best			Worst	1987	Worst			Best
1950	Best		Worst		1988	Best			Worst
1951		Best	Worst		1989		Best		Worst
1952		Best	Worst		1990	Worst			Best
1953	Worst		Best		1991	Best			Worst
1954	Best			Worst	1992	Best			Worst
1955		Best	Worst		1993	Best			Worst
1956		Best	Worst		1994			Worst	Best
1957	Worst		Best		1995		Best		Worst
1958	Best		Worst		1996		Best	Worst	
1959	Best		Worst		1997		Best		Worst
1960	Worst		Best		1998	Worst	Best		
1961	Best		Worst		1999	Best		Worst	
1962	Worst		Best		2000		Worst	Best	
1963	Best		Worst		2001	Best	Worst		
1964	Best		Worst		2002		Worst	Best	

Source: Hagin Investment Research, Inc.

TABLE 38.3 Best and Worst Total Return Comparisons: 1927–1964

Year	Best-Performing Asset Class	%	Worst-Performing Asset Class	%
1927	S&P 500	37.5	30-Day Treasury bills	3.1
1928	S&P 500	43.6	Long-term bonds	0.1
1929	30-Day Treasury bills	4.7	Small-cap stocks	(51.4)
1930	Long-term bonds	4.7	Small-cap stocks	(38.1)
1931	30-Day Treasury bills	1.1	Small-cap stocks	(49.8)
1932	Long-term bonds	16.8	S&P 500	(8.2)
1933	Small-cap stocks	142.9	Long-term bonds	(0.1)
1934	Small-cap stocks	24.2	S&P 500	(1.4)
1935	S&P 500	47.7	30-Day Treasury bills	0.2
1936	Small-cap stocks	64.8	30-Day Treasury bills	0.2
1937	30-Day Treasury bills	0.3	Small-cap stocks	(58.0)
1938	Small-cap stocks	32.8	30-Day Treasury bills	(0.0)
1939	Long-term bonds	5.9	S&P 500	(0.4)
1940	Long-term bonds	6.1	S&P 500	(9.8)
1941	Long-term bonds	0.9	S&P 500	(11.6)
1942	Small-cap stocks	44.5	30-Day Treasury bills	0.3
1943	Small-cap stocks	88.4	30-Day Treasury bills	0.3
1944	Small-cap stocks	53.7	30-Day Treasury bills	0.3
1945	Small-cap stocks	73.6	30-Day Treasury bills	0.3
1946	30-Day Treasury bills	0.4	Small-cap stocks	(11.6)
1947	S&P 500	5.7	Long-term bonds	(2.6)
1948	S&P 500	5.5	Small-cap stocks	(2.1)
1949	Small-cap stocks	19.7	30-Day Treasury bills	1.1
1950	Small-cap stocks	38.7	Long-term bonds	0.1
1951	S&P 500	24.0	Long-term bonds	(3.9)
1952	S&P 500	18.4	Long-term bonds	1.2
1953	Long-term bonds	3.6	Small-cap stocks	(6.5)
1954	Small-cap stocks	60.6	30-Day Treasury bills	0.9
1955	S&P 500	31.6	Long-term bonds	(1.3)
1956	S&P 500	6.6	Long-term bonds	(5.6)
1957	Long-term bonds	7.5	Small-cap stocks	(14.6)
1958	Small-cap stocks	64.9	Long-term bonds	(6.1)
1959	Small-cap stocks	16.4	Long-term bonds	(2.3)
1960	Long-term bonds	13.8	Small-cap stocks	(3.3)
1961	Small-cap stocks	32.1	Long-term bonds	1.0
1962	Long-term bonds	6.9	Small-cap stocks	(11.9)
1963	Small-cap stocks	23.6	Long-term bonds	1.2
1964	Small-cap stocks	23.5	Long-term bonds	3.5

Source: Hagin Investment Research, Inc.

TABLE 38.4 Best and Worst Total Return Comparisons: 1965–2002

Year	Best-Performing Asset Class	%	Worst-Performing Asset Class	%
1965	Small-cap stocks	41.8	Long-term bonds	0.7
1966	30-Day Treasury bills	4.8	S&P 500	(10.1)
1967	Small-cap stocks	83.6	Long-term bonds	(9.2)
1968	Small-cap stocks	36.0	Long-term bonds	(0.3)
1969	30-Day Treasury bills	6.6	Small-cap stocks	(25.1)
1970	Long-term bonds	12.1	Small-cap stocks	(17.4)
1971	Small-cap stocks	16.5	30-Day Treasury bills	4.4
1972	S&P 500	19.0	30-Day Treasury bills	3.8
1973	30-Day Treasury bills	6.9	Small-cap stocks	(30.9)
1974	30-Day Treasury bills	8.0	S&P 500	(26.5)
1975	Small-cap stocks	52.8	30-Day Treasury bills	5.8
1976	Small-cap stocks	57.4	30-Day Treasury bills	5.1
1977	Small-cap stocks	25.4	S&P 500	(7.2)
1978	Small-cap stocks	23.5	Long-term bonds	(1.2)
1979	Small-cap stocks	43.5	Long-term bonds	(1.2)
1980	Small-cap stocks	39.9	Long-term bonds	(3.9)
1981	30-Day Treasury bills	14.7	S&P 500	(4.9)
1982	Long-term bonds	40.4	30-Day Treasury bills	10.5
1983	Small-cap stocks	39.7	Long-term bonds	0.7
1984	Long-term bonds	15.5	Small-cap stocks	(6.7)
1985	S&P 500	32.2	30-Day Treasury bills	7.7
1986	Long-term bonds	24.5	30-Day Treasury bills	6.2
1987	30-Day Treasury bills	5.5	Small-cap stocks	(9.3)
1988	Small-cap stocks	22.9	30-Day Treasury bills	6.3
1989	S&P 500	31.5	30-Day Treasury bills	8.4
1990	30-Day Treasury bills	7.8	Small-cap stocks	(21.6)
1991	Small-cap stocks	44.6	30-Day Treasury bills	5.6
1992	Small-cap stocks	23.3	30-Day Treasury bills	3.5
1993	Small-cap stocks	21.0	30-Day Treasury bills	2.9
1994	30-Day Treasury bills	3.7	Long-term bonds	(7.7)
1995	S&P 500	37.6	30-Day Treasury bills	5.4
1996	S&P 500	23.0	Long-term bonds	(0.8)
1997	S&P 500	33.4	30-Day Treasury bills	4.9
1998	S&P 500	28.6	Small-cap stocks	(7.3)
1999	Small-cap stocks	29.8	Long-term bonds	(8.7)
2000	Long-term bonds	20.3	S&P 500	(9.1)
2001	Small-cap stocks	22.8	S&P 500	(11.9)
2002	Long-term bonds	17.0	S&P 500	(22.1)

Source: Hagin Investment Research, Inc.

CHAPTER 39

Beware of Taxes

Poor investment management and the 2000–2002 bear market, like the other bear markets before it, once again drove hoards of investors out of the stock market and into low-interest savings or money-market accounts.

During the third quarter of 2002[1] the Dow Jones Industrial Average reached its lowest point since October 27, 1997[2]—nearly five years earlier. The decline eclipsed the Dow's 36 percent drop during the 1987 crash—making it the worst bear market for the Dow since it was down 45 percent in 1974. The more broad-based S&P 500 stock index was almost 50 percent off its record high of 11,722.98, making this the worst bear market since the 1930s. The Nasdaq Composite index was off 78 percent from its record high. At the same time the yield on the 10-year U.S. Treasury note, which falls when bond prices rise, dropped to 3.571 percent—its lowest level in 44 years.

In this climate of widespread pessimism the *sine qua non* once again became "the only way to make a small fortune in the stock market is to begin with a large one."

Unfortunately, this is no laughing matter. Hunkered down in low-interest savings accounts, investors have no escape from ongoing inflation and no chance to reap the rewards that eventually accrue to investors in equity markets.

Question 39.1.   You live in an imaginary country where there is no income tax. You invest $10,000 for one year; your income is $500 (5 percent). During the year, inflation is 4 percent.

Your former college roommate, Lois, lives in a country where there is no inflation. She, too, invests $10,000 for one year and her *income is $500 (5 percent). She is, however, required to pay income tax.*

What income-tax rate would Lois have to pay to leave each of you with the same after-inflation, after-tax purchasing power?

a. Four percent.
b. Five percent.
c. Neither of the above.

Table 39.1 compares inflation tax with income tax. It shows that you and Lois make an initial investment of $10,000 and have an annual income of $500 each (paid on December 31). In your case, if the inflation rate is 4 percent, the purchasing power of your $10,000 initial investment is reduced by 4 percent or $400. With the $500 tax-free income offset by the $400 bite from inflation, at year-end your purchasing power has increased by only $100.

Lois's column in Table 39.1 shows that she, too, invests $10,000 and has $500 income. In this illustration, Lois lives in a world where inflation is zero. What income tax would Lois have to pay to leave her with only $100 after-inflation, after-tax purchasing power? Would you believe that 80 percent of her income would have to be taxed away for her to end up in exactly the same after-inflation, after-tax position as you? Thus the correct answer to Question 39.1 is "c"—neither of the above.

After inflation taxes can reduce the returns that taxable investors earn from mutual fund investments. Jack Bogle, founder of the Vanguard Group, Inc.—the world's largest no-load mutual fund group with more than 10 million investors—calls taxes the "black sheep" of the mutual-fund industry.[3]

As managers of actively managed mutual funds continually buy

TABLE 39.1 Inflation Tax versus Income Tax

	You	Lois
Initial investment	$10,000	$10,000
Annual income (5%)	500	500
Less: Inflation	400 (4%)	0
Less: Income tax	0	400 (80%)
Year-end purchasing power	$100	$100

and sell stocks in their ongoing attempts to beat the market, the tax issue is exacerbated because fund shareholders pay taxes on a mutual fund's dividend and capital gains distributions and because mutual fund managers spend their time agonizing over the tax consequences of their decisions. The resulting tax burden falls squarely on the shoulders of taxable shareholders.

The large negative impact that taxes have on relative returns is documented in an outstanding article by Robert H. Jeffrey and Robert D. Arnott, "Is Your Alpha Big Enough to Cover Its Taxes?"[4] Their conclusion is that it is not—raising another large hurdle for active management to overcome versus the minimal tax burdens that flow from index funds to their shareholders.

CHAPTER 40

Beyond Active versus Passive

Question 40.1. Which of the following investment strategies is guaranteed to provide you with above-average long-term investment returns?
  a. Small-capitalization stocks.
  b. Technology stocks.
  c. Low-cost stock-index funds.

Question 40.2. Assume that you have a sizable investment in a broad-based equity mutual fund. Your friends dazzle you day in and day out with tales of their winning stocks.
  You have had enough. You decide to move some of the money in your index fund into an actively managed portfolio. The moment the composition of your portfolio strays from the market portfolio, you land in the new world of active management.
  What do you know with absolute certainty about the average return that you and your active-management cohorts will earn?
  a. You are guaranteed to earn investment returns that are on a new, higher plateau.
  b. You are guaranteed that the average return earned by you and your active-management brethren will be below that of a low-cost passive investment in the market portfolio.

The correct answer to Question 40.1 is "c"—low-cost stock-index funds are guaranteed to provide you with above-average investment returns. This is because the market is made up of investors who incur trading costs *and* investors who minimize costs by buying and holding low-cost index funds. When the costs incurred by these two types of investors are aggregated, the investors who hold low-cost stock-index funds are "guaranteed" long-term above-average investment returns. Similarly, the answer to Question 40.2 is "b"— you are guaranteed that the average return earned by you and your active-management brethren will be below that of a low-cost passive investment in the market portfolio.

Important changes are under way in the way Wall Street analysts provide research to the investment-management community. These changes are having—and will continue to have—a profound impact on professional investors and fiduciaries.

In 1975 the era of fixed (and, by today's standards, particularly fat) commissions that were charged by Wall Street broker-dealers ended. Since then the huge sums Wall Street firms have spent on their research departments have not been covered by commissions. To solve this problem Wall Street analysts were allowed to jump over the so-called Chinese wall and become useful resources for the investment-banking arms of their firms. From my firsthand experience, the highest bonuses were paid to analysts who helped the firms land investment-banking business. In fact, this was so much the case that analysts did everything they could to curry favor with the dealmakers on the other side of the "wall."

There is no doubt that the way research is delivered to investment-management professionals is changing. And more significant changes are on the horizon. Even though people have been talking about the end of soft-dollar research (research provided by Wall Street firms, or third parties, in exchange for directing commissions their way) for years, it is difficult for me to believe that it can stand the heat from increasingly enlightened fiduciaries who, in ever-increasing numbers, are coming to realize that investment managers are paying for their research *out of their clients' pockets*. The way out of this dilemma is to have investment-management clients of Wall Street firms pay real ("hard" in investment jargon) dollars for research.

Like the two blades on a closing pair of scissors, on one hand, if institutional investors have to start paying hard dollars for research, they will pay less for research that they are now receiving; only the research that investment managers perceive as the best will survive. On the other hand, Wall Street broker-dealers—having lost the significant financial subsidy from the firm's investment-banking group—will have to charge more to make investment research a profitable cost center. The so-called "care and feeding" of high-priced economists, strategists, and security analysts is very expensive.

It certainly looks as if when the dust settles that there will be much less research slushing around the institutional-investor marketplace. Less conflicting research and fewer opposing expert opinions could mean less trading on noise. At some point—even though we are miles away from it today—less trading could mean less efficient markets.

The Nobel-winning professor William F. Sharpe explains how passive investors (who buy and hold index funds) benefit from the efficiency brought to financial markets by active investors (who seek to earn above-index returns):

> Should everyone index everything? The answer is resoundingly no. In fact, if everyone indexed, capital markets would cease to provide the relatively efficient security prices that make indexing an attractive strategy for some investors. All the research undertaken by active managers keeps prices closer to values, enabling indexed investors to catch a free ride without paying the costs. Thus there is a fragile equilibrium in which some investors choose to index some or all of their money, while the rest continue to search for mispriced securities.
>
> Should you index at least some of your portfolio? This is up to you. I only suggest that you consider the option. In the long run this boring approach can give you more time for more interesting activities such as music, art, literature, sports, and so on. And it very well may leave you with more money as well.[1]

Question 40.3. Benjamin Graham—known as the "father of security analysis"—recanted his bedrock belief in the usefulness of security analysis.
   a. Fact.
   b. Fiction.

The following quotation stands as a memorial to the professional stature and intellectual integrity of a remarkable friend. In 1976 Graham wrote:

I am no longer an advocate of elaborate techniques of security analysis in order to find superior value opportunities. This was a rewarding activity, say, 40 years ago, when *Graham and Dodd* was first published; but the situation has changed. . . . [Today] I doubt whether such extensive efforts will generate sufficiently superior selections to justify their cost. . . . I'm on the side of the "efficient market" school of thought.[2]

Thus the correct answer to Question 40.3 is "a"—fact. Benjamin Graham recanted his bedrock belief in the usefullness of security analysis.

I should mention, however, that several researchers have pointed to apparent contradictions in the efficient market hypothesis. Leopold A. Bernstein[3] has reasoned: If prices embed all information, why would presumably sane investors go to the expense of analyzing companies with no expected reward? This sets up a conundrum whereby if there is no reward for investment analysis, no analysis will take place; if everyone indexes, market prices will cease to be efficient.

Grossman and Stiglitz[4] believe that the traditional definition of market efficiency is inconsistent with a "rational expectations equilibrium"—as described by Nobel prizewinning economist Robert Lucas. In a rational expectations equilibrium investors will not incur the costs of gathering data and processing it into information unless they expect to be rewarded by higher returns than they can earn by just accepting the market price, where there is no cost for information. According to Lucas, investors will gather and process data until, at the margin, the return from the resultant information equals the return from accepting the market price.

According to Grossman and Stiglitz's interpretation, prices should reflect sufficient mispricing (relative to full-information prices) to allow active investors to recover their expenses. Whereas the traditional efficient market perspective expects the average risk-adjusted returns earned by professional money managers to be negative, the "rational efficient markets" perspective expects the same returns to be neutral (i.e., to break even).

In my view, the belief that active investors would not exist if, on average, they could not earn positive risk-adjusted market-relative returns and the other belief that if there is no reward it is irrational to spend time and money gathering data and processing it into information come apart when we consider two real-world explanations. The first is a behavioral finance perspective. Hope springs eternal. Each active investor wholeheartedly believes that he or she will earn above-average returns. Those who are lucky enough to earn above-average returns will believe that whatever they did caused their success. If they fail they will rationalize their failure and try again, and again, and again. Second, and just as important, investment success or failure is difficult to measure. Most investors do not know how well or poorly they are doing.

Back in the salad days for Johnny-come-lately investors—before the bubble burst in 2000—I had the misfortune to be seated on an airplane next to a self-described day trader. As I tried to read, he was eager to tell me of his successes. As part of his tale he told me that he had made a profit on 11 of his last 12 trades. I asked, "How are you doing overall?" Rather sheepishly he replied, "I'm even." Happily, that was the last time he interrupted my reading.

CHAPTER 41

Long-Term Capital Management

Question 41.1.   You run into an acquaintance at a cocktail party who manages the investment management subsidiary of a large, well-known Wall Street broker-dealer. You tell him that you are reading a book that explains the relevance of the work of Nobel laureates and other academics to real-world investing.

Your acquaintance exclaims, "After the Long-Term Capital Management debacle, everyone should know that the views of Nobel laureates have absolutely no place in the real world."

What was the Long-Term Capital Management debacle?

The history of Wall Street is fascinating in large part because it is dotted with fascinating people. The story of Long-Term Capital Management (LTCM)—and the people who brought it to life—is one such story.

This truth-is-stranger-than-fiction story is well told by Roger Lowenstein in his unauthorized book *When Genius Failed: The Rise and Fall of Long-Term Capital Management.*[1] The story of Long-Term Capital Management is really a story about John Meriwether. Raised on Chicago's South Side, he attended Catholic high school and excelled in math—and in his spare time golf. He had an early passion for games and gambling—when he could tilt the odds sufficiently in his favor. After graduating from Northwestern University, spending a year teaching high school mathematics, and receiving an MBA from the University of Chicago, he joined Salomon Brothers.

Soon after he arrived at Salomon the dull world of "buy a bond and earn the interest" changed dramatically as inflation cut the value of many bondholders' once safe investments in half. During the tumultuous years that followed, Meriwether's status grew, and in 1977 he formed Salomon's Arbitrage Group. In Lowenstein's words it

> marked a subtle but important shift in Salomon's evolution. It was also the model that Long-Term Capital was to replicate, brick for brick, in the 1990s—a laboratory in which Meriwether would become accustomed to, and comfortable with, taking big risks. Although Salomon had always traded bonds, its primary focus had been the relatively safer business of buying and selling bonds for customers. But the Arbitrage Group, led by Meriwether, became a principal, risking Salomon's own capital.[2]

By the 1980s Meriwether was one of Salomon's brightest young stars. He was also the hero of Michael Lewis' *Liar's Poker*.[3] Like many people in the investment business who buy and sell multimillion-dollar amounts of securities in a matter of seconds, Meriwether and his traders liked to gamble when they were not trading. Their game was liar's poker.

The game is played with the serial numbers on dollar bills. Each player (there can be from 2 to 10 players), holding a dollar bill, attempts to fool the other players about the serial number on his or her bill. The game begins when one player makes a bid. Suppose a player bids "two fives." This is a bet that among all of the serial numbers on all the bills held by all of the players there are at *least* two fives. The second player, moving clockwise, has two choices: bid higher or challenge the previous bid. The player can bid higher in two ways. The player can bid the same quantity (in this example the quantity is two) of a higher number—in this example a number greater than five. Or the player can bid a larger quantity of any number—in this example three fours, three eights, and so on. If the player does not wish to bid higher, the player can challenge. Play continues until all of the players have challenged a single player's bid.

Good players not only know the likelihood of the occurrence of two fives in eight randomly drawn numbers from zero to nine but also the numbers that, because of the quirks of the U.S. Treasury, are more or less likely to appear on a dollar bill. For the best players, however, calculating the probability of different sequences on the fly is not that difficult. The advantage, as in regular poker, is in knowing how to bluff. Up to a point Wall Street traders and liar's poker players ask themselves the same questions. In Lewis' words,

> Is this a smart risk? . . . How cunning is my opponent? Does he have any idea what he's doing, and if not, how do I exploit his ignorance? If he bids high, is he bluffing, or does he actually hold a strong hand? Is he trying to induce me to make a foolish bid, or does he actually have four of a kind himself? Each player seeks weakness, predictability, and pattern in the others and seeks to avoid it in himself.[4]

Meriwether, who was held in awe by many for his business acumen and his trading skill, was also the acknowledged champion of liar's poker within Salomon. John Gutfreund was the firm's high-profile chairman, who some speculate wanted badly to "be one of the boys" like Meriwether. During this period Gutfreund would routinely drop by to play one-on-one liar's poker with Meriwether. As the story goes, one day in 1986 Gutfreund stopped at Meriwether's desk on the trading floor and said: "One hand, one million dollars, no tears." The "one hand" was liar's poker, the "one million dollars" was *one million dollars*, and the "no tears" meant there would be no whining by the loser.

This was not Meriwether's kind of bet. Even though he was by far the better player, the odds of winning a *single game* were still close to 50–50—not the kind of odds Meriwether usually enjoyed. As the story goes, Meriwether said, "No, John, if we are going to play for that kind of numbers, I'd rather play for real money. Ten million dollars. No tears." After a long period of silence, Gutfreund's response was "You're crazy." Meriwether, the "priest of the *calculated* gamble," had bluffed Gutfreund out of the game.[5]

In 1983 Meriwether—always seeking an edge in the extremely competitive, pressure-packed arena of investing Salomon's capital—had an idea. He would raid universities for cool, disciplined scholars who could bring their rigorous and highly quantitative approach to markets to Salomon's trading desk. In rapid succession he hired Eric Rosenfeld, an MIT-trained Harvard Business School assistant professor; Victor Haghani, a trader with a master's degree in finance from the London School of Economics; Gregory Hawkins, with a

Ph.D. in financial economics from MIT; William Krasker, a mathematical economist with a Ph.D. from MIT; and Lawrence Hilibrand, who had *two* advanced degrees from MIT.

Like most quantitatively oriented investors, Meriwether's team loved to gamble. In Lowenstein's words:

> Meriwether . . . made gambling an intimate part of the group's shared life. The arbitrageurs devised elaborate betting pools over golf weekends; they bet on horses; they took day trips to Atlantic City together. They bet on elections. They bet on anything that aroused their passion for odds. When they talked sports, it wasn't about the game; it was about the *point spread*.
>
> Meriwether loved for his traders to play liar's poker. . . . He liked to test his traders; he thought the game honed their instincts [for trading].[6]

Suddenly Salomon was in trouble. In a quirk of fate the illegal activities of a government bond trader who was supervised by Meriwether forced Gutfreund and Meriwether to resign. To quell the unrest Warren Buffett became the interim CEO.

Meriwether decided to form Long-Term Capital Management. LTCM's business plan was based on the accepted academic notion that financial markets are reasonably efficient. In such a market when from time to time a relationship gets out of whack, market forces restore the "normal equilibrium" relationship. LTCM's plan was to search global markets for relationships that were out of whack. When such relationships were found, LTCM would buy the assets that were cheap and simultaneously sell the assets that were overpriced. So structured, LTCM was betting on the spreads to narrow. LTCM would (at least theoretically) be unaffected if markets rose or fell—or even if they crashed.

Because the temporary opportunities that LTCM planned to exploit are usually minuscule, the plan was to borrow money (collateralized by the underlying bonds) and leverage transactions 20 to 30 times. With such leveraging LTCM could earn (or lose) a return on its own capital, as well as the borrowed capital. Investors who wanted in on the deal would have to pay LTCM a 2 percent annual management fee and 25 percent of any profits. Plus, in an almost unheard-of "lockup," investors would have to agree to a minimum holding period of three years.

Meriwether's lofty goal was to launch LTCM with $2.5 *billion* under management. To accomplish such a feat, he needed more cachet than his scholarly traders could deliver. To position LTCM in the marketplace as a firm known for its genius, Meriwether returned to academia—but this time he went for its stars. He recruited Harvard's Robert C. Merton, whose name would instantly open doors, not only in America but also in Europe and Asia. (In the late 1960s, working under the wing of the famed Paul Samuelson, Merton literally invented a new field—"continuous time finance.")

In the summer of 1993 Meriwether recruited a second academic star: Myron Scholes, known on Wall Street for his co-discovery of the Black-Scholes option pricing formula.

LTCM opened for business in early 1994 with $1.25 billion. Even though this was half of Meriwether's lofty goal, it was by any metric a huge sum.

It was an especially tumultuous time for financial markets. The Federal Reserve under Alan Greenspan's direction stunned investors with an unexpected increase in interest rates—the first such hike in five years. Investors rushed out of bonds. Super-leveraged investors bled: George Soros lost $650 million of his investors' money in two days; Michael Steinhardt lost $800 million of his investors' money in four days. The ever cunning Meriwether seized the moment. Bond prices had, in LTCM's view, overreacted to a mere one-quarter-point nudge in rates—unless it was the "cockroach theory" (if you see one, you will certainly see more) at work.

With bond spreads wide from the panic selling, LTCM bet on convergence. It did not care if rates moved up or down, only that spreads narrowed. LTCM earned 28 percent in 1994. In the firm's year-end letter to clients, Merton and Scholes calculated that 12 percent of the time (12 years out of 100) the firm would lose at least 5 percent of its money.[7]

In 1995 LTCM earned a 59 percent return before fees and 43 percent after fees. In two years investors who had been invested from the start earned 71 percent. In two years 16 partners and 96 employees had earned a phenomenal $1.6 *billion*.[8] Real money by anyone's metric!

Virtually all of these earnings were from highly leveraged—

between 20 and 30 times—transactions that, on average, went LTCM's way. The bankers who provided this leverage were happy, *and very intertwined*, partners. As for LTCM's partners and key employees, instead of taking the firm's profits as taxable income they elected to let the money ride so that their wealth could compound tax-free. On cue, LTCM earned a 57 percent return in 1996 (41 percent after deducting partners' fees). The partners with employees now numbering over 100 earned $2.1 *billion*. Using Lowenstein's comparison,

> To put this number into perspective, this small band of traders, analysts, and researchers, unknown to the general public and employed in the most arcane and esoteric of businesses, earned more that year than McDonald's did selling hamburgers all over the world, more than Merrill Lynch, Disney, Xerox, American Express, Sears, Nike, Lucent, or Gillette—among the best-run companies and best-known brands in American business.
>
> And they had done it with stunningly little volatility. Not once in 1996 did Long-Term suffer a monthly loss of 1 percent.[9]

There were, however, clouds on the horizon. Competitors had started to play the same game, and LTCM had a problem: Its easy pickings were gone. Previously LTCM had sought relationships that were out of whack. To stay ahead of the game LTCM started making *information-sensitive* trades.

In an unprecedented move, as investment opportunities dried up, LTCM announced it would return all *profits* to its clients on money they had invested during 1994, its first year, and *all* money (both principal and profits) invested after 1994. This excluded the investments by partners and employees.

After accepting their Nobel prize in economic science, Merton and Scholes returned to find that—because the "easy-fish" trades had vanished as competitors rushed to fish in LTCM's waters—the firm had moved dangerously away from the tried-and-true convergence trades (i.e., finding relationships that were out of whack and betting that the spreads would narrow).

In a matter of a few months a "crisis of fear became a self-fulfilling prophecy. . . .As prices fell, banks backed away from hedge funds. And as banks backed away, hedge funds had to keep selling."[10]

Even though it would drag on, LTCM was finished. In Lowen-stein's words, "The fund was immobilized by its sheer mass. Long-Term was helpless, a bloated whale surrounded by deadly piranhas."[11]

LTCM owed enormous sums of money to the bankers who, during the good times, had been more than eager to lend it staggering sums. Now, if LTCM went under, "its 17 biggest counterparties—banks such as Merrill [Lynch], Goldman [Sachs], Morgan [Stanley], and Salomon [Smith Barney]—would stand to lose a total of $2.8 billion."[12] The imperative was to keep LTCM alive long enough to dismantle it. Sidestepping a global catastrophe, the bankers each made contributions measured in the hundreds of millions of dollars. Your acquaintance at the cocktail party in Question 42.1 without doubt had his bonus cut—as did his compatriots at other investment banks.

There are obvious lessons to be learned from LTCM's debacle. It doesn't, however, mean that "the views of Nobel laureates have absolutely no place in the real world." They had brilliant ideas that made themselves, their partners, and their employee's superrich. They were not so smart, however, when they left their winnings "on the table."

CHAPTER 42

To Win the Game

Question 42.1.   You are a member of a group of 20 people. Each of you agree to play "Arnie's card game"[1] whereby:

- *You each wager $1; winners are paid $100.*
- *Arnie shuffles a standard 52-card deck, removes a card, shows the card to everyone in the room, and replaces the card in the deck.*
- *Arnie allows you, if you so choose, to offer to sell your wager to anyone in the group at a one-time price that you specify. You can sell your wager or purchase any of the other wagers that are offered for sale.*

Before the first wager is settled you play another game that is the same in all respects except that Arnie asks each of the players to remove a card, look at it, show it to their witnesses, and replace the card in the deck.

Of the people who have played this game, when Arnie selects the card roughly 80 percent are willing to sell their wagers. What is the average price at which the players in your group offer to sell their wagers?
   a. $1 (the amount of the wager).
   b. Slightly above $1.
   c. Midway between $1 and $2.
   d. Slightly below $2.
   e. Slightly above $2.
   f. Between $2 and $3.
   g. Between $3 and $4.
   h. Between $4 and $5.

    i. Between $5 and $6.

    j. Above $6.

In probability terms you have a 1-in-52 chance of winning $100. This means that your $1 wager is instantly worth $\frac{1}{52}$ of $100, or $1.92. Statistically this is a great bet—you pay $1 for a wager that has an expected value of $1.92. Nonetheless, you have only a 1-in-52 chance of winning the $100.

Broadly speaking, players of Arnie's card game fall into three groups. Risk-averse players will offer to sell their wagers at what they believe is a reasonable price. Players who enjoy taking risks will not offer to sell their wagers. A third group—made up of middle-ground investors—will gamble on the outcome unless they can sell their wagers for what they deem to be an attractive price.

Over many iterations of this game, when Arnie selects the card the average price at which the players offer to sell their wagers is slightly below $2, making the correct answer to Question 42.1 "d."

Question 42.2. Does the percentage of players who are willing to sell their wagers change in the slightly modified version of Arnie's card game in which each of the players selects a card?

    a. Yes. Fewer than 80 percent of the players are now willing to sell their wagers.

    b. No. Roughly 80 percent of the players are still willing to sell their wagers.

    c. Yes. More than 80 percent of the players are now willing to sell their wagers.

Question 42.3. What is the average price at which these players offer to sell their wagers?

    a. $1 (the amount of the wager).

    b. Slightly above $1.

    c. Midway between $1 and $2.

    d. Slightly below $2.

    e. Slightly above $2.

    f. Between $2 and $3.

    g. Between $3 and $4.

    h. Between $4 and $5.

    i. Between $5 and $6.

    j. Above $6.

Something very interesting happens with the variation of Arnie's card game that allows players to select their own cards. First, the percentage of players who offer to sell their cards falls from roughly 80 percent to around 60 percent. It appears that the cards that the players have touched are worth more to them than the cards that Arnie drew in the earlier game. Thus the answer to Question 42.2 is "a"—fewer than 80 percent of the players are now willing to sell their wagers.

How about the average price at which the players in the slightly revised game are willing to sell their $1 wagers? Now the average price usually goes from slightly less than $2 to slightly less than $8. Yes, this is not a typo—*slightly less than $8*. Amazingly, the cards that players touch are perceived to be worth considerably more than the cards that Arnie drew for the players. This makes the correct answer to Question 42.3 "j"—above $6.

Question 42.4. Does the average price at which players are willing to sell their wagers change with the educational levels of the players? If so, how does the price change?
  a. More educated players offer to sell their wagers at lower prices.
  b. There is no change.
  c. More educated players offer to sell their wagers at higher prices.

Surprisingly, there is a difference in the price at which more and less educated players offer their wagers. The most popular answer is "a"—more educated (and presumably more astute) players offer to sell their wagers at lower prices.

If you are reading this while running on your treadmill, be careful not to fall. In fact, more educated players consistently offer to sell their wagers at *higher* prices. This makes the correct answer to Question 42.4 "c." At the risk of overgeneralizing, Arnie's card game shows (at least to me) that more educated players enjoy the risk and the chance of the big payoff. Thus, *when they touch the cards*, they are willing to sell their wagers only at many times the wagers' value of $1.92.

The issue here is one where the illusion of skill (touching the card) distorts our judgment. You risk a dollar at the expectation of winning $100. This is a game of risk (1-in-52 odds), not uncertainty where the odds are imprecise. In the second version of the game you are allowed to pull "your card" from the deck. You impart skill on this game of luck.

Arnie's card game has important implications. Are security analysts, portfolio managers, and investors at large influenced by face-to-face meetings and a handshake with high-level corporate officers and all-American analysts? Are fiduciaries influenced by face-to-face meetings and handshakes with real portfolio managers?

Years ago I spoke with a gentleman in Southern California who was planning a trip to New York. There, he planned to meet with members of the trust department of a distinguished New York bank, for whom he had little regard.

Recapping his meeting upon his return, he described in detail a luncheon in one of the bank's private dining rooms—the place settings, the appetizer, the entrée, the dessert—as well as his tour of the trust department and the trading floor. His conversation was sprinkled heavily with the names—and especially the titles—of a long list of "important" people he met. He added, his chest swelling with pride, that they were very interested in the source of his family's money. This, of course, afforded him the opportunity to talk about his favorite subject—his family's pedigree. The account was followed by his observation that "Bob, they don't take just anybody."

When I asked him about our earlier discussions in which he had expressed his dissatisfaction with their investment results, he brushed my query aside and asked, "Have you ever been in their dining room?" I remember thinking that they may not "take" just anybody but they had certainly "taken" him. Using the parallel to Arnie's card game—he "touched the card."

In my view the first thing to remember as you strive to win the game is to remember that you are a different person after you *touch the card*.

The first question in Chapter 2 asked, "Imagine you are a portfolio manager who buys and sells stocks over time in your quest for above-average investment returns. Also, imagine that you have a computer-based system at your disposal that can provide you with any up-to-the-minute data about the economy, your portfolio, or individual securities. (Given today's technology and the myriad sources for historical and up-to-the-minute financial data, this is not a hypothetical question.)"

If you want to own the Markowitz-Sharpe optimum portfolio

you *do* not need any data, news, or information. You merely need to buy and hold broad-based low-cost index funds. As the character of the market ebbs and flows from value to growth, from technology to health care, your portfolio will adjust *automatically*.

If you take the active management path, in spite of the fact that at the end of any day, week, month, or year not everyone can turn in above-average investment results, I fervently believe there is a small number of professional and skilled amateur investors who can consistently deliver above-average investment results. It is *not easy* to provide such returns; it is *not easy* to find people who can.

To win this highly competitive negative-alpha game you need to be keenly aware of the important differences between *information* and *noise*. You need to know the difference between financial analysts who *analyze* and those who *report*.

Whether you are an investor or a fiduciary, you should never lose sight of the fact that the objective of investment management is to fund liabilities, either current or future, either known with precision or estimated. Your goal is not to outperform an index, a specially designed passive portfolio, or a composite of similar portfolios.

I am doubtful that you and the investment managers you hire can sit around a conference table and using the prognostications of Wall Street analysts and online data from every conceivable source—consistently pick winning stocks. Eugene Fama, a respected academic who is on many people's short lists for a Nobel prize, has said rather frankly, "I'd compare stock pickers to astrologers, but I don't want to bad-mouth the astrologers."[2] The reason: When you or the managers you hire are discussing which stocks to buy and which to sell, virtually the same process is being repeated tens of thousands of times around your competition's conference tables.

Peter Bernstein startled some members of the audience in his keynote presentation to the Association of Investment Management and Research's 2003 Annual Conference when he said, "Long only investing is obsolete." I agree with him wholeheartedly.

Long only investing involves owning stocks. Long/short strategies—practiced by a growing number of long/short hedge funds—seek to cancel out market swings by holding long positions in stocks that the fund managers like and short positions in the stocks they do not like. Because the simultaneous long and short positions cancel out the market-related return, the investor is left with an alpha—which, of course, can be either positive or negative—without the up or down movement of the market.

Going further, Bernstein asked, "Why should [the fiduciaries at] institutions continue to tolerate the kind of volatility that conventional long investing inflicts upon their portfolios?" The answer is, of course, they should not!

Harry Markowitz taught us that optimal portfolios balance the trade-offs between expected risks and returns. Properly constructed long/short portfolios can virtually remove a portfolio's systematic (market-related) risk. Adding a portfolio that has expected returns that are uncorrelated with broad-based market returns makes sense.

Managing—and finding people who can manage—hedge funds is difficult. These can be very treacherous waters.

Yet the use of hedge funds is growing at a staggering clip. Dow Jones estimates that the number of hedge funds increased from approximately 610 in 1990 to 5,329 in the first quarter of 2003 and that the assets under management increased from approximately $39 billion in 1990 to a staggering $619 billion in the first quarter of 2003. Dow Jones estimates that hedge-fund assets will increase to $2 trillion by 2010.[3]

Morgan Stanley[4] estimates that in the United States 22 percent of pension plans and 43 percent of endowments are currently invested in hedge funds. Recent announcements of new allocations to hedge-fund strategies include these: California Public Employees Retirement System (CalPERS) initiated a $1 billion hedge-fund program and is making initial allocations of $20 million to $50 million to individual managers; Seventh Swedish National Pension Fund has allocated 4 percent of its $2.4 billion to hedge funds; and Stanford University has recently committed itself to allocate between 5 and 10 percent of its $8 billion endowment to hedge funds and absolute-return strategies.

I close with a quotation from the late Carl Sagan's last book, *Billions and Billions.*[5] Sagan was the author of 30 books, and his Peabody Award–winning public television series, *Cosmos,* has been seen by more than 500 million people in over 60 countries. As we contemplate the future of investment management and bring into focus the important role played by fiduciaries, Sagan's words seem equally applicable whether we seek to understand the keys to successful investment management or we strive to understand the cosmos.

If you know a thing only qualitatively, you know it no more than vaguely. If you know it quantitatively—grasping some numerical measure that distinguishes it from an infinite number of other possibilities—you are beginning to know it deeply. You comprehend some of its beauty and you gain access to its power and the understanding it provides. Being afraid of quantification is tantamount to disenfranchising yourself, giving up on one of the most potent prospects for understanding."[6]

CHAPTER 43

Highlights

The problem with most investment books is that they do not tell you "why you need to know. . . ." For this reason I have organized each chapter in this book around the kinds of everyday questions faced by investors, consultants, and fiduciaries. With the caveat that the next few pages are intended as a review of the highlights for persons who have already invested the time to understand the fictions these facts replace—and who appreciate the weight of evidence supporting these facts—I offer a few highlights of important things to remember.

Readers who have read the earlier chapters should find these highlights useful; readers who start with these highlights will be disappointed. There are no quick fixes or "10 minutes to becoming a better investor" here or elsewhere.

This said, the biggest problem facing investors is having too much irrelevant information. "Noise" abounds. Remember: if you cannot articulate how a particular news item relates to the decision at hand, it is *noise*. Noise traders—who, when it is said and done, are basically guessing which stocks will go up and which will go down—dominate the trading activity in financial markets. We live in a world in which millions of investors pay commissions (and often taxes) to *sell* shares at a price that other investors find attractive enough to pay commissions so that they can *buy* the identical shares at the identical price.

We are eternal optimists. Ninety percent of us believe we are above-average drivers. One hundred percent of all active investors (more appropriately called speculators) believe they will earn above-average returns. Yet, using Nobel laureate William Sharpe's words, "it must be the case that before costs, the return on the average actively managed dollar will equal the return on the average passively managed dollar and, *after costs, the return on the average actively managed dollar will be* less *than the return on the average passively managed dollar* [emphasis added]."[1]

It is useful to think of the active versus passive debate in the following terms: Passive investors have a near 100 percent chance of attaining above-average long-term returns; active investors have something on the order of a one-in-four chance of beating the above-average returns of low-cost index funds.

As normal individuals, we are plagued by a tendency to see patterns where none exist. We too often confuse being lucky with being skillful. It is important to remember that, in perfectly random games such as coin tossing, selecting stocks with a dartboard, or any of a large number of noise-based strategies, winners and losers emerge. Moreover, once the winners are ahead they are unlikely to relinquish their winner positions.

There is persuasive evidence that financial markets are remarkably "efficient." This means that information is embedded into prices so quickly that it becomes useless. In such a world there is no advantage or disadvantage to trading with or without news because market prices reflect all that is known at that instant of a trade.

Technical analysts use historical price data to predict the direction and magnitude of price changes. Under the well-documented weak form of the efficient market hypothesis (also known as the random walk hypothesis), historical price data cannot be used to predict either the magnitude or the direction of subsequent price changes. Thus, the weak form of the efficient market hypothesis is directly opposed to the basic premise of technical analysis.

Fundamental analysts use data that are fundamental to a company's income statement and balance sheet to select investments that are expected to have better-than-average investment returns. The semistrong form of the efficient market hypothesis—for which there is much supporting evidence—is diametrically opposed to the concept of fundamental analysis.

In the face of poor odds—and much evidence in support of extremely efficient financial markets—I believe it is possible for a few informed investors to exploit "pockets of opportunity." There is absolutely no doubt, for example, that if you knew next year's earnings for a large number of actively traded stocks you could use this information to attain significantly above-average investment returns. The concurrent earnings-change/return-change effect provides a remarkable insight in how the stock market works. Efficient markets embed everything that is known today into today's security prices. One of the things the market does not know, however, is which companies will report the best and worst earnings changes 12 months down the road.

Thus, even though analysts can forecast next year's earnings in a statistical sense, you cannot use analysts' average forecasts to earn consistently above-average investment returns. This is because "torpedo stocks" (high-expectation stocks that are rocked by earnings disappointments) consistently sink the returns of high-expectation portfolios. In this topsy-turvy world, portfolios with the *worst* forecasted earnings growth rates end up having the *best* returns; portfolios with the *best* forecasted earnings growth rates end up having the *worst* returns.

Nobel laureate Harry Markowitz has shown the benefits of owning well-diversified portfolios and, conversely, the poor combination for expected return and expected risk you have when you mirror the many individual investors who hold only a few stocks.

Nobel laureate William Sharpe has shown us that at any instant the market portfolio reflects everyone's best thinking. Thus, in an efficient market, there is no other combination of securities, held in these proportions, at these prices, which can have a higher expected return or a lower variance than the market.

There is much confusion about the compensation that investors in the stock market expect to receive and the compensation they actually receive. A fundamental truth is that, in the long run, you are compensated for taking market risks. As you move from an investment in risk-free securities, such as T-bills, to the risk inherent in the stock market, you demand—and over the long run you can expect to receive—a higher rate of return. Earning this market return is easy: All you need to do is invest in low-cost index funds.

Earning positive returns from nonmarket risks is not easy. Above-market returns that you earn must come from the negative returns of your competitors. This truth is so often forgotten, it bears repeating. One person's above-market return *must* come from another person's below-market return. To earn above-market returns you must be smarter than other investors. You must consistently discover and exploit investment opportunities that have been missed by other investors due to their errors, incompetence, and/or inattention. You must hold a portfolio that is different from the market portfolio, and you must be right!

Understanding the competitive nature of financial markets, the well-known economist John Maynard Keynes and Nobel laureate John Nash have shown that it is important to base our decisions on how we expect our competitors to decide—when facing the same decisions, with the same information. Here one rational solution is not to compete.

In this regard Charles Ellis makes an important distinction between a "winner's game" and a "loser's game." In a winner's game the outcome is determined by the actions of the winner. Points are won. In a loser's game the outcome is determined by the actions of the loser. Points are lost. Investing is usually a loser's game: The harder investors try to produce above-average investment returns, the more they trade; the more they trade, the more likely they are to end up with below-average long-term returns.

We know a lot about how investors behave. Trading lowers returns for both men and women. Because men (and particularly single men) trade more than women, men earn measurably lower returns. Other fascinating studies show that the stocks that individual investors sell typically perform better than the stocks they purchase.

Also, when considering the impact of trading, it is useful to remember that there are significant differences between the returns earned from investments and the returns earned by investors. Because many investors *do not hold their investments for an entire year*, the returns earned by investors in equity and fixed-income mutual funds are well below the returns earned by the mutual funds.

Because all of the excess return (the return above that of T-bills) comes in sudden spurts, "market timing"—shifting investments between risky and risk-free asset classes—is an inordinately risky strategy. Also, much can go wrong between the time a portfolio manager decides to buy or sell a stock and the time the necessary purchases or sales are completed. Factoring in estimates of commissions, market impact, trading delays, and missed trades, the average round-trip (sell-buy or buy-sell) cost of trading for large investment management organizations is on the order of 2.6 percent per trade. With the burden of such costs it is not surprising that the leading mutual-fund rating services do not appear to be able to discern better-performing funds.

Over time, the characteristics of the market change—sometimes significantly. In turn, the indexes we use to describe the market also change—sometimes significantly. In this context it is interesting to discover that managers that adhere to a rigid style with above-index returns over three years are likely to deliver below-index returns over the next three years; managers that adhere to a rigid style with below-index returns over three years are likely to deliver above-index returns over the next three years. This is obviously due to style persistence—not manager persistence.

Two odds and ends: First, the so-called law of active management shows that an investor with a little information about a lot of securities stands the better chance of success than an investor with a lot of information about a few stocks. Second, in a laboratory setting, the kinds of circuit breakers instituted by market regulators to minimize the severity of abrupt market declines apparently give market participants a false sense of security. The laboratory evidence shows that the presence of circuit breakers makes investors feel safer, which, in turn, causes bubbles to grow even faster.

I fervently believe there is a small number of professional and skilled amateur investors who can consistently deliver above-average investment results. It is *not easy* to provide such returns; it is *not easy* to find people who can.

Notes

CHAPTER 1 INTRODUCTION

1. The "Reno" and "Rome" examples, with similar examples drawn from South America and Italy, appear in Massimo Piattelli-Palmarini's fascinating book, *Inevitable Illusions: How Mistakes of Reason Rule Our Minds*, translated by Massimo Piattelli-Palmarini and Keith Botsford, John Wiley & Sons, Inc., 1994.
2. The latitude (the angular distance north and south of the earth's equator) and the longitude (the angular distance east or west measured from Greenwich, England) for Los Angeles are 34°3′ N by 118°15′ W and for Reno are 39°32′ N by 119°49′ W. *Source:* National Geographic.
3. The latitude for these cities is Rome 41°53′ N; Boston 42°20′ N; New York 40°42′ N; Atlanta 33°45′ N; Miami 25°45′ N; and San Juan, Puerto Rico 18°15′ N. *Source:* National Geographic.

CHAPTER 2 WHAT YOU NEED TO KNOW

1. Russell L. Ackoff, "Management Misinformation Systems," *Management Science*, vol. XIV (December 1967), pp. 147–156.

CHAPTER 3 INFORMATION OR NOISE?

1. See Chris Mader and Robert Hagin, *Information Systems: Technology, Economics, and Applications* (Chicago: Science Research Associates, Inc. [Subsidiary of IBM], 1974).
2. In my view the information age is poorly named. "Information" implies "usefulness" to me. Yet I would agree that the "noise

age" and the old term "data processing" lack the cachet of "information age" and "information technology."

3. Fischer Black, "Noise," *Journal of Finance*, vol. 41, no. 3 (July 1986), pp. 529–543.
4. Ibid.
5. Richard Bernstein, *Navigate the Noise: Investing in the New Age of Media and Hype* (New York: John Wiley & Sons, 2001), Introduction p. xix.
6. Ibid., pp. 21–22.

CHAPTER 5 RANDOM OCCURRENCES

1. Peter Bernstein, *Against the Gods: The Remarkable Story of Risk* (New York: John Wiley & Sons, Inc., 1996).
2. Ibid.
3. A variation of this question appears in Massimo Piattelli-Palmarini, *Inevitable Illusions: How Mistakes of Reason Rule Our Minds*, translated by Massimo Piattelli-Palmarini and Keith Botsford (New York: John Wiley & Sons, 1994).
4. Gambling parlance distinguishes between payoffs stated as *for* and *to*. In a 35-*for*-1 payoff the casino keeps the wagered amount and pays the bettor $35 for each dollar wagered. In a 35-*to*-1 bet, in Atlantic City or Las Vegas, the winning bettor keeps his or her wager and is paid $35 for each $1 gambled.
5. The house expects to lose one single-number bet out of each 38 and to pay $35 to $1. By taking in $37 from losing bettors while paying out $35 during these 38 bets, the house expects to win the difference of $2, or 5.26 percent ($2/_{38}$), out of each $38 wagered. At the end of any day, week, or month, as long-run expected and actual results narrow, casinos take in almost exactly 5.26 percent of every dollar wagered on roulette.
6. Two consecutive coin tosses will land in one of four possible sequences (which is $2^2 = 4$); three consecutive coin tosses will land in one of eight possible sequences (which is $2^3 = 8$); six consecutive tosses will land in one of 64 possible sequences (which is $2^6 = 64$).

CHAPTER 6   LAW OF SMALL NUMBERS

1. A similar example appears in John Paulos, *A Mathematician Plays the Stock Market* (New York: Basic Books, 2003), pp. 64–65.
2. Ibid.
3. Adapted from T. Gilovich, R. Vallone, and A. Tversky, "The Hot Hand in Basketball: On Misperception of Random Sequences," *Cognitive Psychology*, vol. 24, pp. 1110–1126. Also in Thomas Gilovich, *How We Know What Isn't So—The Fallacy of Human Reason in Everyday Life* (New York: Free Press, 1991), pp. 11–12.
4. Gilovich, *How We Know What Isn't So*, p. 15.
5. Ibid, pp. 15–16.
6. Ibid., p. 21.
7. Ibid.
8. A similar example appears in Massimo Piattelli-Palmarini, *Inevitable Illusions: How Mistakes of Reason Rule Our Minds*, translated by Massimo Piattelli-Palmarini and Keith Botsford (New York: John Wiley & Sons, 1994), pp. 30–32.

CHAPTER 7   AVERAGE IS AVERAGE

1. Here market is intended to be a large number of approximately normally distributed securities. If you imagine a 10-stock market in which nine stocks earned 1 percent and one stock earned 25 percent, half would *not* be above average.
2. It should be noted that the time it takes for buy and sell orders to arrive in continuous financial markets gives rise to temporal imbalances between buy and sell orders. Given these imbalances, the clearing price may be significantly away from the current bid or ask prices. This causes the bid or ask prices to change to match buyers and sellers at acceptable prices. However, when prices are set there cannot be an imbalance between buyers and sellers.
3. Technically, assume that you and the other investors purchased the shares in proportion to each stock's capitalization weighting in the S&P 500 index.

CHAPTER 8 EFFICIENT MARKETS

1. A friend and respected long-time colleague, Philip Nelson, abhors the increasing use of "impound" to refer to earnings or other expectations that have been "pounded" into the price of a company's stocks. In Nelson's view, which agrees with my dictionary's view, "impound" conjures up images of the local dogcatchers taking my dogs off to the pound or, worse yet, the attorney general impounding my collection of skeet guns. Nelson suggests that I use "embed" in the place of "impound."

    I must confess that, to me, "embed" conjures up images of fossils in rocks. Thus, embed connotes to me a certain permanence. Embed does not (at least for me) conjure up images of a blacksmith, covered with perspiration, hammering (in the "pounding" sense) and shaping iron that can, if necessary, be reshaped anytime we deem appropriate.

    That notwithstanding, "embedded" is used in the place of "impounded" throughout this book.

CHAPTER 9 RANDOM WALK

1. Named after Robert Brown, the Scottish botanist who first observed the phenomenon, Brownian motion is the name given to the random movement of microscopic particles that are suspended in liquids or gases. This motion is caused by the collision of such particles with surrounding molecules and is of great interest to physicists. In 1905 Albert Einstein presented the renowned paper in which he "discovered" the mathematical equation that describes the phenomenon of Brownian motion. Einstein reportedly regarded this discovery as one of his greatest contributions. Yet Einstein died not knowing that Bachelier five years earlier had discovered that the same equation could be used to describe the random behavior of stock prices.

2. The first modern-day reference to Bachelier's work was published by Sidney S. Alexander, "Price Movements in Speculative Markets: Trends or Random Walks," *Industrial Management Review*, vol. 2, no. 2 (May 1961), pp. 7–26. Reprinted (and ex-

panded) in Paul H. Cootner, ed., *The Random Character of Stock Market Prices*, (Cambridge, MA: MIT Press, 1964), pp. 199–218 and 338–372.

3. Eugene Slutsky, "The Summation of Random Causes As the Source of Cyclic Processes," *Econometrica*, vol. 5, no. 2 (April 1937), pp. 105–146.

4. Holbrook Working, "A Random-Difference Series for Use in the Analysis of Time Series," *Journal of the American Statistical Association*, vol. 29, no. 185 (March 1934), pp. 11–24.

5. Alfred Cowles and Herbert F. Jones, "Some *Á Posteriori* Probabilities in Stock Market Action," *Econometrica*, vol. 5, no. 3 (July 1937), pp. 280–294.

6. Maurice Kendall, "The Analysis of Economic Time Series—Part I: Prices," *Journal of the Royal Statistical Society*, Series A (General), vol. 116, pt. 1 (1953), pp. 11–25. Reprinted in Paul H. Cootner, ed., *The Random Character of Stock Market Prices*, pp. 85–99.

7. Ibid.

8. Harry V. Roberts, "Stock Market 'Patterns' and Financial Analysis," *Journal of Finance*, vol. 14, no. 1 (March 1959), pp. 1–10. Reprinted in: Paul H. Cootner, ed., *The Random Character of Stock Market Prices*, pp. 7–16; Richard E. Ball, ed., *Readings in Investments* (Boston: Allyn & Bacon, 1965), pp. 369–379; and James Lorie and Richard Brealey, eds., *Modern Developments in Investment Management: A Book of Readings*, 2d ed. (Hinsdale, IL: Dryden Press, 1978), pp. 154–163.

9. M. F. M. Osborne, "Brownian Motion in the Stock Market," *Operations Research*, vol. 7, no. 2 (March–April 1959), pp. 145–173.

10. Roberts, "Stock Market 'Patterns' and Financial Analysis."

11. Holbrook Working, "Note and the Correlation of First Differences of Averages in a Random Chain," *Econometrica*, vol. 28, no. 4 (October 1960), pp. 916–918. Reprinted in Cootner, ed., *The Random Character of Stock Market Prices*, pp. 129–131.

12. Alexander, "Price Movements in Speculative Markets."

13. Alfred Cowles, "A Revision of Previous Conclusions Regarding Stock Price Behavior," *Econometrica*, vol. 28, no. 4 (October 1960), pp. 909–915. Reprinted in Cootner, ed., *The Random Character of Stock Market Prices*, pp. 132–138.

14. Alexander, "Price Movements in Speculative Markets."
15. Hendrik S. Houthakker, "Systematic and Random Elements in Short-Term Price Movements," *American Economic Review*, vol. 51, no. 2 (May 1961), pp. 164–172.
16. Paul H. Cootner, *The Random Character of Stock Market Prices*.
17. Arnold B. Moore, "A Statistical Analysis of Common Stock Prices." Unpublished Ph.D. dissertation, University of Chicago, 1962.
18. Eugene Fama, unpublished Ph.D. dissertation.
19. *Fortune*, vol. 74, no. 1 (July 1, 1966).
20. Michael C. Jensen, "Random Walks: Reality or Myth—Comment," *Financial Analysts Journal*, vol. 23, no. 6 (November–December 1967), pp. 77–85.
21. Michael C. Jensen and George A. Benington, "Random Walks and Technical Theories: Some Additional Evidence," *Journal of Finance*, vol. 25, no. 2 (May 1970), pp. 469–481.
22. Victor Niederhoffer, "A New Look at Clustering of Stock Prices," *Journal of Business*, vol. 39, no. 2 (April 1966), pp. 309–313.
23. Victor Niederhoffer and M. F. M. Osborne. "Market Making and Reversal on the Stock Exchange," *Journal of the American Statistical Association*, vol. 61, no. 316 (December 1966), pp. 887–916.
24. Charles Lee and Bhaskaran Swaminathan, "Price Momemtum and Trading Volume," *Journal of Finance*, vol. 55, no. 5 (October 2000), pp. 2017–2070.

CHAPTER 10 PERFECT EARNINGS FORECASTS

1. When studying annual earnings data a common mistake is to assume that earnings for periods ending on December 31 are known on December 31. In fact, earnings for periods ending on December 31 are not known until some time later. To avoid introducing a "look-ahead bias"—which can render research results useless—I make the very conservative assumption in this study that actual year-end earnings are not available until the end of the next calendar quarter. For this reason, the holding periods in Table 10.1 start and end on March 31.

This study analyzed consensus earnings forecasts for companies with December fiscal years, beginning-year stock prices of at least $5.00 per share, and trailing-year earnings per share of at least $0.50, for which Institutional Brokers Estimate Service (I/B/E/S) had earnings forecasts.

Philip Nelson programmed the software that was used for the calculations in Chapters 10 through 15. We designed this software so we can study the relationship between any specifiable factors (such as P/E or size) and any specifiable categories (such as technology or utility stocks) *without* reprogramming. All that is necessary is to change the underlying data.

Initially the software was dubbed "Fact Cat" for its ability to study the relationship between any specifiable factors or categories. It did not take long, however, before its name became "Fat Cat."

Philip also programmed the rebalancing simulator (Reb Sim) software that we use to understand trading strategies. It is not enough to know that stocks with certain factors (say, low P/Es) in certain categories (say, small capitalization) tend to have better-than-average returns. How many stocks should you hold? How frequently should you trade? What is the best definition of a low-expectation stock? These are only a few of the questions that must be answered before successfully implementing an investment strategy.

2. To increase readability, I will refer to "return." Unless otherwise noted, "return" in this context means "average 12-month universe-total relative total return."

3. Most of these data are contemporaneous. That is, they were gathered over time so that the 1980 data, for example, were taken from I/B/E/S immediately following 1980.

4. It should be noted that it is incorrect to derive the 25-year average universe-relative return by either averaging or linking the universe-relative returns for each of the years. Instead, the 25-year average universe-relative return for each of the five portfolios was derived from the difference between the 25-year geometric-average return of the universe (14.2 percent) and the 25-year geometric-average return for each of the five portfolios.

5. Even so, the differences between each of the five periods are statistically significant using a chi-squared test.

6. *Technical Note:* Some researchers make a serious mistake when they "link differences." Assume investor A earns a two-period return of 10 percent and 20 percent. Investor B earns a two-period return of 5 percent and 10 percent.

Investor	Return Period 1	Return Period 2	Wealth Index
A	10%	20%	1.320
B	5%	10%	1.155
Incorrect: Linked Differences	5%	10%	1.155
Correct: Difference between Wealth Indexes			1.165

It is incorrect to calculate investor A's success relative to investor B's by linking the differences between their returns—1.05 times 1.10 = 1.155. When, in fact, investor A turned $1.00 into $1.32, investor B turned $1.00 into $1.155. The correct way to calculate the difference between investor A's and investor B's wealth is to *subtract* $1.155 from $1.320. Investor A outperformed investor B by 16.5 cents—not the 15.5 cents implied from linking the differences between investor A's and investor B's returns.

CHAPTER 11 CAN ANALYSTS FORECAST EARNINGS CHANGES?

1. I used chi-square analysis to compare the actual numbers of the companies with the numbers that we would expect if there were no relationship between forecasted and actual earnings changes. I also used regression analysis to compare the forecasted and actual changes.

CHAPTER 12 EARNINGS FORECASTS (AND TORPEDO STOCKS)

1. Although the joint-classification scheme used in Figure 12.1 has the advantage of being relatively simple and easy to use, it has a

shortcoming in the upper left and lower right cells. This is that a company ranked worst has no way to become even worse. Similarly, a company ranked best has no way to be ranked better than best. Imagine a case, for example, in which a company's earnings were expected to grow at 30 percent and the company was classified in the best forecasted earnings change row. Then, suppose that one year later the actual earnings change was 40 percent. By the 5-by-5 classification scheme this pleasant surprise would end up in the "perfect" cell in the bottom right corner.

Thus, even though I have not altered the symbols in Figure 12.1, I would not be surprised to find poor relative performance in the cell in the upper left corner as some low-expectation stocks provide even lower than expected earnings growth. Conversely, I would not be surprised to find above-average relative performance in the cell in the lower right corner as some high-expectation stocks provide even higher than expected earnings growth.

2. The naming and first documentation of the torpedo effect appeared in Robert L. Hagin, "The Subtle Risk of High Expected Earnings Growth—the Torpedo Effect," Kidder Peabody & Co., Inc., July 1982.

CHAPTER 15   PRICE-EARNINGS EFFECT

1. For ease of interpretation I refer here to P/E ratios. All analysis, however, was done with earnings-price ratios. To ensure that this data would be available *ex ante*, I calculated P/E ratios using actual earnings for the period ended December 31 but did not construct portfolios based on these P/E ratios (and begin to measure returns) until the following March 31. So that prices would be as fresh as possible, I used March 31 prices in the P/E calculation.

CHAPTER 16   THE MAGIC OF GROWTH

1. Martin L. Leibowitz and Stanley Kogelman, "Inside the P/E Ratio: The Franchise Factor," *Financial Analysts Journal*

(November–December 1990), appears in Frank Fabozzi, ed., *Investing: The Collected Works of Martin L. Leibowitz* (Chicago: Probus Publishing Company, 1992), pp. 287–289.

2. Ibid., pp. 288–289.

CHAPTER 17 ESTIMATE REVISIONS

1. To the extent that year-ahead earnings expectations are the expectations that are correctly embedded into today's stock prices, the expectations are correct. They are "wrong" in that today's expectations for year-ahead earnings are wrong.

2. I believe this term was coined originally by Melissa Brown (currently at Goldman Sachs Asset Management).

3. E. H. Hawkins, S.C. Chamberlin, and W. F. Daniel, "Earnings Expectations and Security Prices," *Financial Analysts Journal*, vol. 41 (September–October 1984), pp. 24–38.

4. E. J. Elton, M. J. Gruber, and M. N. Gultekin, "Professional Expectations: Accuracy and Diagnosis of Error," *Journal of Financial and Quantitative Methods Analysis*, vol. 19 (December 1984), pp. 351–363.

5. Edwin J. Elton, Martin J. Gruber, and Mustafa Gultekin, "Expectations and Share Prices," *Management Sciences*, vol. 27, no. 9 (September 1981), pp. 975–987.

6. D. van Dijk, *Almost Everything You Ever Wanted to Know about Consensus Earnings Revisions*. Unpublished MBA thesis, Baruch College–CUNY, New York, NY (June 1986).

7. Robert D. Arnott, "The Use and Misuse of Consensus Earnings," *Journal of Portfolio Management* (Spring 1985), pp. 18–27.

8. Patricia C. O'Brien, "Analysts' Forecasts as Earnings Expectations," *Journal of Accounting and Economics*, vol. 10 (1988), pp. 53–83.

9. D. Givoly and J. Lakonishok, "The Information Content of Financial Analysts' Forecasts of Earnings," *Journal of Accounting and Economics*, vol. 1 (1991), pp. 165–185.

10. Scott Stickel, "Common Stock Returns Surrounding Earnings Forecast Revisions: More Puzzling Evidence," *Accounting Review*, vol. 66, no. 2 (April 1991), pp. 402–416.

11. Langdon B. Wheeler, "Changes in Consensus Earnings Estimates and Their Impact on Stock Returns," in Brian Bruce and Charles Epstein, eds., *The Handbook of Corporate Earnings Analysis: Company Performance and Stock Market Valuation* (Burr Ridge, IL: Probus Publishing Company, 1994), pp. 63–83.

12. O'Brien, "Analysts' Forecasts as Earnings Expectations."

13. Scott Stickel, "Predicting Individual Analyst Earnings Forecasts," *Journal of Accounting Research*, vol. 28, no. 2 (Autumn 1990), pp. 409–417.

14. Lawrence Brown, "Forecast Selection When All Forecasts Are Not Equally Recent," *International Journal of Forecasting*, vol. 17, no. 3 (November 1991), pp. 349–356.

15. Haim Mozes and Patricia Williams, "Evidence of Mimicking in Analyst Forecasting Behavior," Working paper, Fordham University, 1998.

16. Sandip Bhagat, "Impact of Earnings Prenannoucements," Presentation at the Third Annual Corporate Earnings Analysis Seminar, New York, 1997.

17. Leonard Soffer, Ramu Thiagaragan, and Beverly Walther, "Earnings Preannouncements," Working paper, Northwestern University, 1998.

18. Parveen Shinka, Lawrence Brown, and Somnath Das, "A Reexamination of Financial Analysts' Differential Earnings Forecast Accuracy," *Contemporary Accounting Research*, vol. 14, no. 1 (Spring 1997), pp. 1–42.

19. Ronald Kahn and Andrew Rudd, "Leaders, Followers and Rebels: A Classification Scheme for Analysts," Presented at the Q-Group Seminar, Spring 1998.

20. Martin Herzberg, James Guo, and Lawrence Brown, "Enhancing Earnings Predictability Using Individual Analyst Forecasts," *Journal of Investing* (Summer 1999).

21. Richard Bernstein, *Navigate the Noise: Investing in the New Age of Media and Hype* (New York: John Wiley & Sons, 2001).

CHAPTER **18** **NOBEL LAUREATE MARKOWITZ**

1. Harry M. Markowitz, "Portfolio Selection," *Journal of Finance*, vol. 7, no. 1 (March 1952), pp. 77–91.

2. Harry M. Markowitz, *Portfolio Selection: Efficient Diversification of Investments.* (New York: John Wiley & Sons, 1959).
3. Adam Smith, *An Inquiry into the Nature and Causes of the Wealth of Nations.* 2d ed., vol. 1, bk. 2 (London: Methuen & Company, 1904).

CHAPTER 19   NOBEL LAUREATE SHARPE

1. William F. Sharpe, "Capital Asset Prices: A Theory of Market Equilibrium under Conditions of Risk," *Journal of Finance*, vol. 19, no. 3 (September 1964), pp. 425–442. Reprinted in James Lorie and Richard Brealey, eds., *Modern Developments in Investment Management: A Book of Readings*, 2d ed. (Hinsdale, 'IL: Dryden Press, 1978), pp. 366–383.
2. John Lintner, "Security Prices, Risk, and Maximal Gains from Diversification," *Journal of Finance*, vol. 20, no. 12 (December 1965), pp. 587–615.
3. Jack L. Treynor, "Toward a Theory of Market Value of Risky Assets." Unpublished manuscript, 1961.
4. Jan Mossin, "Equilibrium in a Capital Asset Market," *Econometrica*, vol. 34, no. 10 (October 1966), pp. 768–783.
5. Meir Statman, "Bubbles and Portfolios: Investment Lessons from Kahneman and Smith, Winners of the 2002 Nobel Prize in Economics," Association for Investment Management and Research, Inc., Annual Conference, Arizona, 2003.

CHAPTER 20   COMPENSATION FOR BEARING RISKS

1. Because the standard deviation of the distribution of a security's expected excess returns quantifies the likelihood that deviations of certain magnitudes will occur, it is an appropriate measure of risk. The problem with this conceptually accurate representation is that, mathematically, standard deviations are not additive. However, given the relationship standard deviation^2 = variance and the fact that variances of two independent sources of risk—nonmarket and market—can be combined, it is possible to square the two standard deviations and then combine the two resulting variances.

2. Technically, R-squared is the coefficient of determination (R^2).
3. Barr Rosenberg and James Guy, "Prediction of Systematic Risk from Investment Fundamentals," *Financial Analysts Journal*, vol. 32, no. 3 (May–June 1976), pp. 60–72, and vol. 32, no. 4 (July–August 1976), pp. 62–70.
4. Barr Rosenberg, Michel Houglet, Vinay Marathe, and Walt McKibben, "Components of Covariance in Security Returns." Research Program in Finance Working Paper No. 13. (Berkeley: Institute of Business and Economic Research, University of California, 1973; rev. 1975).
5. Eugene Fama and Kenneth French, "The Cross-section of Expected Stock Returns," *Journal of Finance*, vol. 47 (1992), pp. 427–465.
6. Eugene Fama and Kenneth French, "Common Risk Factors in the Returns on Stocks and Bonds," *Journal of Financial Economics*, vol. 33 (1993), pp. 3–56; Eugene Fama and Kenneth French, "Size and Book-to-Market Factors in Earnings and Returns," *Journal of Finance*, vol. 50 (1995), pp. 131–155.
7. John Cochrane, "Portfolio Advice for a Multifactor World," *Economic Perspectives*, Federal Reserve Bank of Chicago, vol. 23, no. 3 (1999), pp. 36–58; John Cochrane, "New Facts in Finance," *Economic Perspectives*, Federal Reserve Bank of Chicago, vol. 23, no. 3 (1999), pp. 59–78.
8. Cochrane, "New Facts in Finance."

CHAPTER 21 DARING TO BE DIFFERENT

1. Drawn from Charles D. Ellis, *Investment Policy: How to Win the Loser's Game* (Homewood, IL: Dow Jones–Irwin, 1985).

CHAPTER 22 LAW OF ACTIVE MANAGEMENT

1. Technically, this analysis assumes that what is known about each security is independent of what is known about each of the other securities. This is usually not the case, causing the number of securities to be greater than the number of independent decisions. Given the caveats about the specific calculations, the insights

gained from understanding the laws of active management are important for both investors and fiduciaries.

2. An excellent and more detailed explanation of the fundamental law of active management and of information ratios appears in: Richard C. Grinold and Ronald N. Kahn, *Active Portfolio Management: Quantitative Theory and Applications* (New York: McGraw-Hill, 1995).
3. The approximation is caused by ignoring the benefits of reducing risk when forecasts are accurate. The assumptions behind this equation are discussed in detail in Grinold and Kahn.
4. Grinold and Kahn, *Active Portfolio Management*. p. 119.
5. Ibid.

CHAPTER 23   NOBEL LAUREATE NASH AND KEYNES

1. John Maynard Keynes, *The General Theory of Employment Interest and Money* (London: Macmillan & Company, 1936).
2. This question was adapted from a question in John Paulos, *A Mathematician Plays the Stock Market* (New York: Basic Books, 2003).
3. Charles D. Ellis, *Investment Policy—How to Win the Loser's Game* (Homewood, IL: Dow Jones–Irwin, 1985).
4. Ellis, *Investment Policy*, pp. 16–17.
5. Ibid., p. 11.

CHAPTER 24   NOBEL LAUREATES KAHNEMAN AND SMITH

1. Daniel Kahneman from the Nobel web site.
2. Variations of this and the following question originally appeared in Kahneman and Tversky's seminal 1979 paper, "Prospect Theory: An Analysis of Decision under Risk," *Econometrica*, vol. 47 (March 1979); the questions are also reprinted in Richard Thaler's outstanding book, *Quasi Rational Economics* (New York: Russell Sage Foundation, 1994), p. 5.

3. Variations of this and the following question originally appeared in Richard H. Thaler and Eric J. Johnson, "Gambling with the House Money and Trying to Break Even: The Effects of Prior Outcomes on Risky Choice," *Management Science* vol. 36, no. 6 (June 1990), pp. 643–660; the questions are also reprinted in Thaler, *Quasi Rational Economics.*

4. Paul A. Samuelson, *Economics*, 10th ed. (New York: McGraw-Hill, 1976), pp. 474–475.

5. Variations of the following four questions appear in Richard Thaler, "Mental Accounting and Consumer Choice," *Marketing Science*, vol. 4 (Summer 1985), pp. 199–214. The questions are also reprinted in Thaler, *Quasi Rational Economics.*

6. The MacArthur Fellows Program awards unrestricted fellowships to talented individuals who have shown extraordinary originality and dedication in their creative pursuits and a marked capacity for self-direction. There are three criteria for selection of fellows: exceptional creativity, promise for important future advances based on a track record of significant accomplishment, and potential for the fellowship to facilitate subsequent creative work. The MacArthur Foundation does not require or expect specific products or reports from fellows, and does not evaluate recipients' creativity during the term of the fellowship. The fellowship is a "no strings attached" award in support of people, not projects. Each fellowship comes with a stipend of $500,000 to the recipient, paid out in equal quarterly installments over five years. See also www.macfound.org.

7. Meir Statman, Glenn Klimek Professor of Finance, Santa Clara University, "Bubbles and Portfolios: Investing Lessons from 2002 Nobel Prize Winners Kahneman and Smith," speech at Association for Investment Management and Research 2003 Annual Conference, Arizona; Ross M. Miller, *Paving Wall Street* (New York: John Wiley & Sons, 2002).

8. Vernon L. Smith, Gerry L. Suchanek, and Arlington W. Williams, "Bubbles, Crashes, and Endogenous Expectations in Experimental Spot Asset Markets," *Econometrica*, vol. 56, no. 5 (September 1988), pp. 1119–1151.

9. Gunduz Caginalp, David Porter, and Vernon L. Smith, "Momentum and Overreaction in Experimental Asset Markets,"

International Journal of Industrial Organization, vol. 18, no. 1 (January 2000), pp. 187–204.

10. Ronald R. King, Vernon L. Smith, Arlington W. Williams, and Mark van Boening, "The Robustness of Bubbles and Crashes in Experimental Stock Markets," in *Nonlinear Dynamics and Evolutionary Economics*, edited by Richard H. Day and Ping Chen (New York: Oxford University Press, 1993), pp. 183–200.

11. Miller, *Paving Wall Street*.

CHAPTER 25   WHAT GUIDES INVESTORS

1. Terrance Odean, "Volume, Volatility, Price, and Profit When All Traders Are Above Average," *Journal of Finance*, vol. 103 (1998), pp. 1887–1934.

2. Brad Barber and Terrance Odean, "Boys Will Be Boys: Gender, Overconfidence, and Common Stock Investment," *Quarterly Journal of Economics*, vol. 116, issue 1 (February 1, 2001).

3. Mary A. Lundeberg, Paul W. Fox, and Judith Punccohar, "Highly Confident but Wrong: Gender Differences and Similarities in Confidence Judgments," *Journal of Educational Psychology*, vol. 86 (1994), pp. 114–121.

4. Melvin Prince, "Women, Men, and Money Styles," *Journal of Economic Psychology*, vol. 14 (1993), pp. 175–182.

5. Barber and Odean, "Boys Will Be Boys."

6. Odean, "Volume, Volatility, Price, and Profit."

7. Hersh Shefrin and Meir Statman, "The Disposition to Sell Winners Too Early and Ride Losers Too Long: Theory and Evidence," *Journal of Finance*, vol. 60 (1985), pp. 777–790.

8. Odean, "Volume, Volatility, Price, and Profit."

CHAPTER 26   LUCK OR SKILL?

1. John Paulos, *A Mathemetician Plays the Stock Market* (New York: Basic Books, 2003), p. 5.

2. Technically, investment returns are not normally distributed. In practice there are too many large deviations—above and below

the mean—which cause distributions of investment returns to have inordinately fat tails. This lack of normality in the context that it is used here *increases* the number of years of above-benchmark returns that are required to have confidence that the returns are derived from skill.

3. James T. McClave and George P. Benson, *Statistics for Business and Economics* (San Francisco: Dellen Publishing Company, 1991).

CHAPTER 27 MEASURING INVESTMENT RETURNS

1. The questions and answers dealing with infrequently priced assets were adapted from Robert Merton's presentation to the Association for Investment Management and Research's Annual Conference in Phoenix, Arizona, May 12, 2003.

CHAPTER 28 ANATOMY OF THE S&P 500

1. Further discussion of these criteria can be found in "Focusing the S&P 500 on U.S. Large Cap Stocks and the Removal of Non-U.S. Companies in the S&P 500" at Standard & Poor's web site (www.spglobal.com/research.html). See "Standard & Poor's U.S. Indices."
2. David M. Blitzer and Srikant Dash, "The Tale of an Index in Bubble and Bear Markets: S&P 500 from 1997 to 2002," August 24, 2002, www.sandp.com.

CHAPTER 29 RETURNS EARNED BY INVESTORS

1. Statistics reported in this section were taken from the press release on Dalbar's web site (www.dalbar.com).
2. Laurence Siegel's research is, as yet, unpublished. These quotations are from an e-mail addressed to me and a telephone conversation on July 14, 2003. Siegel's research was also the subject of an article by Jason Zweig in "What Fund Investors Really Need to Know," *Money* (June 2002), pp. 110–124.

CHAPTER 31 MARKET TIMING: RISK VERSUS REWARD

1. Robert H. Jeffrey, "The Folly of Stock Market Timing," *Harvard Business Review* (July–August 1984), pp. 100–102.
2. There is nothing magical about 112 quarters. Two and one-half years ago—when I first decided to replicate Jeffrey's 1984 study—I quite arbitrarily downloaded 100 quarters of historical returns. Even though 1974 was an excellent time to own equities, the conclusions drawn from this analysis hold for other periods.
3. One dollar invested for 9 years at 10 percent per year appreciates to 1.10^9 or \$2.36; \$1.00 invested for 10 years at 10 percent per year appreciates to 1.10^{10} or \$2.59.

CHAPTER 32 KNOW THE ODDS BEFORE YOU PLAY THE GAME

1. This format was used by Robert "Tad" Jeffrey in Robert H. Jeffrey, "The Folly of Stock Market Timing," *Harvard Business Review* (July–August 1984), pp. 100–102.
2. Technically, the rank is on R^* where $R^* = \log [1 + \max(R1, R2)] - \log [1 + \min(R1, R2)]$ where R1, R2 are the stock and bond returns, respectively.

CHAPTER 34 TRADING COSTS

1. Wayne H. Wagner, "The Nature of Institutional Order Flow: The Hurdles to Superior Performance," research paper presented at the Institute for Quantitative Research in Finance Spring Conference, March 2003.

CHAPTER 35 MUTUAL FUNDS

1. Mark M. Carhart, "On Persistence in Mutual Fund Performance," *Journal of Finance*, vol. 52 (1997), pp. 57–82.
2. Dave Kovaleski, "Record Number of Funds Bit the Dust in 2002," *Investment News*, vol. 7, no. 1 (January 6, 2003), p. 25.

3. Standard & Poor's Indices versus Active Funds Scorecard, Fourth Quarter 2002. See www.sandp.com.
4. Carhart, "On Persistence in Mutual Fund Performance."
5. James Dow and Gary Gordon, "Noise Trading, Delegated Portfolio Management, and Economic Welfare," _Journal of Political Economy_, vol. 105 (1994), pp. 1024–1050.
6. Matthew R. Morey, "Rating the Raters: An Investigation of Mutual Fund Rating Services," _Journal of Investment Consulting_, vol. 5, no. 2 (November–December 2002), pp. 30–50.
7. Ibid., p. 30.

CHAPTER 36   ADVANTAGES OF . . .

1. David M. Blitzer and Srikant Dash, "Does Active Management Work for Small-Cap Stocks?" _A Guide to Small-Cap Investing_ (a publication of Institutional Investor, Inc.) (Spring 2003).
2. Ibid.
3. William F. Sharpe, "The Arithmetic of Active Management," _Financial Analysts Journal_, vol. 47, no. 1 (January/Febreuary 1991).
4. Rosanne Pane and Srikant Dash, _Standard & Poor's Indices versus Active Funds Scorecard_, First Quarter 2003, January 21, 2003.
5. G. Brinson, R. Hood, and G. Beebower, "The Determinants of Portfolio Performance," _Financial Analysts Journal_, vol. 47, no. 3 (May–June 1991).
6. Mark Kritzman and Sebastian Page, "The Hierarchy of Investment Choice: A Normative Interpretation," _Journal of Portfolio Management_, vol. 29, no. 3 (Spring 2003).

CHAPTER 37   STYLE PERSISTENCE

1. Richard Bernstein, _Navigate the Noise: Investing in the New Age of Media and Hype_ (New York: John Wiley & Sons, 2001).

CHAPTER 39   BEWARE OF TAXES

1. On October 9, 2002, the Dow Jones Industrial Average low was 7,286.27.

2. On October 27, 1997, the Dow Jones Industrial Average low was 7,161.15.

3. John C. Bogle, *Common Sense on Mutual Funds: New Imperatives for the Intelligent Investor* (New York: John Wiley & Sons, 1999), p. 279.

4. Robert M. Jeffrey and Robert D. Arnott, "Is Your Alpha Big Enough to Cover Its Taxes?," *Journal of Portfolio Management* (Spring 1993), pp. 15–25.

CHAPTER 40   BEYOND ACTIVE VERSUS PASSIVE

1. William F. Sharpe, presented at the Spring Presidents' Forum, Monterey Institute of International Studies, May 2002.

2. Benjamin Graham, *Financial Analysts Journal*, vol. 32, no. 5 (September–October 1976).

3. Leopold Bernstein, "In Defense of Fundamental Analysis," *Financial Analysts Journal* (January/February 1975), pp. 56–61.

4. Sanford Grossman and Joseph E. Stiglitz, "On the Impossibility of Informationally Efficient Markets," *American Economic Review* (June 1980), pp. 393–408.

CHAPTER 41   LONG-TERM CAPITAL MANAGEMENT

1. I am indebted to Roger Lowenstein and Random House for the extensive references to Roger Lowenstein's *When Genius Failed: The Rise and Fall of Long-Term Capital Management* (New York: Random House, 2000) throughout this chapter.

2. Ibid., p. 9.

3. Michael M. Lewis, *Liar's Poker: Rising through the Wreckage on Wall Street* (New York: W.W. Norton & Company, 1989).

4. Ibid., pp. 16–17.

5. Lowenstein, *When Genius Failed*, p. 10.

6. Ibid., p. 14.

7. Ibid., pp. 61–62.

8. Ibid., p. 77.

9. Ibid., p. 94.

10. Ibid., p. 152.

11. Ibid., p. 169.
12. Ibid., p. 188.

CHAPTER 42 TO WIN THE GAME

1. Arnold Wood, Presentation to The New York Society of Security Analysts and The Institute of Psychology and Markets, November 2002 in New York; Arnold Wood, "Fatal Attractions for Money Managers," *Financial Analysts Journal* (May–June 1989), pp. 3–5.
2. Shawn Tully, "How the Smart Money Really Invests," *Money* (July 6, 1998).
3. Dow Jones newswire December 3, 2002.
4. Morgan Stanley Investment Management webcast, Pension Strategies Group, May 15, 2003.
5. Carl Sagan, *Billions and Billions: Thoughts on Life and Death at the Brink of the Millennium* (New York: Random House, 1997). (This book was completed posthumously by Sagan's wife, Anne Druyan.)
6. Ibid., p. 21.

CHAPTER 43 HIGHLIGHTS

1. William F. Sharpe, "The Arithmetic of Active Management," *Financial Analysts Journal* (January–February 1991), p. 7.